de Vinck

Et ma charge
de Conseller

Prelude to Terror

Prelude to Terror

The Constituent Assembly
and the
Failure of Consensus,
1789-1791

NORMAN HAMPSON

Basil Blackwell

Copyright © Norman Hampson 1988

First published 1988

Basil Blackwell Ltd
108 Cowley Road, Oxford OX4 1JF, UK

Basil Blackwell Inc.
432 Park Avenue South, Suite 1503
New York, NY 10016, USA

British Library Cataloguing in Publication Data

Hampson, Norman
    Prelude to terror: the Constituent Assembly and the failure of consensus, 1789-91.
    1. France—History—Revolution, 1789-1794   2. France—Politics and government—Revolution, 1789-1799
    I. Title
    944.04 DC161
    ISBN 0-631-15237-7

Library of Congress Cataloging in Publication Data

Hampson, Norman
    Prelude to terror: the Constituent Assembly and the failure of consensus, 1789-91 / [Norman Hampson]
       p. cm.
    Bibliography: p.
    Includes index.
    ISBN 0-631-15237-7
    1. France. Assemblée nationale constituante (1789-1791)
    2. France—History—Revolution, 1789-1791 3. France—Politics and government—Revolution, 1789-1799
    I. Title.
    DC165.H35 1988
    87-35576 CIR
    944.04' 1—dc19

Typeset in 10 on 12pt Garamond
by Downdell Ltd., Abingdon, Oxon
Printed in Great Britain by T. J. Press Ltd, Padstow, Cornwall

Endpapers: *The genius of Rousseau enlightens the National Assembly*, engraving published by Chapuy, Paris, 1789, Bibliothèque Nationale, is reproduced by kind permission.

To my brother

I hate these absolute systems which make all events of history depend on great first causes by a chain of fatality, and which, as it were, exclude man from the history of mankind . . . I believe . . . that many important historical facts can only be accounted for by accidental circumstances and that many others remain inexplicable.

Alexis de Tocqueville

Contents

Introduction:
On Trying to Understand
the French Revolution

THE subject of this book is one of the great tragedies of modern times. In the spring of 1789 a considerable number of French people, perhaps even the majority of the population, were convinced that they had entered a new and better age. Even those who had profited from the privileges, anomalies and inequalities of the old order seemed ready to abandon them in order to create a brave new world. From the bleak and cynical viewpoint of our own times, it may be difficult to take these professions at their face value, but those who dismiss them as insincere will never begin to understand the French revolution. What was at issue was much more than a matter of politics: it involved the belief that an entire society was being regenerated and that the millennium had already begun. An intelligent middle-aged nobleman, the marquis de Ferrières, who had been elected to the Estates General, wrote to his wife about the religious ceremony that inaugurated its session,

I had not realized the extent of the common bond that links us with the soil, with men who are our brothers; I learned it at that moment. I take this oath: beloved France, where I was born, where I spent the happy days of my youth, where my moral life took shape, constant source of all that I have felt in the course of my existence, never will I betray the honourable trust of those who confided your interests to my hands; never shall my judgement or my will be determined by anything but the common good.[1]

Even the savage and sanguinary Marat, in the only optimistic pamphlet that he ever wrote, caught the general mood of concord and optimism: 'Blessed be the best of kings. Hope is born again in our hearts . . . Let priests and nobles continue to enjoy their honourable distinctions, but let all the Orders of the state draw together.'[2] The journalist Brissot, recently returned from the

---

[1] *Correspondance inédite*, ed. H. Carré (Paris, 1932), p. 43.
[2] *Offrande à la patrie*, in C. Vellay, *Les Pamphlets de Marat* (Paris, 1911), p. 21.

United States, was less convinced of the universal harmony but equally optimistic:

I had scarcely left you ten months, to cross the Atlantic, and you have changed beyond recognition; you have crossed an immense gap. You were languishing in slavery and now you are free . . . The debasement and ignorance of the people are merely the accidental products of bad government which will gradually disappear under a free regime. It follows that the idea that a people cannot be regenerated is not true.[3]

It was not merely a question of how people felt but of what they wanted to do. If, in 1788, one had asked the protagonists who were soon to be fighting each other so fiercely to describe their hopes for the future, their responses would have been remarkably similar. Almost all of them believed that sovereignty belonged, in some sense, to the people as a whole. They wanted to replace the nominally absolutist regime by a constitutional monarchy and they believed themselves very lucky to have 'the best of kings' on the throne. The great majority of those with fiscal privileges were resigned to giving them up, even if they disagreed about how far social equality ought to go. All of those who were to exercise any kind of political power in the coming years thought property to be sacred, even if they were not unanimous about how far rights and privileges should be held to be forms of property. They were all agreed about civil liberties: freedom of speech and of the press and habeas corpus, although some of the clergy had reservations about freedom of religion. Everyone took it for granted that a reformed Roman Catholic Church would continue to preside over the spiritual welfare of the nation. They were, in other words, rather more in agreement about what should be done than the rival wings within most present-day political parties.

Throughout the western world, what was happening in France in that miraculous summer of 1789 seemed a triumph for humanity as a whole. The British Ambassador in Paris reported to his government, 'The greatest revolution that we know anything of has been effected with, comparatively speaking, if the magnitude of the event is considered, the loss of very few lives: from this moment we may consider France as a free country.'[4] The House of Commons proposed to the Lords 'a day of thanksgiving for the French Revolution'.[5] In far away Koenigsberg the philosopher Kant broke the habit of a lifetime and abandoned his afternoon walk to read about the taking of the Bastille.

Two years later these same Frenchmen were at each other's throats and the country was heading for civil war and the Terror; Burke was preaching a crusade against what he saw as a threat to civilization and Europe had taken the

---

[3] *Plan de conduite pour les députés du peuple aux Etats-Généraux de 1789* (n.p., 1789), pp. i, vi.

[4] *Despatches from Paris*, ed. O. Browning (London, 1910), 2 vols, II/243.

[5] I am indebted for this information to my friend, Dr John Addy.

first steps towards a war that was to last for twenty years and to spread destruction from Portugal to Moscow.

I should like to know why. This book is a search for an answer. If I could discover an explanation, it might tell us about much more than the French revolution.

The first step in any such inquiry is to test one's initial assumptions. It becomes clear at once that my picture of universal euphoria is over-simplified. From the second half of 1788 onwards there was a shrill outcry against what people were beginning to refer to as the 'privileged Orders', in other words, the nobility and the clergy. In the most famous of all the pamphlets published at the time, *What is the Third Estate?* the abbé Sieyès wrote that 'One is obliged to consider the privileged class in a nation as one would some horrible disease eating the living flesh on the body of some unfortunate man.'[6] This is a far cry from Marat's appeal for national unity and I seem to have been exposed in the elementary mistake of basing my argument for a general consensus on the selection of such bits of the evidence as happened to confirm my own prejudices. That may be true, but things are not so simple.

A few months before he wrote *What is the Third Estate?*, in the late summer of 1788, Sieyès had published another pamphlet, *Views on the Means available to the representatives of France in 1789*. This contains some political theory and a sketch of how the Estates General ought to conduct itself – and not a word of criticism of the clergy or nobility. When he re-edited this pamphlet, Sieyès was somewhat embarrassed by his total omission of what he was later to present as the central issue. Rather disingenuously, he wrote that his first work 'contains nothing about the unfortunate discussions (*sic*) that have *since* (my italics) arisen between the orders'.[7] In between the two he produced an *Essay on privileges*, that included a relatively measured criticism of the clergy and nobility. When he re-edited *this*, he sharpened the attack quite considerably. In other words, Burke could have been right when he argued in his *Reflections on the Revolution in France* that the attack on the nobility was a put-up job that was invented as a matter of political tactics. The initial consensus had been there but it had been broken by men who hoped to make capital out of discord.

If one tries to test this new hypothesis, there is little evidence for any general hostility towards the 'privileged Orders' before the late summer of 1788. After that there is a good deal. One can explain this in one of two ways: either the lack of evidence means that there was a lack of animosity, or the vehemence of 1789 reveals the existence of feelings that had had to be bottled up for a long time. Each argument strikes me as about equally plausible – and equally incapable of proof or refutation. One's preference is liable to be determined by reasons that have very little to do with the French revolution. This is not very helpful.

---

6 ed. P. Campbell (London, 1963), p. 164.
7 *Collection des ecrits: edition à l'usage de l'Allemagne* (Paris, n.d.), p. 4.

We have stumbled up against the basic dilemma in all historical explanation. One cannot leave it to the evidence to oblige us by explaining itself. Much of it was never recorded or has since disappeared and the quantity of what survives and could perhaps be relevant is too great for anyone to assimilate. The computer offers no way out of this difficulty since one would have to feed it with inferences and interpretations and it could only repeat, in a deceptively objective-looking way, the subjective lessons that one had taught it. Where the reader, rather than the historian, is concerned, things are even more unsatisfactory since he or she cannot even know what the writer has chosen to omit as implausible or irrelevant.

If one steers away from the Scylla of empiricism one encounters an even more hazardous Charybdis. If one could set out with a knowledge of the laws that regulate historical processes, one could hope to penetrate beneath the surface confusion of events and reveal the underlying forces that made things happen in the way they did, to X-ray the French revolution, so to speak, and bring to light an inner structure of which the participants themselves were unaware. This is more of a hazard to navigation than Scylla. A philosophy of history has to come from somewhere and if it does not originate in the evidence it presumably rests on some kind of act of faith. It may be spendid but it is only one way of looking at things and the past is littered with the wrecks of too many discarded theories to offer much ground for the belief that a new one will fare any better. Besides, the people who make history have one important advantage over those who write it: when they changed their minds, things took a different course. When the historian changes his, they don't. A writer who is wedded to his theory cannot offer his characters much scope to tamper with it. If the theory is to make sense it cannot allow much room for 'Chance, kings and desperate men'; the end must be implicit in the beginning. There is, of course, an obvious sense in which one thing led to another but to assume that it could not have led anywhere else is to opt for a degree of determinism in the past that we would never admit in our own lives.

When Alfred Cobban wrote his *Social Interpretation of the French Revolution*, he amused himself in a couple of brilliant introductory chapters by demonstrating the absurdity of both the empirical and what he saw as the sociological approaches to history. This left him without any third leg to stand on, unless one opts for the Macbeth theory of history as a 'tale told by an idiot, full of sound and fury, signifying nothing'. This may be true, but it is discouraging.

What then is one to do and what kind of credentials can I offer my readers? They are at least entitled to know the principles on which this book has been constructed. It seems to me that public affairs are usually regulated by the interplay of three interacting forces: the pursuit of material self-interest by individuals or groups; the realization of systems of belief that may, but need not be, religious; and the provision of solutions to political problems, which includes the pursuit of political power. These factors are usually present in any historical situation, although one or another may predominate at any particular time. They continually interact with each other and I see no reason for supposing that any one of them plays a basic role, in the sense of determining the operation of the other two.

What I have done has therefore been to look at what seemed the most important evidence and try to interpret it in terms of the play of these three forces. Right or wrong, that sounds fairly straightforward. In fact, the technical problems are formidable. My method implies putting a good deal of emphasis on conscious human motivation, which implies that we are in a position to find out what this was. This is less easy than one might think.

If one reads Mirabeau's speeches (which, to complicate matters, were usually written for him by other people), one gets the impression that he saw the French revolution in essentially constitutional terms and that his main concern was to establish the right balance between the power of the king and that of the assembly. If one turns to his correspondence, it looks as though what really mattered to him was to outsmart his rivals and to persuade the king and queen that he was actually earning the considerable reward they had promised him. His contemporaries, well aware of the public evidence and suspicious of the private, could never make up their minds about where he actually stood. The historian, with access to more of the evidence, is tempted to wonder whether Mirabeau himself knew. Juggling with so much intrigue and equivocation, telling each man what he wanted him to believe that he thought, keeping everyone in play and all his options open, he may have ended up unable to distinguish between subterfuge and purpose. Mirabeau is, admittedly, an extreme case, but when other people made speeches or wrote pamphlets they were more concerned to persuade and convert than to behave as though they were in some kind of a political confessional.

A second problem is more general. As I read the reports of debates in the Assembly I realized that, to understand them properly, one had to follow them day by day. The deputies might be taking up again the discussion of a subject that they had begun to consider days or weeks before, and in one sense the new debate was a continuation of the old. Its outcome, however, was liable to be affected by what had happened in the meantime, perhaps by a violent dispute over an entirely different matter or the receipt of news from Paris or the provinces. Thirsty for synthesis, the historian who divides everything into topics is liable to miss the many-splendoured thing. If, on the other hand, he has the patience and ability to take in the whole picture and to keep it all in perspective, he cannot expect anyone to follow him through volume after volume. If I had put it all in, the reader might reasonably have complained that I was making him or her do my job for me.

My attempt to escape from this particular dilemma explains the structure of the book. At the beginning and the end of the period the flow of events was of prime importance. If one does not follow the sequence one cannot make much sense of what was going on. These chapters are therefore treated chronologically. By the autumn of 1789 the way had been cleared for the Assembly to set about the reconstruction of most of France's institutions. This seemed to call for a pause, in which I could survey the consequences of class conflict, ideology and politics over the period as a whole. To illustrate the practical results of this, I have selected two areas for more specialized treatment: foreign policy and religion. Various others might have been chosen, such as local government, the law or finance, but since my objective was to explain the breakdown of consensus rather than to write the history of the Assembly, these two seemed sufficient for my purpose.

I chose to centre the book round the Constituent Assembly, which sat (originally as the Estates General) from May 1789 to September 1791. This was the body that took the decisions that remade France. There was, of course, a world outside the Assembly that influenced – sometimes deliberately – what went on within it, but much of what happened outside was either a response to the actions of the Assembly or an attempt to persuade or intimidate it. If there is any answer to the question of why France tore itself apart, this is where it must be sought. Limiting the book to the period of the Constituent Assembly involves stopping in the autumn of 1791 when the war and the Terror lay in an avoidable future. By that time, however, most of the constructive work of the revolution had been done and the attempt to do it by compromise and consensus had already failed.

Since I hope that what I have to say will be of interest to people with little or no previous knowledge of the French revolution, I have tried to take as little as possible for granted. This involves explaining, especially in the introductory chapters, what will already be familiar to some readers. I hope they will be patient and perhaps find enough that is new or unexpected to sustain their interest. My main concern has been that others should not be unnecessarily confused by my forgetting to tell them what they could not be expected to know in advance. Things are quite difficult enough as it is.

The book incorporates the substance of the Sir D. Owen Evans Memorial Lectures, delivered at the University College of Wales, Aberystwyth, during the session 1986 to 1987.

1

The State of the Nation

THE ways in which most educated Frenchmen in the late eighteenth century thought about the relationships between man, nature and society were largely determined by the intellectual movement known as the Enlightenment. This rested on two main assumptions: that all ideas were the result of the mental processing of information derived from the senses, and that the methods of empirical science could allow men to apprehend the laws that regulated all phenomena, from the orbits of the planets to the functioning of human societies. Both of these beliefs were startling novelties when they became generally accepted in the late seventeenth and early eighteenth centuries. The first of them, at least by implication, disposed of Original Sin, together with the belief that ideas were innate and to some extent divinely inspired. If all ideas, including moral principles, were rational conclusions drawn from exposure to similar experiences, it would follow that, as Lord Chesterfield put it, 'the same matter occurs equally to everybody of common sense'. Whatever departed from this general consensus was to be explained as the product of over-hasty jumping to conclusions or to peculiarities of individual experience that led people to draw rational but erroneous conclusions on the basis of insufficient evidence. Originality and enthusiasm were both suspect. Reasonable men ought not to disagree. Evil, from this perspective, was to be explained as the product of exposure to the wrong sensations, or in other words, to a defective social environment. In a properly regulated society the esteem conferred on socially useful behaviour would incline all rational people to find their personal fulfilment in the pursuit of the common interest. At least until the middle of the eighteenth century, the most spectacular triumphs of the scientists had been in physics. This probably encouraged people to assume that scientific laws related to static situations, that they were explanations of how things worked and not of how they changed. A more general inference from the scientific model was the belief that all problems were soluble, at least in theory, and that if one solution was correct, all the others must be wrong.

This is not to suggest, of course, that all educated Frenchmen thought in the same way. Helvétius, who had not much use for 'sensible people, those idols of the mediocre', pioneered what was to become the Romantic concept of the unrecognized genius. Diderot's restless and inquisitive mind responded to the findings and speculations of the biologists, which were already pointing in the direction of evolution. Rousseau rejected the whole basis of Enlightened rationalism for intuition and reliance on conscience as a truer guide than reason. All of them, however, were affected, consciously or not, by the prevailing orthodoxy and they incorporated some of its assumptions into their own systems. Their works shaped the minds of most of the future revolutionaries. Other people still clung to older ideas and continued to see the world in terms suggested to them by the Church. The historian has to beware of his tendency to isolate as especially significant those elements of one age that were to become characteristic of the next. Despite such reservations, when men spoke or wrote about politics during the French revolution they shared common assumptions that derived from the Enlightenment.

With the benefit of hindsight it is easy to see that many of the new creeds were undermining the foundations of the official order. They left no room for belief in divine sanction behind authority of any kind. Few people were atheists but the majority of the educated, whether still nominally Christian or not, conceived of God in increasingly abstract terms as a First Cause who had created the universe but left it to its own devices. Similarly discredited was the idea that tradition conferred authority, that things should go on being done in traditional ways. It was only too easy for the critics to point to discredited 'scientific' beliefs and superstitious practices like the burning of witches. Indeed those who were dissatisfied with the status quo were inclined to believe that whatever was traditional was out of date in an Enlightened century. If political authority was sanctified neither by God nor by precedent all it had to fall back on was utility. Its legitimacy therefore depended on its ability to provide satisfaction. Thanks to the emerging social sciences of economics and sociology, it looked as though it should be possible to work out the right way to make the most of the possibilities inherent in any situation. Inefficiency, corruption, economic recession or widespread crime were therefore proof that the government was not doing its job properly. This was heady stuff and the absence of a free press or any representative institutions meant that such issues had to be debated more or less surreptitiously and in a political void. None of the writers risked having his ideas put to the practical test and Frenchmen - unlike their rivals across the Channel - were not exposed to the chastening parliamentary experience of getting rid of Tweedledum only to find that Tweedledee was not much better. This made for optimistic theorizing, and the assumption that everything, or almost everything, was remediable made people impatient with what had not been remedied.

When the question at issue was how states should be governed, virtually all the revolutionary generation turned for guidance to Montesquieu and

Rousseau.[1] What concerns us here is not what these authors intended, which, especially in the case of Rousseau, is still hotly contested, but what the men of 1789 understood them to have meant. Montesquieu's major work, *The Spirit of the Laws*, was published in 1748. It began as a treatise on comparative government, comparing the institutions appropriate to republics, monarchies and despotisms. For the first of these Montesquieu turned to classical Greece and Rome, seeing the ancient polis as animated by the *vertu* of its citizens, by which he meant their readiness to seek self-fulfilment in total dedication to the welfare of the community. Montesquieu implied that such behaviour was morally good and the republic therefore rested on a moral foundation that made it superior to every other kind of state. Despite the help of institutions designed to foster the idea of public service, the practice of *vertu* involved the continual subordination of inclination to duty and the republic therefore rested on the continuing triumph of will and principle over convenience. It was, in other words, if not too good to be true, too demanding to be relevant to the Europe of his day. One gets the impression that Montesquieu abandoned his republics with some reluctance and his idealized picture of Athens, Sparta and early Rome reinforced, if it did not initiate, a cult of the republican virtues. Despotism he wrote off from the start as the negation of civilized government. That left monarchy, a practicable rather than an exemplary form of government. Its main weakness was the inclination of kings to become despots. This was countered, not by any opposing moral principle but by the sense of honour natural to the nobility. Montesquieu insisted that this had no moral foundation but amounted to a bizarre collection of prejudices perpetuated by aristocratic breeding, which was supposed to make nobles *prefer* death to dishonour. Since, in one of its senses, honour was conferred by the king, he could buy service cheaply in return for medals, decorations or honorary titles – but it was service on the nobility's terms and not on his own. Their obedience was conditional on the king's acceptance of the proper limits to his own authority. To be effective, restraint by the nobility was best exercised by powerful corporate bodies, such as the provincial Estates or sovereign courts of appeal, known as Parlements, whose judges had bought their offices and could therefore not be removed by the king. This was, of course, exactly what the Parlements and the few provincial Estates that survived in France wanted to hear, since it cast a glorious cloak of constitutional principle over resistance to the king that might otherwise have looked like naked self-interest. Until the convocation of the Estates General in 1789, these bodies, together with the Assembly General of the Clergy, were the only sources of constitutional opposition. During the political crisis of 1788 the pamphlets by which their members whipped up each other's enthusiasm resounded with invocations of *The Spirit of the Laws*. In 1789 this aristocratic offensive gave way to a very different political conflict and the whole argument became irrelevant.

[1] On this subject, see N. Hampson, *Will and Circumstance: Montesquieu, Rousseau and the French Revolution* (London, 1983).

This by no means disposed of Montesquieu who, after serving the purposes of the nobility, went on to become the hero of radical revolutionaries like Brissot and Marat. In Book XI of *The Spirit of the Laws*, when he came to deal with the question of liberty, Montesquieu gave up the attempt at neutrality and brought forward an entirely different theory of government, which he mistakenly believed to be exemplified in England. As he developed this in the rest of his work it came to rest upon the belief that attitudes and principles were largely the product of environmental conditioning by social, religious, economic and geographical factors. These diverse and interacting forces were partly external to society and partly the product of its previous decisions. Individuals therefore differed not merely in their material interests but in their beliefs. For him, the sum of these divergences constituted the 'general spirit' of a society. The function of government was to reflect them and to hold them in balance. To achieve this, each had to be given political representation within a constitution whose constituent parts held each other in check. He imagined this to be the case in England, with the Commons representing the numerical mass of the people and the Lords defending the interests of birth and property. Each restrained the other and both united to frustrate any despotic intentions on the part of the king. The right of everyone to trial by an independent jury protected the individual from any unholy alliance of executive and legislature. Rightly or wrongly, he was thought to have argued that the different powers within a constitution must be kept wholly separate from each other.

Montesquieu's fascinated sense of the complexity of things made him reluctant to sacrifice insight to consistency and he was never quite clear about whether governments should conform to what they perceived to be the general spirit of their peoples or whether they should try to counter an unfavourable environment by institutions that inclined people in an opposite direction. His general preference for relativism coexisted uneasily with his commitment to certain absolute values: freedom, justice and a tolerable standard of living for all. Despite his obscurities and contradictions, when Frenchmen in 1789 thought about constitutions they did so in the terms that he had taught them. Whatever circumstances might oblige them to practise, the revolutionaries believed in the separation of the powers. When they invoked the example of England, as the more moderate were much given to doing, as a warning against going to theoretical extremes, it was Montesquieu's England that they had in mind. Only at the height of the Terror, in 1794, did Robespierre challenge him, and even then in a way that suggested a certain uneasiness. Saint-Just, another radical, wrote that he was endlessly finding new reasons to 'obey' him. Brissot wanted a statue erected to him and Marat, who had written a eulogy of him in 1785, regretted six years later that he was not still alive to be tutor to the Dauphin. For almost everyone he was the man who had explained how constitutions worked. Some of them understood his warnings about what was liable to happen when they did not.

If men were convinced by Montesquieu, they were converted by Rousseau. Both writers saw liberty as the objective of politics but Rousseau's temperament was religious where Montesquieu's was secular. For Rousseau man had once lived in a state of primitive grace. His Fall was due to the quest, not for knowledge, but for material progress. This had given rise to civil society, inequality and the corruption of man's natural goodness by meretricious social pressures that estranged him from his true nature. This looked backward towards the Enlghtenment's belief that values were socially conditioned and forward in the direction of Marx's vision of the ideal society. What false social values had destroyed, true ones could restore, although Rousseau was very pessimistic about the chances of corrupted men being willing to effect their own regeneration. Redemption could come only from society but its objective and the safeguard for its continuing was the inner transformation of individuals. Rousseau's conception of freedom was a secularized version of Christian doctrine: it consisted in man's willing self-surrender to a higher power, in the service of which the individual would realize his full potentiality. In other words, if men could be persuaded to seek self-fulfilment in total dedication to the welfare of their communities, all that they would have to abandon was what was selfish or meretricious in their present lives (the world, the flesh and the devil) and they would then be free to live in accordance with their true natures. The problem, of course, was to persuade corrupted men to will their own redemption, which called for the intervention of a kind of superman, the Legislator, who would understand what was needed and have the moral authority to induce people to accept the institutions that would condition them to tread in the paths that they were helpless to follow of their own accord. As examples of the kind of men he had in mind he quoted Moses, Mahomet and Calvin.

Most of his readers were probably unaware of all the implications of this secularized religion; a good many of them still are. They responded to Rousseau as a preacher. His hypnotic prose was totally unlike the rational clarities of Montesquieu. Even those who never read his political works could sense his message from his other writings. Within the space of a couple of years, in 1761-2 he published a best-selling novel, the *Nouvelle Héloïse*, an educational classic, *Emile* and a fundamental work on political theory, the *Social Contract*. In the process he transformed the perceptions of a generation and it would scarcely be exaggerating to describe most of the revolutionary leaders as 'born-again Rousseauists'. It was the cumulative impact of his works that mattered. Brissot was converted to deism by *Emile*. His future political ally, Madame Roland, found in the *Nouvelle Héloïse* a liberation from what, in her precocious adolescence, she had come to regard as the sterility of the Enlightenment. Robespierre, although he had been familiar with some of Rousseau's works before then, seems to have been swept off his feet by the publication of the *Confessions*, just before the revolution began. Whereas Montesquieu gave people new ideas about government, Rousseau made them feel differently about themselves and society. In the process they may well have misunderstood his political message. In some respects, perhaps in essentials, he was a conservative and a traditionalist. His novel suggested that he had a good deal of sympathy for a paternalist and pastoral society. He was certainly no revolutionary, especially where France was concerned, and his *Social Contract* was written with his native city-state of Geneva in mind. He denounced the kind of representative government that was practised in England as a sort of elective dictatorship. He was almost equally critical of the Athenian type of direct democracy and his personal preference was for an elective aristocracy. Superficially, this might look rather like the British Parliament. The essential difference for Rousseau lay in the location of sovereignty, which resided in the general will of the nation as a whole and not in any of its institutions. This was all very well in theory. When practical politicians tried to follow Rousseau, they had to locate the general will rather more positively. The more radical used his theories to argue that popular sovereignty was inalienable and a people that believed itself to be misgoverned was always entitled to revolt. This tended to appeal more to those in opposition than to those in office. The more moderate or ministerial maintained that, by the process of election, the mass of the population transferred the exercise of its sovereignty to its representatives – which was precisely what Rousseau had denounced in the case of England.

The first lesson that Rousseau's devotees learned from him was to despise the society in which they lived as false, unjust and morally rotten. This offered more consolation to the discontented than the Enlightened view of the eighteenth century as well advanced on the road from medieval obscurantism towards a brighter future. Politics must therefore be primarily concerned with 'regeneration', the most over-worked word of 1789. Rousseau, like other preachers, insisted that what mattered was the will to change: 'The limits of the possible, in moral matters, are less narrow than we think; we are confined by our own weakness, vice and prejudice.' This became easier to believe in 1789 when the old order was visibly collapsing and the inconceivable had actually happened. Regeneration implied radical change, inspired by an abstract conception of what the future ought to be, rather than the cautious adjustment of institutions to circumstances that had more appeal to men of Montesquieu's temperament.

Since, from Rousseau's point of view, what mattered about people was their moral stature rather than the size of their stake in a country conceived as a kind of joint-stock company, run by and for its shareholders, all adult males (Rousseau, like the future revolutionaries, was a furious anti-feminist) were equally entitled to a share in decision-making. One of the constituents of freedom for him was independence of others, which led him in his wilder moments to advocate a pastoral economy of agrarian self-sufficiency. His followers rarely went so far as that but they shared his idealization of peasant values and his curious belief that wealth for some implied poverty for others.

Both he and they were ambivalent about the status of private property, but inclined to take it for granted that the rich were suspect if not necessarily vicious. Both had their doubts about the very poor, who were corrupted by the loss of their independence, and they felt most confidence in the small independent producer who neither sold his own labour nor hired that of others.

Rousseau's insistence on locating sovereignty in the general will went much further than saying that governments ought to be responsible to public opinion. The general will was not what the majority thought they wanted but what was actually good for society as a whole. We are mercifully spared the need to entangle ourselves in the questions of how far this is a meaningful concept and how the general will is to be identified; for the men of 1789 it meant, in the first instance, that France was to be treated as an organic whole and not as a collection of semi-autonomous provinces or distinct social orders. In other words, there was a national interest which was morally as well as legally binding on everyone. This was sovereign in the sense that it took precedence over constitutional rules, international treaties or past practices. As Sieyès put it in *What is the Third Estate?*, 'A nation is independent of any procedures; no matter how it exercises its will, the mere fact of its doing so puts an end to positive law.'[2] To allow this general will to emerge, no local foci of political loyalty - provinces, assemblies of the clergy or political parties - could be tolerated since they would become centres of sectional interest. Once the general will was known, in relation to any particular issue, those who had initially advocated different policies must acknowledge their mistake and not merely comply with the verdict as legally binding but adopt it as their own. Debate was legitimate, indeed necessary, to enable the sovereign will to emerge; once it had done so, opposition was not. The general will, Rousseau had said, 'by the mere fact of its existence, is always what it ought to be'. He himself had probably believed it to manifest itself in terms of a few basic decisions of principle concerning the organization of society. His followers were inclined to extend its empire to include any resolutions of the national legislative body. Anyone who persisted in resisting it must, as Rousseau had explained, be 'forced to be free', for his own good. Since the general will was what was actually best for the community, whether its members appreciated this or not, it was not necessarily the same thing as the result of a majority vote. What this tended to mean in practice was that politicians in opposition denounced the government as illegitimate since it did not reflect public opinion; once in office themselves, they became more appreciative of the need to educate the public about what its true interests really were.

One could argue that British politicians who have never read Rousseau have been known to think along similar lines, but this would not actually be true of the great majority of them. Her Majesty pays the leader of her opposition and no prime minister expects the other parties to disband when they lose an election. Whatever the posturing, politics in England is seen as offering the

2 ed. P. Campbell, (London, 1963), p. 128.

public a choice between legitimate alternatives. Whatever governments like to pretend about their monopoly of virtue and wisdom, the electorate makes a hard-headed attempt to decide which of the groups competing for its favours will prove the least incompetent. Superficially, the Constituent Assembly looked more like the British House of Commons than anything that existed elsewhere in contemporary Europe, but the real differences of attitude behind the similarities of procedure were deep and decisive, and they derived to a great extent from Rousseau.

SOCIETY

France is a much bigger country than the United Kingdom and in the eighteenth century the effect of geography was accentuated by poor communications, at a time when the cheap transport of goods in bulk was only possible by sea. The range of climates in France is also much greater, which meant a more diversified agriculture. Much land was given over to wine-growing and the South formed part of a Mediterranean economy that had little in common with the cereal-growing North-East. History had reinforced geography, in the sense that the lands ruled by the French kings were less unified than England in 1789. Mirabeau and Robespierre, in their electoral literature, referred to their 'nations' as Provence and Artois, and the French provinces differed so widely from each other in every respect that generalizations about the country as a whole are almost bound to be misleading.

Like the rest of Europe, France was an overwhelmingly agrarian country, with something like 85 per cent of the population living in villages and scattered hamlets and making a living from the land.[3] The harvest was the regulator of the entire economy: poor crops meant a shortage of work for casual labourers and when peasants had less to spend on clothes there was a slump in the textile industry. The result was an increase in vagrancy, food rioting and banditry. Mass starvation was a thing of the past, which meant that the population had risen steadily during the eighteenth century until it stood at about 26 million. The country was therefore bulging at the seams. Since there had been no corresponding increase in agricultural productivity and virtually all cultivable land was actually being cultivated, life was getting more difficult for the poor. A contemporary British observer, Arthur Young, found much of France similar to Ireland. Even in good years, millions depended on charity to stay alive. There was no equivalent of the British Poor Law and survival was the result of a precarious victory for abstinence, hard work, desperate ingenuity, good luck and, when necessary, occasional crime.

In such a society wealth tended to correspond to land ownership. Conditions varied so much that national figures make little local sense but in a general sort

[3] See W. Doyle, *Origins of the French Revolution* (Oxford, 1980), chs 6, 7, 9 and 12, and P. Goubert and D. Roche, *Les Français et l'Ancien Régime* (Paris, 1984), 2 vols, II/295-339.

of way one can think of the nobility and the urban middle classes owning about 30 per cent each with the clergy in possession of about half as much. France was unusual if not unique in Europe in the sense that the peasantry owned perhaps as much as a quarter of the land. The term, of course, is not very meaningful since it takes in everyone from the yeoman to the cottager, but the widespread ownership of small parcels of soil was enough to prevent the kind of agricultural improvements, based on enclosure, that were gradually transforming British farming. Much of the best cornland consisted of open fields in which individuals owned scattered strips. Substantial landowners could therefore not enclose unless holdings could be consolidated. This could not be done by consent and there was no French equivalent to the Enclosure Acts - perhaps because France did not have a parliament controlled by landowners. Smallholders retained their land but agricultural productivity was probably not much more than half that of England.

Most of what industry there was took place in the countryside. It tended to be small-scale and backward in its techniques. British textile machinery was beginning to be imported, but not to any significant extent, and iron was still smelted by charcoal rather than by coke. Heavy industry - mining, quarrying and iron-smelting - was more a branch of estate management than an autonomous economic activity. Much of it was conducted by the nobility, who owned many of the forests and mineral deposits.[4] With occasional local exceptions, most of French industry was therefore scattered, domestic and important mainly as a supplement to agriculture.

Towns were mostly clerical or administrative centres, dependent for their prosperity on a cathedral or important law court, which provided them with their wealthiest citizens and main sources of employment. They were not very dynamic places: a royal official in Angers reported in 1783, 'The present generation vegetates just as that which preceded it vegetated and the succeeding one will vegetate.' To this there was one striking exception: the ports, especially those on the Atlantic coast. Bordeaux in particular had grown spectacularly in the eighteenth century. Its merchant princes built themselves the sort of palaces that few nobles could emulate. It had its own opera and Arthur Young exclaimed that Liverpool was nothing in comparison. Much of this wealth was founded on transporting slaves to the French colonies in the West Indies, which was beginning to pose a problem. Some of the writers of the Enlightenment who, on other grounds, had much to attract enterprising and secular-minded merchants, had damned the slave trade as inhuman. This was especially true of the local hero, Montesquieu. Just before the revolution a society of *Amis des Noirs* was founded in Paris to campaign against slavery and the slave trade.

Like any other country, France had an economic structure in which some people owned the means of production - land, ships, machines etc. - and others

---

[4] See G. Chaussinand-Nogaret, *The Nobility in Eighteenth-century France* (Eng. trans., London, 1985), ch. 5.

worked for wages, at least for part of their time. This generated particular attitudes, vested interests and frictions. As a result of the increase in population, wages had gone up less than prices and prices less than rents. This implied a squeeze on the less prosperous, probably a tendency for land ownership to become more concentrated, and an increase in tension all round. The relative prosperity of the middle years of the century had been interrupted, about the time of the accession of Louis XVI in 1774, by poorer harvests, epidemics of animal disease and over-production of wine. The sluggishness of the economy may have been reinforced by the fact that massive borrowing by the government kept interest rates very high, but with little fixed capital or incentive to invest, this may not have made much difference.

On this economic foundation rested a society based in theory, and to some extent in fact, on older and quite different assumptions. Traditionally, society was conceived as divided into three Orders: clergy, nobility and commoners, differentiated by birth or, in the case of the clergy, by vocation. Men, in other words, were created *un*equal. Nobles, as Montesquieu had explained in the first part of *Spirit of the Laws*, regulated their lives in accordance with principles of honour peculiar to themselves. Within such a society status was determined by length of lineage and proximity to the king, rather than by the extent of one's wealth or possessions. Honour implied hierarchy and at the top of the social tree was the Court nobility, restricted in theory to those who could prove that their noble ancestry dated back before 1400 and in fact to such of the ancient families as could afford the high cost of living at Versailles. The second tier of the nobility, at least in terms of political importance and in their own estimation, comprised the legal and administrative nobles, especially the judges in the Parlements. They could sometimes, boast of a lineage as ancient as that of the Court nobility but their influence was less personal and more an expression of the corporate strength of the institutions to which they belonged. The majority of the nobles had probably never seen Versailles, except perhaps as tourists, and belonged to no powerful corporations. They lived in the country or in provincial towns, served in minor offices or in the lower commissioned ranks of the army, or cultivated their estates.[5]

In the distant past the nobility had exercised a good deal of public authority in return for which they had been given – or had helped themselves to – rights of a semi-public kind. By the eighteenth century the French kings had deprived them of their powers while leaving most of their privileges intact. These were of many kinds. They could be 'useful', such as exemption from some forms of taxation, or purely honorific, such as the right of duchesses to be seated at Court or a seigneurial pew in a country church. The latter were none the less tenaciously held for bringing in no financial return: many people today would prefer a knighthood to a pension. The virtual monopoly of army commissions might almost be put in the honorific category since a military career was not

[5] For a study of the last category, see R. Forster, *The Nobility of Toulouse in the Eighteenth Century* (Baltimore, Md, 1960).

much of an investment, except to the Court nobility who received accelerated promotion. Seigneurial justice too was often more trouble than it was worth, at least as regards criminal cases. There were other seigneurial rights of a very different character, often associated with land ownership, but sometimes amounting to a kind of local sovereignty. These could include a monopoly of mill, oven and wine-press, all of which could be leased out for a useful income. The whole collection of rights and privileges was often described by contemporaries as 'feudal'. This was not strictly accurate, but what was good enough for them may conveniently serve for us.

Theoretically distinct, the economic and the 'feudal' societies coexisted, overlapped, combined and occasionally conflicted, to create a society unique in eighteenth-century Europe. Wealth in sufficient quantities had always been able to bend the 'feudal' rules. Those at the top needed it to sustain life at Court or to buy an important office (offices and army commissions all had to be bought) and those who had it found little trouble in providing noble husbands for their well-endowed daughters. Sons were a different matter since nobility descended on the male side. Seigneurial rights could be a means of acquiring wealth, as well as a source of social status. As always, conditions over the country varied from one extreme to the other: some nobles derived most of their income from seigneurial rights, others scarcely any. To some of those still occasionally described as 'vassals', manorial dues were a heavy burden; to others they hardly mattered. Conversely, wealth could be a means of acquiring seigneurial rights, since they were regarded as a form of property and could be bought by anyone with the means to do so. It was unusual but not rare for the seigneur to be a commoner. Local studies suggest that a proportion of about 15 per cent of non-noble seigneurs was fairly common. In a village where a commoner was one of the lords of the manor, renting land from one noble and leasing some to another while being himself the 'vassal' of a third, the relationship between the social and the economic could become rather confused.

The social values of 'feudal' society tended to be accepted by those whose day-to-day preoccupations were primarily economic. The most respectable forms of wealth were what the American historian G. V. Taylor has described as 'proprietory': land, office and annuities.[6] The professions conferred more status than trade, even when trade brought in more money: there were no merchants in the Bordeaux Academy. The ultimate objective of most successful commoners was to acquire nobility. There were various ways of doing this. If one had enough money, hereditary nobility could be purchased outright. There were also ennobling offices which conferred the much-desired status after a family had held the same office over three generations. France therefore contained a great many families who, at any time, were part way up

6 'Types of capitalism in eighteenth-century France', *English Historical Review*, 79 (1964) and 'Non-capitalist wealth and the origins of the French Revolution', *American Historical Review*, 72 (1967).

the ladder towards hereditary nobility. The claim of the nobility to genetic distinction was therefore a myth. If they had not recruited new members they would have become extinct. Most of them knew when their families had ceased to be commoners. The king had always ennobled men for distinguished service but in the eighteenth century most of those who took the escalator paid for the journey.

If one compares French society with British, the differences were often matters of definition rather than of substance. Everything tended to appear in sharper focus in France, as it still does, but the British were quite well aware of who was and who was not a gentleman and the gentry were treated very differently from other folk. In both countries promotion owed more to influence than to merit and all kinds of legal and social relationships took inequality of status for granted. What will perhaps never be known is whether France was evolving in the British direction, towards more fluidity and the gradual replacement of social by economic status or whether, within a more rigid and legalistic system, growing economic pressures were producing a closing of ranks and a hardening of arteries. A century of internal peace and invasive royal bureaucracy meant that French nobles were more likely to regard themselves as intellectuals than as warlords. In Parisian salons and provincial academies and cultural societies, nobles and commoners were mixing more. They often shared an attachment to the new values of the Enlightenment and they were becoming harder to distinguish from each other: until he decided to break with conventional society, Rousseau wore a sword. On the other hand, it has been argued that the nobility were closing the avenues to social promotion and that, as the demand for ennoblement rose and the supply of ennobling offices did not, and perhaps actually fell, the disappointed were increasingly inclined to challenge what they could not realistically aspire to join. On the whole this looks unlikely. If one considers some of the most radical of the future revolutionaries, Marat actually claimed to be noble and Brissot, Danton, Robespierre and Saint-Just all tinkered with their names to give them a rather more aristocratic appearance. The successful had often prospered by exploiting the innumerable privileges and anomalies of the *Ancien Régime*. Its critics were usually disappointed men of letters, maverick nobles or men like Marat who felt that their talent had been denied recognition by their envious inferiors. There were plenty of men like that in England too. Some of them might have enjoyed a revolution, but they did not get one.

This is not to suggest, of course, that there were no stresses within French society. That would indeed have made it unique. Court society was renowned for its interminable intrigue. It was not unknown for landlords and tenants to disagree about leases and seigneurs and 'vassals' about obligations, or employers and their workmen about wages. Some tensions were the result of economic relationships and some arose from the nature of 'feudal' society. Often the two were indistinguishable, as when villagers opposed a squire who was both seigneur and landlord. There was possibly a tendency for seigneurs to become more businesslike in exploiting their manorial rights, although if this was the case it was perhaps more likely to apply to those who had recently invested in manors than to those who gloried in their position as hereditary squires. Resistance to rapacious seigneurs did not call the social system into question: it was not until 1789 that riotous peasants were to burn manorial rolls. Peasant anger was, in any case, as likely to be directed against the miller or the bailiff as against the magnate. Granted the difficulty of publicizing social protest, it may be that the surviving evidence conceals the kind of generalized hostility towards 'feudalism' that was to erupt in 1789, but one cannot simply assume that this was the case. Especially where the middle classes and the towns were concerned, there are no serious grounds for assuming the existence of severe and intensifying social tensions that were building up towards a crisis. The social revolts that did occur look more like a consequence than a cause of the revolution.

What is quite clear is that a 'feudal' landed nobility did not find itself confronted by a class-conscious industrial and commercial bourgeoisie, contemptuous of aristocratic values and about to turn its economic superiority into political mastery. That would be false on just about every count. Revulsion against the artificiality of polite society, fanned by the new passion for sensibility, might burst out in social criticism: Madame Roland, the future revolutionary, when taken to Versailles as an adolescent, claims that she consoled herself with thoughts of classical republics. Marat had denounced the whole social order, but that was before he was appointed physician to the household troops of the king's brother and claimed noble ancestry. One could accumulate plenty of evidence to show that adolescents postured, journalists declaimed and the unsuccessful thought that it was all the fault of society. They may have become rather shriller and more numerous in the 1780s, but there was nothing in all this that would have cost a British magistrate much sleep and no suggestion that France was moving towards a major upheaval.

Things were rather different where the Church was concerned. In addition to its rents and seigneurial dues it levied tithes on most of the products of agriculture. Since tithes often went to support distant abbeys and produced no local benefit, they were frequently a source of bitter resentment. Where educated townsmen were concerned, the Enlightenment challenged a good deal of what the Church stood for and encouraged caustic contrasts between the wealth and worldliness of the clergy and the message of the Gospels. Celibacy was anathema to people obsessed with the idea of conforming to nature and worried - even if wrongly - about depopulation. To utilitarians, monasticism, at least in the case of the contemplative orders, looked like subsidized idleness and a threat to morals. Some of the criticism came from within the Church itself, either from parish priests increasingly resentful of their humiliation by the upper clergy or from Jansenists, Puritans who believed the Church to have been corrupted by loose living and lax doctrine.

The French clergy, the first Order of the state, formed an autonomous corporation. Self-financing and exempt from taxation, they made regular gifts to the Exchequer, which gave them a hold over the government. In addition to exercising a religious monopoly – it was not until 1787 that Protestants were officially tolerated – the Church controlled education, public health and organized charity besides acting as a kind of Ministry of Information, since the government's only form of nationwide publicity for its policies was to have them promulgated in the parish churches. The Assembly General of the Clergy, which regulated its affairs, was dominated by the bishops, all of whom were noble in 1789. There was therefore a considerable overlap between the spiritual and lay hierarchies and it is sometimes suggested that there were, in effect, only two Orders, the nobility and the commoners. This was to become a theme of revolutionary pamphleteers, but it was at best an over-simplification. As events were to show, the ultimate allegiance of the bishops was to canon law and one did not have to be noble to benefit from clerical privileges. An anonymous life of Sieyès – that enemy of the 'privileged Orders' – claims that he 'never preached and never heard a confession'. He was also said to have been free from 'every kind of superstitious idea and sentiment', whatever that was meant to imply.[7]

Like all the other institutions of the *Ancien Régime*, the Church was involved in a complex system of political relationships. Its bishops had all been appointed by the king, which did not stop them from opposing royal policy whenever they felt like it. They were nevertheless dependent on the civil power to enforce their decisions and to suppress blasphemous or anti-clerical writings. Despite being composed of nobles, the Assembly of the Clergy, as a corporate body with that excessive *esprit de corps* that was the plague of the *Ancien Régime*, was frequently at odds with Parlements and provincial Estates. Alternatively, it might ally with them to challenge the royal government. The upper clergy regarded themselves and were regarded by others as distinct from the lay nobility, many of whom were more aggressively anti-clerical than the great majority of commoners.

What was not obvious at the time was the dangerous gap that had opened up between the Church as an institution and public opinion, especially in the towns, but also in parts of the countryside where religious indifference, if not actual incredulity, was widespread. Elsewhere, particularly in western France, religion of a sort took precedence over almost everything else, sometimes to the embarrassment of parish priests to whom its rituals, pilgrimages and sacred sites smacked of superstition. Educated men agreed about the need for religious instruction, whether to recall all men to their moral duties or to discipline those too ignorant to regulate their behaviour by rational principle. They were sympathetically disposed towards the parish clergy, but on their own terms. What they wanted was what they were to describe during the revolution as

7 Anonymous, *Notice sur la vie de Sieyès* (Switzerland/London, 1795), pp. 15-16.

'officers of morality'. How far this conception of the role of the parish priest was compatible with his own view of his function, time was to show.

The Church therefore found itself in a very vulnerable situation, retaining and even flaunting the benefits derived from former piety in a secular-minded age that rejected many of its assumptions. Even those who accepted its dogma were increasingly resentful of what happened to the tithes they paid. This was all the more serious since the Church was the only really national institution. In secular matters Frenchmen belonged to provinces, towns and corporations, each with its separate identity and sectional interests. From the government's point of view they were all subjects of the king, but they never met each other in order to transact public business, except under the thumb of royal officials. There were, as always, partial exceptions to this: in the Breton Estates, for example, clergy and nobility exercised some effective authority, but although they spoke for the province, they represented only themselves. In the Estates of Artois the representatives of the commoners were chosen by the other two Orders. If the Church lost its moral authority, all that was left to hold the country together was the royal bureaucracy. For this dangerous situation the responsibility lay with the monarchy.

POLITICS

In politics, as in society, new ways had been superimposed on the surviving practices of an older order of things. Traditionally, the great magnates had regarded the king as their leader, in some sense God's chosen ruler, to whom they owned service and to whom they were both obliged and entitled to offer counsel. He ruled over possessions, acquired by inheritance, marriage or conquest, that were united only by their allegiance to him, which had sometimes been granted on written conditions. As late as 1788 the Rennes bar argued that even a law voted by the Estates General was applicable to Brittany only if endorsed by the local Estates.[8] The same argument was put forward in Normandy, which had lost its autonomy centuries before the revolution. Norman lawyers claimed that the province's treaty of association with France 'has all the characteristics of the social contract of the Normans.[9] From the traditionalist point of view, although the king's will was law, he was morally bound to rule in accordance with custom, and all laws had to be registered in the Parlements, which were entitled to remonstrate against them.

By the seventeenth century such ideas had been largely superseded by the development of a new kind of bureaucratic absolutism. The king chose his own advisers. Most of the provincial Estates disappeared; Parlements were

[8] *Très-humbles et très-respectueuses représentations de l'Ordre des Avocats au Parlement de Bretagne au Roi* (Rennes, 1788).

[9] *Extrait des respectueuses représentations à Monseigneur le Garde des Sceaux des Officiers du Bailliage d'Orbec* (n.p., n.d.).

instructed to register first and remonstrate afterwards. Louis XIV asserted his authority over the Church, restricting Papal power to matters of dogma. Government became a professional business: the king determined policy with the help of ministers of his own choice and implemented it by means of his agents in the provinces (the intendants), who looked to the central government at Versailles for reward and promotion. The institutions of the older order of things lost much of their importance but were allowed to survive. Distinguished members of the Court nobility served as provincial governors. The Estates of Languedoc and Brittany remained powerful enough to need tactful handling. Old attitudes survived, as well as old institutions. The king did not actually regard all Frenchmen as equal subjects. When he deprived the magnates of their power and functions he respected their social pretensions. Versailles housed a Court as well as a civil service and the king's view of himself as the first gentleman of his kingdom imposed psychological limitations on his role as chief executive.

One consequence of this was interminable trench warfare between the old institutions and the new. Parlements, provincial Estates and the Assembly of the Clergy played an endless game of precedents against each other and against the royal government. Ministers were often rivals if not enemies and Court factions struggled to advance the interests of competing clans. If the king himself failed to impose his unifying will, the government was incapable of pursuing a resolute and coherent policy for long. After the death of Louis XIV in 1714 none of his successors proved able or willing to fulfil the role that he had created for the monarchy. At the same time, resistance to royal authority was sapped by the conflicting claims and exaggerated *amour propre* of the various corporate bodies and the royal bureaucracy was continually extending its authority. During the eighteenth century both sides resorted to increasingly grandiloquent hyperbole in justification of their claims but all they actually did was to try to push the frontier a little further forward whenever they got the chance. There was an element of ritual ballet about the recurrent protests of the Parlements, their exile to some uncomfortable market town and the eventual compromise that ensured the resumption of judicial business. As in the case of present-day strikes, there had to be a settlement in the end and no one expected matters to get out of hand. Public attitudes did not always correspond to private policies. If the intendant of Brittany, Bertrand de Moleville, and the editor of his memoirs can be believed, Sieyès made such a nuisance of himself at the local assembly at Orleans that the finance minister, Brienne, was persuaded to buy him off with the offer of an abbey worth 12,000 livres a year. The reward was never paid, either because of a misunderstanding or because Sieyès was unable to deliver the vote. A few months later he published the first of his pamphlets, which included a diatribe against Brienne, 'the French vizir'. Soon after this Sieyès heard that he could not be given a post to which he aspired, because of his humble birth. This was followed by *What is the Third Estate?* with its denunciation of privilege.[10]

[10] A. F. Bertrand de Moleville, *Histoire de la Révolution de France pendant les dernières années du Règne de Louis XVI* (Paris, 1801), 10 vols, I/366-76.

During the second half of the eighteenth century these stylized tournaments began to take on a new tone. The Parlements seized on the message of the first part of *Spirit of the Laws* and declared themselves to be the restraining force that prevented the monarchy from degenerating into despotism. They were increasingly prone to the use of 'republican' language, speaking of the nation rather than the kingdom and of citizens rather than subjects. Both sides were more and more inclined to court public opinion. In the absence of a free press and representative institutions, the scope for an informed public opinion was severely limited but both ministers and their opponents played to the gallery, as when a Parlement denounced 'the axes of the soldiery, raised against the temple of the laws'. The Paris parlementaire d'Eprémesnil, when packed off to a brief exile on a part of the Mediterranean coast much favoured by present-day tourists, apostrophized the soldiers who arrested him: 'Let them come and sully this temple with carnage; let them butcher the ministers and glorious martyrs of justice under its own eyes and upon its very altars.'[11] This was admittedly in 1788, by which time people had become rather excited. A good many of the favourite clichés of revolutionary rhetoric were already stale before the revolution began. *Fauteurs du despotisme* who *encensaient les tyrans* and oppressed the *enfants de la patrie* were being denounced as *infâmes et traîtres à la patrie* before 1789. What is not clear is how far this sort of grand opera anticipated the political crisis that opened in 1787. If one reads certain publicists one gets the impression of a growing restlessness, a desire for change and a tendency to toy with radical or millenarian ideas in the 1780s; but how many people did read them? It is impossible, in the present state of knowledge, to decide whether one should think in terms of a groundswell of discontent that would sooner or later impose some kind of change, or of Grub Street snapping and snarling of the kind that was familiar enough in England where it had no political consequences of any significance. It seems clear that the radical pamphleteers were powerless on their own, without the help of the incautious language and rash tactics of men who were fighting a very different battle for the recovery of their ancient powers and status. One reason for the success of the French revolution was the fact that no one thought it possible.

Throughout the eighteenth century the Achilles heel of the monarchy was finance. It has never been satisfactorily explained why French governments could not balance their budgets. Part of the reason is the fact that they did not have one. An antiquated system of tax collection by private entrepreneurs, the farming out of indirect taxes, payments in arrears and anticipations of taxation, meant that it was almost impossible for the minister responsible to understand what the financial situation actually was. Frequent wars, which involved extensive armaments on land and sea, had generated a heavy national debt – but one that was no greater than the British debt in 1789, in a country with three times the population. France was heavily, if inefficiently taxed and the exemptions of the nobility were nothing like so extensive as was generally believed. One of the main reasons for France's fiscal problems may lie in the

[11] Included in the *Recueil de diverses pièces concernant la révolution du 8 mai 1788*, in the John Rylands Library, Manchester.

way that its financial institutions worked. In a country where the king's will
was theoretically absolute (and his habit of using public resources to reward
personal protégés virtually incorrigible) and where the greatest nobles were
almost above the law, it was impossible to enforce the kind of universal rules
that would have made possible the operation of a national bank. Credit was
roughly twice as expensive in France as in England. Having borrowed
extensively and expensively, the government had therefore to go on borrowing
more in order to meet the interest on previous loans. Parlements could be
bullied into registration but investors were free agents who had to be tempted
by high interest rates. Much of the debt was placed abroad, which meant that
the predecessors of the 'gnomes of Zurich' were in a position to precipitate a
financial crisis in France if they decided that further investment was too risky.
In the meantime the government blundered along from one expedient to
another, obliged to negotiate where it had not the power to dictate and unable
to embark on long-term reforms that would involve an immediate loss of
revenue. Bureaucratic absolutism had expanded the state's capacity to spend
beyond its ability to tax. As the years went by, the extent of the changes that
would be needed to re-establish the monarchy on a stable financial base became
more than ministers cared to contemplate. The question of whether or not they
could be implemented without imposing changes so drastic that they would
alter the nature of French society and provoke massive resistance and unrest,
was the sort of question that politicians prefer not to ask themselves. After half
a dozen years of extravagant spending by the finance minister, Calonne,
perhaps in the hope of generating confidence, the money ran out at the end of
1786 and the day of reckoning had arrived.

In any absolute monarchy the character of the king is a prime political factor,
especially when the going becomes difficult. Louis XVI, who came to the
throne in 1774, was endowed with a peculiar collection of virtues and vices that
ensured that he would make the worst of every possible world. He was an
earnest man who took very seriously his divinely imposed obligation to rule in
the interest of his subjects. This made him disinclined to hand over his
authority to a chief minister who might have wielded it more effectually. He
was not lacking in knowledge or common sense but he was totally devoid of
self-confidence and resolution. Pathetically anxious to do what was best, he was
never sure what it was. His lack of the social graces of his predecessors
prevented him from imposing himself on a Court society where how things
were done and said could matter as much as the things themselves. When he
came to the throne he was only twenty, with little to rely on beyond his good
intentions. He turned for guidance to Maurepas, an able enough minister in
his time but a man who had been out of office for thirty years and who, at the
age of seventy-three, was mainly intent on a quiet life. Maurepas encouraged
Louis to get rid of any minister who provoked controversy and disagreement.
After Maurepas' death in 1781 the king managed on his own, too benevolent
to be ruthless and too indecisive to be effective. At Versailles he inspired

neither respect nor fear and if his concern for reform proved inconvenient it was not very difficult to deflect him by discrediting its agents. He was deeply conscious of his duty to God to be a good ruler, but his conventional education had left him hostile to the Enlightenment and unable to conceive that his subjects might believe themselves to have political rights that were independent of what he chose to give them. Ruling was his responsibility and he would do it to the best of his ability, even if he did not enjoy it very much or do it very well.

The queen of France, who was always a foreign princess, was expected to provide an adequate number of male heirs and otherwise to remain inconspicuous. If a dazzling female presence was required at Court, it was provided by the king's mistress. Louis XVI had no mistresses and Marie Antoinette was not very good at either of her roles. For the first eight years of her marriage she was childless and she did not provide France with a Dauphin until 1781. She was never inconspicuous. Like her husband, she had the wrong combination of qualities and defects. As an Austrian, she was the living symbol of an unpopular alliance that had reversed traditional French foreign policy with unfortunate consequences during the Seven Years War of 1756-63. Obedient to her mother, Maria Theresa, she tried to act as a representative of Austrian interests at Versailles, which did not commend her to the French foreign ministry. With Louis as something of a social cypher, the animation of the Court rested upon her. Too wayward to accept the dehumanizing discipline that her station demanded, she had not the intelligence to appreciate the consequences of disregarding it. Her extravagance, which might have been overlooked in easier times, contrasted with Louis's ineffectual attempts at economy. To escape from the stifling ceremonial of Versailles she retired to the Trianon with a handful of lavishly rewarded favourites. What went on there was probably nothing more reprehensible than amateur theatricals and indiscreet gossip but the great nobles who were excluded from the charmed circle revenged themselves by paying hack pamphleteers to libel the queen as a monster of depravity. During the revolution they were to resort to more political vengeance. By 1789 Louis was still regarded with affection by the great majority of the population, if without much respect by those in contact with him. His wife was already an object of general hatred. She supplied the resolution that Louis lacked; she had the personal authority in which he was deficient; but her lack of judgement and consistent misreading of the political situation meant that she did him much more harm than good.

There was therefore little evidence of a deepening social crisis in France in the mid 1780s, although there was perhaps a more critical spirit in the air. The Enlightenment had sapped the traditional bases of authority and created the impression that the right policies could make all things new. In default of the chastening realities of party politics, abstract speculation acquired a certain plausibility. Old opponents of absolutism were beginning to fight their traditional campaigns with new theories, open to more radical interpretations than those who proclaimed them intended. A growing population dependent on inefficient agriculture was exceptionally vulnerable to bad harvests, and the harvest of 1788 was to be very bad indeed. If a crisis were to develop, the destruction of the public role of local gentry would make everything depend on the skill and strength of the government. None of this implies that a revolution was inevitable, still less the kind of revolution that actually happened, but the worsening deficit was driving France towards a lee shore, the ship was none too seaworthy, the man at the wheel was bewildered and irresolute and the wind was rising.

2

The Political Crisis of 1787–8

I T is virtually impossible for anyone at the present time to think of the
years immediately preceding 1789 without seeing everything in terms
of that memorable vortex into which French society was soon to be
plunged. Contemporaries, of course, had a different perspective. It was only
gradually that they became aware that they were approaching a real turning-
point, very different from the political crises of the past, which had been affairs
of much rhetoric but little change, except for the individuals who rose or fell
with them. No one knew what was going to happen next and historians must
beware of the tendency to assume that it could not have happened differently.
There were times when it looked as though the most likely development would
be a reinforcement of royal absolutism and the term 'revolution' was first
applied to the royal *coup d'état* of 8 May 1788 which virtually abolished the
political role of the Parlements. To understand how the men of 1789
conceived of their revolution one must therefore discover how they became
gradually aware of the dimensions of the crisis and the extent of the
opportunities it offered them. Some were involved, at the national level, as
early as 1787; others became drawn in, through local politics, at a later date.
All of them were marked by the experience of these preparatory years, but that
experience was very different in different parts of the country and contrasting
strata of society. The marquis de Lafayette, a Court nobleman, was already
sitting in a quasi-political national assembly when obscure provincial barristers
like Robespierre in Arras and Le Chapelier in Rennes were playing a
subordinate role in support of their local Parlements, and the abbé Sieyès was
still looking for clerical preferment. To understand why people behaved as they
did in 1789 one must therefore begin rather earlier.

In August 1786 the finance minister, Calonne, told the king that the
monarchy was heading for bankruptcy. Special taxation, voted during France's
intervention in support of the colonists during the American War of
Independence, was due to expire at the end of the year, after which the
situation would become rapidly worse. Calonne, believing the problem to be
too serious to be dealt with by the time-honoured palliatives, proposed an
ambitious programme that was designed to set the royal finances on a stable

footing and also to associate public opinion with a reformed fiscal policy. Internal tolls were at last to be abolished, some Crown lands alienated and the obligation to repair roads replaced by a money payment. The salt tax was to be reduced and distributed more evenly between the different provinces. The clergy were to be invited to liquidate their corporate debt by selling off their seigneurial rights. The main item in Calonne's package was a new land tax that was to continue indefinitely and was to be levied on all land, whether owned by Church, nobility or commoners. The support of public opinion was to be enlisted by the creation of new provincial assemblies in those areas where the old local Estates had not survived.

This was not a revolutionary programme, in the sense that it would not have made a radical change in the existing distribution of wealth, but it did involve innovation and challenged some old attitudes, in a country where such things were regarded with suspicion as liable to upset the balance between rival corporate authorities – Parlements, provincial Estates and clergy – and were resolved only after long and acrimonious horse-trading. The Parlements, in particular, could be expected to resist policies intended to make the Crown less dependent on their willingness to register loans. The new provincial assemblies would create a rival focus of public interest and might challenge the Parlements as the taxpayers' friends. Calonne therefore decided to call a meeting of some of the most important people in the country in the hope of winning their support for his proposals. Such a body of Notables had not met since 1626, which emphasized the exceptional seriousness of the occasion and could be taken as hinting that the government was turning its back on a century and a half of bureaucratic centralization and picking up the threads of what some conservatives believed to have been the traditional French constitution.

Louis XVI, who was not short of common sense, seems to have scented trouble and it was not until the end of the year that he agreed to Calonne's plan. When the Notables met, in the spring of 1787, they justified his apprehensions. Times had changed since 1626. Even Dillon, the imperious archbishop of Narbonne, spoke of the 'nation' rather than the kingdom, and Brienne, the politically ambitious archbishop of Toulouse, said that the clergy were primarily citizens. From Calonne's point of view, the function of the Notables was to advise him on how best to implement the policy that the king had authorized. The Notables, seeing themselves as spokesmen for the nation, insisted on discussing the policy itself. When the king forbade this, one of his brothers, Provence, tolerated it in the bureau over which he presided, while the other, Artois, made no attempt to stop criticism of Calonne. From the start, the Notables were inclined to claim something of the role of a British parliament and the king could not even rely on his brothers to defend royal authority.

The Notables began by accepting the principle that all sections of society should be equally liable to the new taxation. What they contested was the need for it. In view of Calonne's record of lavish expenditure, they implied that the fiscal crisis was due to his mismanagement and they were disinclined to allow him more money to waste. This forced Calonne, in order to vindicate himself, to blame the deficit on his predecessor, Necker. He said that, at the beginning of the reign, in 1774, the debt had amounted to no more than 37 million livres. Necker, who had tried to finance the American war by borrowing, had raised it to 80 million. If he was to disengage his own responsibility, Calonne had no alternative but to blame Necker, but this did not do him much good, for the Swiss banker was not a man who could be provoked with impunity.

Necker had resigned in 1781 when, as a Protestant, he had been refused a seat on the royal Council. In itself this was a rather 'republican' action. Royal ministers were expected to serve at the king's pleasure. When dismissed they were officially 'disgraced' and frequently ordered into temporary exile on their estates. Necker, however, forced his own retirement and immediately constituted himself as an unofficial leader of the opposition. Whether from pride or political ambition, he insisted on breaching accepted views of confidentiality by publishing accounts of the fiscal situation, intended to show that he had left a budget surplus of 10 million livres. With the help of his wife's salon, he built up an interest group of influential friends and allies, like de Cicé, the archbishop of Bordeaux. In distant Arras a very uninfluential lawyer, who then called himself de Robespierre, was said to be flourishing a letter from Madame Necker, to impress his friends.

Predictably enough, Necker and his partisans in the Notables turned on Calonne as the man responsible for the deficit. It was impossible then, as it still is, to know for certain which side was nearer to the truth. It does not matter, in the sense that the evidence was obscure enough for everyone to convince himself of what he wanted to believe. Knowing Necker, the king forbade him to go into print. When he defied this he was ordered out of Paris. It was perhaps a sign of the times that he did not find himself in the Bastille.

In addition to the Neckerites, Calonne had also to deal with Brienne, who was after his job. Ambitions of this kind were the stuff of Court politics. Brienne had some backing amongst the clergy and could rely on the support of Marie Antoinette, although not that of Louis, who suspected him of being an atheist and had already blocked his transfer to the see of Paris. In the face of opposition from Brienne and the Neckerites, Calonne lost control of the Notables. He made a rather desperate appeal to public opinion, in the form of an *avertissement* that was read out from the pulpits of parish churches. This informed the public, for the first time, of Calonne's programme and laid all the blame for the opposition to it on the wealthy and privileged who were accused of trying to avoid their fair share of taxation. France was decidedly beginning to learn the English way of politics. It was symptomatic of the bewilderment of men groping their way through uncharted waters that Calonne, after hoping to use the good offices of the Notables to outflank the Parlements, should suddenly have tried to discredit them. His appeal to public opinion seems to have met with virtually no response. It was more plausible – and more convenient – to see the Notables as the protectors of the taxpayer. It was also to be a striking feature of the pre-revolutionary crisis that educated Frenchmen, with the exception of the legal circles that gravitated round the Parlements, were not to become politically active until the autumn of 1788 and the impending elections to the Estates General. This rather reinforces the impression that there was no 'industrial and commercial middle class', seething with discontent.

Those who did react to the *avertissement* were the Notables, who were understandably incensed by Calonne's aspersions. As was usual in the *Ancien Régime*, his enemies included some of his ministerial colleagues. The king agreed to dismiss one of them but when Calonne demanded the sacrifice of another, who was a protégé of the queen, it was the finance minister who fell. Louis had presumably come to the conclusion that the only way to salvage Calonne's programme was by detaching it from its accident-prone author. Brienne then bombarded the king with helpful memoranda about how Calonne's aims could be realized by more accommodating methods, and soon succeeded it getting himself appointed in Calonne's place. He asked for Necker to join him, but this was more than Louis was prepared to stomach. One man, at least, thought that this was the turning-point: Necker claimed in 1797 that if he had been given office in 1787, 'none of what we have since seen would have happened'.[1] It is not a point of view that has won much support from historians.

Brienne then tried to salvage as much as he could of the reform programme, which he diluted in important respects, notably by agreeing to limit the duration of the land tax and to restrict its yield to a specific amount. The Neckerites had no quarrel with him and the clergy were reluctant to oppose their own man, but new sources of opposition appeared amongst the Notables, who were beginning to harbour rather more radical ideas. One of the most prominent exponents of these was the marquis de Lafayette.

Lafayette, although he was only thirty, already had a remarkable career behind him. Ten years earlier he had freighted a ship with munitions, at his own expense, and left France in secret to fight for the American colonists. He eventually became a general in the American army, where he played an important part in the decisive battle of Yorktown. His American experience was the turning-point of Lafayette's life. He became a hero-worshipper of his commander-in-chief and even christened one of his children 'George Washington'. On his return to France he remained something of an American at heart, responsive to the republican dream, while hoping to remain a loyal servant of the French monarch with whom he was on friendly terms. With such a past behind him, he was understandably restless in court society and he participated eagerly in whatever looked likely to improve the state of the country. He travelled to Nîmes to meet the Protestant pastor Rabaut Saint-Etienne and used his influence to help the campaign that won limited toleration

[1] *De la Révolution française* (Paris, 1797), p. 19.

for Protestants in 1787. He was a founder-member of the Franco-American Society and the anti-slavery society, the *Amis des Noirs*. Our cynical age, curiously more responsive to radical declamation than to practical philanthropy, is inclined to patronize the Lafayettes of this world as do-gooders. The marquis may have been naïve but he put his money where his mouth was: he invested 125,000 livres in an estate in Guiana in the hope of demonstrating that if slaves were treated with humanity they would renew their own population and thus make the slave trade unnecessary. In the Notables, it was Lafayette who asserted that any new taxation could only be authorized by an elected assembly, such as the ancient Estates General. 'No taxation without representation' had crossed the Atlantic and the political debate in France was assuming a more constitutional shape.

Brienne, who saw himself as a royal minister of the traditional type, believing that the Notables were not going to give him the moral endorsement that he needed, brought the session to an end. From his point of view it had served its purpose in enabling him to take Calonne's place. It had also revealed the government's lack of authority. Months had gone by, nothing had been done about the deficit, public opinion had been given the example of an assembly arguing about finance and raising issues of constitutional principle – and Brienne still had to face the Parlements. Perhaps the main factor affecting political attitudes, at least amongst the nobility, was age. Everywhere the old hands, who were familiar with the great jousts of the past, were concerned to stop things getting out of control. Everywhere they were challenged by those whom a commentator in Arras described as *têtes sulphureuses*, men who knew their Rousseau as well as their Montesquieu and had fewer inhibitions about carrying things to extremes. Much given to posturing and grandiloquence, some were to retain a cavalier loyalty to the aristocratic cause, as it emerged in 1789, while others became equally committed revolutionaries. In 1787 they united in opposition to the royal government, which was denounced as 'ministerial despotism'. What was at issue was a claim for political representation and the defence of status rather than of property. The clergy accepted fiscal equality but insisted on retaining their corporate right to tax themselves; the nobility made no fuss about commoners having half the seats in the new provincial assemblies but insisted that the president must be either a noble or a clergyman. In the words of Roederer, a future member of the Constituent Assembly, 'It was the revolt of ideas that detonated the revolution of suffering and it was the sufferings of *amour propre* that detonated the revolution of material interests.'[2]

When Brienne presented his proposals to the Paris Parlement, it was young lawyers, led by Duport, a noble of twenty-eight, who induced the court to declare that any new taxation would need the approval of the Estates General, which had not met since 1614. Going much further than the Notables, the Parlement decided to prosecute Calonne – who fled to England – denounced

[2] *L'Esprit de la révolution de 1789* (Paris, 1831), p. 4.

ministerial despotism and demanded the freedom of the press and the abolition of the *lettres de cachet* that allowed ministers to imprison their opponents without having to go through the courts. This set off a long war of attrition between Brienne and the Parlements. On the whole they won. Brienne had to abandon the land tax in return for a loan and the prolongation of existing taxation. He also promised to call a meeting of the Estates General, although not until 1791, by which time he hoped to have restored financial stability and to be able to negotiate from strength. From the autumn of 1787 until the spring of the following year, government and Parlements sparred with each other.[3] This was a struggle between the Crown and the courts. The latter could rely on the support of barristers, solicitors and a whole legal suburbia of clerks and petty officials who were good for a riot but not for a revolution. The Parlements could not bring Brienne down but their resistance could go a long way towards making government ineffective. In August 1787, rather than risk war with England and Prussia, Brienne had to abandon the revolutionaries who had seized power in the Netherlands. As the British ambassador in Paris informed his government, rather smugly, in April 1788, 'either this country must shortly be plunged into the most dreadful state of Anarchy, or an end be put to all pretentions to a Constitution'.

Brienne seems to have arrived at the same conclusion and he had had enough. On 8 May 1788 all of the Parlements were simultaneously presented with a series of royal edicts intended to legislate them out of their political existence. Much of their judicial work was transferred to new courts; reforms were made in judicial procedure, notably by the abolition of torture for those under investigation. The Parlements were deprived of their right to register – and protest against – royal decrees. This was transferred to a new Plenary Court whose members would be nominated by the king. 'Ministerial despotism' was beginning to look like something more than the invention of polemically minded lawyers.

The predictable result was the most violent opposition that the government had yet encountered. The present tendency amongst historians is to emphasize that this was limited, both socially and geographically, and to suggest that Brienne would have been able to survive it if he had not been brought down for other reasons. The question is not one that admits of a positive answer and there is a good deal to be said for this point of view. The new courts offered ambitious lawyers the prospect of attractive jobs that would eventually raise them to the nobility – if they were not frightened off by the threats of the Parlements to have their revenge on those whom they denounced as *infâmes et*

---

[3] For further information about this conflict, J. Droz, *Histoire du Règne de Louis XVI* (Brussels, 1839), is still worth reading, as is A. Chérest, *La Chute de l'Ancien Régime* (Paris, 1884), 3 vols. For more recent accounts, see J. Egret, *La Pré-Révolution française, 1787-8* (Paris, 1962) and A. Goodwin, 'Calonne, the Assembly of the French Notables of 1787 and the origins of the "revolte nobiliaire" ', *English Historical Review*, 61 (1946). I have also drawn extensively on the *Recueil de pièces intéressantes pour servir à l'histoire de la révolution en France* in the John Rylands Library in Manchester.

traîtres à la patrie. Some courts were delighted to be elevated to *grands bailliages*, although others refused to cooperate. Serious rioting was confined to a few areas, especially Brittany, Dauphiné and Béarn, all remote from Paris and from each other. Only the *têtes sulphureuses* amongst the parlementaires challenged the royal order to disperse. All of the Parlements did go into exile and, given time, the new courts would no doubt have begun to function.

All this is true enough but it does not exhaust the question. The edicts of 8 May set off a major crisis that both revealed the inability of the government to get its orders obeyed and accelerated the process. In Brittany, where the provincial Estates were still powerful, they supported the Parlement of Rennes. They and the national Assembly of the Clergy took up the demand for the prompt summoning of the Estates General. In other words, there were signs that the clergy and nobility – the only people who could express any sort of corporate protest – were making common cause with the Parlements, not in order to strike a new bargain with the royal government, but to make a new start. In view of all that was to follow, even more important were the opening up of a nation-wide debate on the principles of the monarchy, the effect on educated opinion of the first high drama of the French revolution, the creation of networks of correspondence and propaganda that were to become an important part of it, and the accumulation of precedents that were to be invoked in 1789.

It was typical of Brienne's difficulties that news of the impending *coup d'état* was leaked in Paris. D'Eprémesnil – at forty-three a middle-aged *tête* – persuaded the parlementaires to anticipate the blow with a declaration that the ministers were subverting the legal basis of the monarchy. 'France is a monarchy governed by the king in accordance with the laws.' These included 'the right of the nation freely to grant subsidies by means of the Estates General', the traditional customs and privileges of the provinces and the right of Parlements to register only such royal decrees as were in conformity with the law. The judges threw in habeas corpus in order to protect themselves against arbitrary arrest and swore never to participate in any other judicial system. When, on the following day, troops entered the building and demanded the identification of d'Eprémesnil and another ringleader, the magistrates replied 'We are all called d'Eprémesnil and Montsabert!'. This was strong stuff, although it did not prevent the arrest of the pair and the dispersal of the court.

Events in the little town of Pau were rather more *folklorique*. When the king's representative ordered the Parlement of Navarre to disperse, several thousand nobles forced him to cancel the order and the court remained in session for some time. The nobles printed a proclamation including the bold statement that 'Peoples must have existed before they had kings'. Enthusiastic crowds paraded the cradle of Henri IV, the local hero and widely regarded as France's last constitutional monarch, through the streets. Brienne was not likely to lose much sleep over that.

Things were altogether more serious in Rennes, where both the Parlement and the Breton Estates had a reputation for defiance of the royal government. The intendant, Bertrand de Moleville, when he discovered the content of the sealed orders for the enforcement of the edicts and the dispersal of the Parlement, assured the parlementaires of his devotion to the principles of the magistracy. He laid most of the blame for what followed on the reluctance of the military commander, the comte de Thiard, to use his troops to maintain order. Thiard's circumspection was understandable since twenty-two officers resigned from one regiment alone in protest against the role they were expected to play. From the start the Breton nobility came out in support of the Parlement. On 26 May, 320 of them signed a protest against ministerial despotism and declared, 'The Plenary Court will not assemble.' Three weeks later the protesters had increased to 2,500. The Parlement itself might have preferred to manage without its over-enthusiastic supporters, but the older magistrates fell in behind the younger and more radical ones. The historian, Cochin, as part of his thesis that the revolution was due to minorities, working through *sociétés de pensée*, political clubs which, by manipulation and intimidation, enforced their will on a passive majority, insisted that the Breton revolt did not reflect public opinion as a whole.[4] This seems to be confirmed by the fact that when the Breton nobility imitated the strategy pioneered in Dauphiné and called an illegal meeting of the three Orders, they got little support from the clergy and the Third Estate. Not more than eighty people turned up in Rennes and only nine of the forty-two towns in the province responded. This did not prevent the nobility and the crowds they could assemble from dominating the streets of Rennes. Fearing that his official residence was about to be attacked and convinced that he could not rely on Thiard for protection, Moleville escaped over his garden wall on 9 July and did not stop until he reached Versailles.

The replacement of Thiard by the more resolute Stainville allowed order to be restored without bloodshed, but the sight of one of his intendants in flight did not do much for Brienne's authority. The Breton revolt was resolutely backward-looking and concerned entirely with the traditional rights of the province. The local lawyers spelled this out emphatically on 9 August: 'Even the Estates General can exercise no authority over the administration of Brittany, because the Bretons meet in a body as a nation . . . because it is there, and nowhere else, it is in that assembly and in the Parlement that the province is represented and defended.' Two of the signatories to this piece of archaism were Le Chapelier and Lanjuinais, who were to sing a very different tune when they were elected to those Estates General whose powers over Brittany they had been so eager to deny, but not many of those politically active in 1787-9 could boast of much consistency. The protest in Rennes was violent and

4 See his very interesting study, *Les Sociétés de pensée et la révolution en Bretagne* (Paris, 1925), 2 vols.

dramatic but, to the extent that it was limited to the demand for local autonomy, it could always be bought off by local concessions.

At the opposite end of the country, in Dauphiné, things began in a similar way but took a very different direction. The Grenoble Parlement greeted the May edicts with the assertion that 'The rights of Subjects are no less sacred than those of the sovereign' and duly denounced all those who accepted posts in the new courts as *traîtres à la patrie*. When the Parlement was ordered into exile there was a riot. One of the two regiments sent to suppress this fired on the crowd but the commanding officer of the other refused to give the order to open fire. When the Parlement had allowed itself to be sent into exile a movement was launched to reconvene the local Estates, which had not met since the seventeenth century. Representatives of the three Orders in Grenoble invited the other towns in the province to a meeting at Vizille. When the governments tried to ban this the local military commander took no action, even though the rebels issued a proclamation that 'municipalities originated before the monarchy'. The response to the appeal from Grenoble was patchy. About half of the towns and 15 per cent of the peasant communities agreed to attend. Many of those expressing support were illiterate, which could either mean that the movement had a wide popular base or that they were obeying the orders of their social superiors. No bishop attended and some towns allowed their jealousy of Grenoble to get the better of their patriotism. The meeting nevertheless took place and produced a Rousseauist declaration to the effect that 'The law must be the expression of the general will . . . if the people detest it, it is not a law . . . The Plenary Court will not be created.' This was going beyond an appeal to local rights.

The revolt in Dauphiné was unique in several ways. Unlike the Bretons, the Dauphinois could not pose as traditionalists and they were not encumbered with actual Estates and quarrels about their domination by the nobility. Even so, when the deputies to the meeting at Vizille originally met as three separate Orders, internal divisions soon appeared. They dealt with this by the radical decision to meet and vote in common. This did much to reduce internal bickering and it helped to protect them from antiquarian particularism; one local pamphleteer had declared the rights of the Dauphinois to be derived from those of the Allobroges! When Béarn wrote to sound Grenoble on the need to preserve local privileges, it was given a lesson in political theory and told that local liberties must be merged in those of the nation. 'Let us not think of what we used to be, but of what we want to be today: free Frenchmen under a King.'

Much of the credit for this forward-looking attitude belonged to Mounier, a Grenoble lawyer of thirty, the son of a merchant, who had already acquired personal nobility. If one can legitimately infer Mounier's attitude then from his conduct in the following year and what he wrote soon afterwards, he was an essentially moderate man, opposed to violent change and a follower of 'the immortal Montesquieu' whose *Spirit of the Laws* he considered to be 'one of the finest works to have honoured the human mind'. He responded to

Rousseau as a moralist – 'Read *Emile* and, in spite of the errors of the book, woe unto you if you do not feel the need to become a better man ' – but was sceptical about the *Social Contract*, although he recognized that it was 'of all political treatises, the one most frequently and favourably quoted'. Mounier thought it was 'The worst work on government ever written.' 'Rousseau was mistaken in arguing that the legislative power should belong exclusively to the people, which would create a despotic or absolute democracy.' It was, however, not Rousseau's fault if people applied to France arguments that had been intended only for a tiny republic and if they mistook his search for a 'chimerical perfection' for a treatise on practical politics.[5] Mounier's moderation was not to become fully apparent until 1789. As the guiding spirit behind the revolt of Dauphiné in 1788 he acquired a national reputation as a bold radical who had not merely defied the government but defeated it.

When the Vizille meeting adjourned, it agreed to reconvene soon afterwards at Romans. This time Brienne made a virtue of necessity and authorized what he was unable to prevent. The government's blessing on the Romans meeting reversed the century-old process of bureaucratic centralization. The story was followed with attentive admiration all over France. It was bound to be imitated elsewhere and the Dauphinois, realizing that their own safety might depend on their enlisting general support, were eager missionaries. As we have seen, they advised Béarn to think nationally. A printed letter from 'a Dauphinois noble to a citizen of Toulouse' urged Languedoc to follow Dauphiné's lead, pointing out that this was already being done by the Bretons 'with whom we are united and with whom we are coordinating all our moves'. At Montélimar a town meeting, held in defiance of a ban by the local authorities, responded to letters from Grenoble and Romans and claimed that the French towns were assuming the role of counterpoise to royal power that had formerly belonged to the Parlements. The nobility of Franche-Comté demanded the restoration of their ancient Estates and when Brienne forbade them to meet they defied the attempt of the local commander to stop them.

These local movements often conformed to the Breton rather than the Dauphinois plan, in demanding the restoration of purely local privileges. This was something that was likely to appeal to the nobility, and noble leadership in the revolt posed the awkward question of the reliability of army officers who were often sympathetic to the point of view of those they were supposed to be disciplining. A Swiss regiment at Dijon was reluctant to suppress a riot. A *militaire* in Dauphiné – if he was not the invention of a pamphleteer – went into print to the effect that 'We are not the vile instruments of the despotic will of the agents of tyranny . . . We deliberated about absurd orders that were an affront to our *délicatesse*.' The baron de P, who claimed to be an officer in the

5 Mounier, *Exposé de la conduite de M. Mounier dans l'Assemblée Nationale et des motifs de son retour en Dauphiné* (Paris, 1789); *Recherches sur les causes qui ont empêché les Francais de devenir libres* (Geneva, 1792); *De l'influence attribuée aux Philosophes, aux Francs-Maçons et aux Illuminés sur la Révolution de France* (Tübingen, 1801).

French Guards, a regiment which shared in the responsibility for maintaining order in Paris, went a good deal further. '*We are all born citizens*; we are all *enfants de la patrie* before being royal subjects.' 'Each and every one of its children is dominated by that moral being, *la patrie*, to whose service the King himself is no less subjected than the least of his subjects . . . The King is only the first subject of his kingdom.'

Inflammatory language of this kind, which could reflect either the *frondeur* attitudes of the seventeenth century or a new approach to politics – or an explosive combination of both – was to be heard everywhere. Months before the passage of the May edicts the parlementaires of Nancy had declared that 'Liberty and property are essential and primitive rights of Citizens. Their preservation is the object and end of society.' Their colleagues at Rouen denounced the ministers as traitors and refused to correspond with them at all. The nobility of Guyenne, Gascony and Périgord, demanding the release of some Bretons who had been arrested, claimed that 'Peoples derive their right to liberty from nature. Their rights are imprescriptible.' All through the eighteenth century the Parlements had been inclined to dress up moderate expectations in resounding language, but in 1788 words were being matched with deeds. There were some curious anticipations of what was to happen in the following year. Parlements, locked out of their meeting places, declared, like that of Dijon, that they would reassemble wherever they could find accommodation. When the government had eventually capitulated and revoked the May edicts, the return of the triumphant parlementaires to Grenoble and Dijon was the occasion for public fêtes which anticipated those of 1793-4, with *jeunes divinités* presenting laurel crowns, 'since *vertu* should be crowned by the hands of innocence', obelisks and triumphal arches. At Grenoble the two regiments provided the music for the procession and all their officers presented their respects to the victorious lawyers.

While this agitation was gathering way came the decision to call the Estates General in 1789 and the fall of Brienne. As was to happen time and again until 1792, there was no decisive confrontation. This makes it possible to argue that the government could have prevailed, but Brienne was losing ground all the time. Even the clergy turned against him, perhaps offended by the fact that, in true eighteenth-century style, he had taken advantage of his office to exchange Toulouse for the more lucrative see of Sens. A special Assembly of the Clergy, invited by the government to make it a grant of 8 million livres, confined itself to 1.8 million and accompanied that with a denunciation of the May edicts, a demand for the confirmation of its traditional immunities and a request for a meeting of the Estates General. Brienne is said to have told the clergy's Agent-Géneral, 'Since the nobles and the clergy are abandoning their natural protector, the king, he will have to throw himself into the arms of the Commons and crush them both.' On 5 July he invited members of the public to advise him on the way to make the coming Estates General a truly national assembly. This was generally taken to signify the suspension of the censorship.

Supporters of the Parlements had not waited for Brienne's permission to begin pamphleteering, but he may have thought that to provoke a wider discussion on the constitution of the Estates General would divide the opposition. If he was reviving the populist policy of Calonne's *avertissement*, he was to have more success than he bargained for, but the press campaign took months to gather momentum and came too late to do him any good. On 8 August he agreed to suspend the introduction of the Plenary Courts and to bring forward the meeting of the Estates General from 1791 to 1789. This was the decisive turning-point and the proof that the ministry was on the run. The Estates General would meet with the government still insolvent and more or less at their mercy. The agitation of the summer of 1788 would merge with the electoral campaign to maintain a continuing atmosphere of political crisis that would leave the government virtually powerless. A week after this capitulation the supply of ready money ran out. This was not so much a sign of general insolvency as a short-term crisis due to the deliberate or accidental failure of the bankers to keep Brienne supplied with the money that he needed for the transaction of day-to-day business. He was forced to pay creditors in paper money, which was seen as a declaration of bankruptcy. Once again Brienne turned to Necker, this time with the king's approval, but the Swiss banker replied, plausibly enough, that public confidence could only be restored if the finance minister resigned and Brienne had to go.

For the second time in little more than a year the opposition had brought down the king's chief minister. The monarchy still had some freedom of manoeuvre but it was less and less in control of events. Necker believed that it would do more harm than good to try to manage the meeting of the Estates General. His colleague, Malesherbes, disagreed and advised the king to draft a liberal constitution and proclaim it on his own authority, but Louis was not that kind of man and Malesherbes resigned. The substitution of Necker for Brienne implied a major change. The archbishop was an *Ancien Régime* politician who had tried to further his own career by defending his master's power. Necker, an outsider, did not have the same commitment to the old order. He was loyal to the king, but after his own fashion. He was also a man who revelled in popularity and he allowed himself to be persuaded that he was the man who could guide France in a new direction. He therefore abandoned Brienne's rearguard action, scrapped the May edicts and recalled the Parlements from exile. The Paris Parlement was only too pleased to register the royal edict for the summons of the Estates General in the following year. What a contemporary described as 'the revolution in France' had failed. 'Ministerial despotism' had been routed and the way was clear for the drafting of a new constitution by the king and his people.

It was then that the political crisis took off in a new and a wholly unexpected direction. The demand for a meeting of the Estates General had appealed to all those opposed to the government. To the parlementaires it signified a return to the old ways of the monarchy, while the more forward-looking saw it as the beginning of a constitutional regime. The reality came as a surprise to everyone. Even before the Estates met, it had become clear that they would put an end to the political pretensions of the Parlements, who were soon hoping for a dissolution. Competition to get elected was fierce: with the recent American example before them, a generation of young hopefuls aspired to become the Founding Fathers of the new France. For a good many of them, that immediately raised the question of whether they were to be classified as belonging to the nobility or to the Third Estate. Noble status which, except in the more backward parts of the country like Brittany, had gradually been tending towards the kind of limited social importance that it had in England, suddenly became a matter of urgent political consequence, especially for the very people whose ambition and success had elevated them into the no-man's-land of personal nobility. Furthermore, as Mounier had observed in Dauphiné, the separation of the three Orders encouraged them to concentrate on their sectional identities and on the issues that divided them. When the time came to draft *cahiers* of grievances and elect deputies, opinion was politicized throughout the entire country and expectations raised that all wrongs would soon be righted. Many regimes later, Frenchmen were to say *Que la république était belle sous l'Empire!* That was even more true of the Estates General.

The Third Estate, or to speak in more realistic terms, educated middle-class opinion, which all through the summer had sympathized with the Parlements in their fight against Brienne, began to suspect that 'aristocrats' were intent on purely political changes that would put an end to absolutism for their own exclusive benefit. When the Paris Parlement approved the convocation of the Estates General, it added 'in accordance with the procedure of 1614'. It probably had no clear idea of what it meant: it certainly did not intend that parlementaires should be classed with the Third Estate, as they had been in 1614. Perhaps it merely wanted to make sure that the Estates were elected and not nominated, as the provincial assemblies had been. What it was assumed to have meant was that the Estates General should consist of three quite separate Orders – clergy, nobility and commoners – each with a veto over the decisions of the other two. Where constitutional issues were concerned, that need not have aroused much alarm, since it was the nobility that had led the fight against absolutism. If the 'procedure of 1614' caused such an outcry within the Third Estate this could only be because its members were beginning to suspect their social superiors of wanting political power for themselves, with no social concessions to their former allies.

In an astonishingly short space of time the united front disintegrated. Perhaps ministerial despotism had lost its terrors now that Necker was in charge. Members of the Third Estate now began to argue that the 'privileged Orders' had only opposed the government because they had been afraid of being made to pay their fair share of taxation. This, of course, was what Calonne and Brienne had said, and the archbishop was suspected of subsidizing some of the pamphlets that attacked his old tormentors. In a society that had never known freedom of the press or political debate, politics had necessarily taken the form of personal intrigue at Court and the habits of suspicion this engendered were to plague the revolutionaries. A 'letter from a citizen' of 8 December complained that 'War is no longer declared against the arbitrary authority of ministers, but amongst the citizens. In his frenzy, everyone fails to recognize his brothers, whose intentions are his own, and he is on the point of invoking against their pretensions that very arbitrary power that he has so much reason to dread but that he no longer fears.'

When Necker reconvened the Notables, to advise him on the way in which the meeting of the Estates General should be organized, those distinguished gentlemen, who had been acclaimed as the champions of liberty in 1787, were now denounced as the embattled defenders of privilege. The immediate issue was whether or not the Third Estate, since it represented the great majority of the population and much of the nation's wealth, should have the same number of representatives as the other two Orders combined. Since this would be of no importance if the Orders voted separately, the advocates of double representation for the Third Estate (*doublement*) assumed it to imply voting by head in a united meeting of the three Orders. To this the Notables were vehemently opposed. Most of the princes of the blood published a memorandum denouncing the pretensions of the Third Estate, reminding the king of all the blood that his loyal nobility had shed on his behalf, and threatening to boycott the Estates General if they did not get their way. To those – and they certainly included the queen – who remembered the events of the previous summer, it looked as though the nobility had nerve as well as courage.

Political alignments might have changed but political temperaments were more stable. Mounier kept his Dauphinois on a moderate course. The Bretons were predictably violent. Sieyès, who had whipped himself into a frenzy about Brienne, now became even more abusive of the 'privileged Orders'. D'Eprémesnil, the melodramatic hero of the Paris Parlement's resistance to the May edicts, was just as swashbuckling in his opposition to the Third Estate. Hyperbole was in the air and it was difficult for anyone to keep a level head. Rabaut Saint-Etienne was one of many who were excited by the uniqueness of the occasion. 'If one consults the annals of all ancient and modern peoples, one will find no period so solemn and remarkable as the one in which we find ourselves today.' Fortunately Necker was the most virtuous and enlightened Frenchman [sic] who had ever lived. With the stakes so high, even moderation had to be defended in violent terms and Rabaut called down 'Eternal hatred on all those who try to divide the Orders.'[6]

One of the latter was Pétion, a lawyer from Chartres who was to sit on the Extreme Left of the Constituent Assemble. Pétion had already distinguished himself by his extreme anti-clericalism, denouncing monks as 'pious idlers' and rather illogically wanting to liberate them from their 'slavery'. He had also advocated suppressing the tithe, selling the estates of the Church, paying the

---

[6] *A la nation Française* (n.p., November 1788).

clergy a salary and introducing divorce. In a subsequent essay he had repeated much of this and struck up a somewhat Rousseauist attitude, although Jean-Jacques would not have approved of Pétion's strictures against excessive wine-growing. Equal inheritance, the prohibition of prostitution, the encouragement of public fêtes and the crowning of virtuous maidens were more in Rousseau's line.[7] Pétion's *Avis aux Francais* put him squarely on the Rousseauist side in the ideological debate that was beginning. Montesquieu was 'a sublime writer' but he had been blinded by his rank and position and his respect for circumstances. 'Why do we need to examine what is done and what has happened, to find out what we ought to do? . . . The science of administration . . . is within the reach of any ordinary man who can think straight.' Nature had made all men free and equal and 'How can a free man be wicked? All moral vices were the product of oppression. He went on to suggest a programme for the Estates General that was an astonishing anticipation of what actually happened. The people – the source of the king's power – would decide on the limits of his authority. Pétion favoured a unicameral assembly since the existence of two Houses had been responsible for the decay of political liberty in England. This assembly, composed of mandated delegates rather than representatives, should decide matters of war and peace and negotiate treaties. 'The Estates General are all-powerful . . . when they are assembled the king has no authority.' It was typical of the times that Pétion should have complained at the lack of response to his appeal for 'perfect unity' from those he maligned. The more extreme revolutionaries were always inclined to see the road to unity as requiring a confession of guilt and a promise of repentance from their opponents.

Sieyès was on a similar tack. In his *Views on the means available to the representatives of France in 1789*, he argued that buying a constitution was like buying a clock, in the sense that the customer was less concerned with the mysteries of horology than with getting the most recent and efficient piece of machinery. He warned his readers against the danger of basing programmes on experience. The Legislator should work out from first principles what was appropriate to a people. 'Never has it been more urgent to give reason its full force.' He went on to describe how the Estates General should set about its business. It should declare all taxation annulled, but extend it for the duration of the session and guarantee the national debt. It should assume sole responsibility for its rules of procedure and declare its members immune from prosecution. Ministers should be excluded from its sessions, to ensure its independence of the executive. The president, who should be changed once a week, was to have purely nominal powers. The old provinces were to be abolished and the country divided on a different basis. All, or almost all of this, the Constituent Assembly was to do. Sieyès rejected the idea of any balance of political forces, since 'We need one common will.' He equated this will with the majority. Even Sieyès realized that it might be awkward if the sovereign

---

[7] *Les Lois civiles et l'administration de la justice, ramenées à un ordre simple et uniforme*; and *Essai sur la mariage*. Both in *Oeuvres* (Paris, an I).

people wanted to interfere with the decisions of its mandatories. Having no
solution to this problem, he assured his readers, rather uneasily, that it would
not arise.

What is the Third Estate?, which Sieyès brought out in January 1789,
reflected the changed atmosphere in being directed not against absolutism, but
against the First and Second Estates, of the former of which he was a nominal
member. By the ingenious expedient of defining the various immunities enjoyed
by many commoners as 'common rights', he was able to denounce the clergy
and nobility as 'the privileged Orders' and to exclude them altogether from the
French polity, although he did have the grace – or was he perhaps thinking of
himself? – to admit that they had provided the commons with its most vigorous
defenders. True to his faith in first principles, he insisted that France should
follow 'ideal models of the beautiful and the good' and 'rise at once to the
challenge of setting ourselves up as an example to the nations'. This would
require the exercise of a single sovereign will. 'The nation is prior to everything. It is the source of everything. Its will is always legal, indeed, it is the law
itself.' The executive power – the name by which the Constituent Assembly
was to refer to the king – was merely 'an ad hoc product of a representative
will'. A body of representatives was the same thing as the nation itself. 'It is
not necessary in this case to take many precautions against the misuse of
power.' This was to opt for Rousseau ('The general will, by the mere fact of its
existence, is always what it ought to be') as against Montesquieu ('Every man
with power is led to abuse it. He pushes on until he encounters some limit.
Who would have thought it? *Vertu* itself needs limits'). Sieyès saw the Estates
General – the repository of the hopes of everyone else – as fatally flawed, since it
was a traditional body, encumbered with historical precedents. Voting by head
would not cure it, since half the members would belong to the 'privileged
Orders' who were no part of the nation. What was needed was the election of a
convention that would have sovereign power and be free from any shackles of
precedent. Just as he had previously asserted that the sovereign people would
not want to dictate to the men it had elected, he now insisted that political
equality would involve no threat to property, again without providing any
proper explanation of why things should turn out so conveniently.

Despite the extremist language and the growing tendency to abuse one's
opponents, Sieyès's reassurances are a useful reminder that the people who
suspected and denounced each other had more in common than they chose to
acknowledge. As veterans of the campaign against ministerial despotism, they
were all in favour of a constitutional monarchy in which executive power
would lie with the king, while the Assembly controlled taxation. If this was to
work properly there would have to be habeas corpus and freedom of the press.
There were disagreements as to what constituted property – radicals were
already saying that the clergy were merely the administrators of the possessions
of the Church, while some nobles considered both their material and social
privileges to be their property – but there was no disagreement about the
sanctity of property itself.

What was at issue was not a competition for power between representatives of rival classes since virtually all those who were to play a political role of any importance belonged to the same class. The quarrel was about attitudes rather than interests. It was about the choice between a society based on a sense of hierarchy that was more or less equated with birth and one conceived on the American (not British) principle that 'all men are created equal'. This divided people who agreed with each other about constitutional and economic policy. Attitudes to the place of the Church within society also cut across other divisions. Everyone assumed that it must have one, but Jansenists, Rousseauists and deists in general saw no need for its continued existence as a wealthy self-governing corporation. Less obviously, but with equally unhappy consequences, educated people were divided between those of a pragmatic bent who thought that France would not be doing badly if it emerged from the crisis with institutions no worse than those of England and those who would settle for nothing less than the New Jerusalem. The former drew their ammunition from Montesquieu, the latter from Rousseau. Since the disagreements arose from attitudes rather than material interests, the lines of division did not correspond to wealth or social status: there was a certain *snobbisme* in advertising one's own enlightenment by rising above the prejudices of one's rank. There was scope here for political leadership but no one with political experience, and there were no precedents. When all groups were repeating the call for national regeneration – often with a genuine acceptance of the need for personal sacrifices – few realized the dangers of the revolutionary movement escaping from everyone's control and no one was able to assert the authority that might conceivably have brought the contending factions to appreciate how much they had in common – and how much they had to lose. If they could have seen where they were all going they would certainly have decided to go somewhere else.

Necker was not the man to dominate the situation by some bold act of statesmanship. When his friends urged him to produce a royal programme for the Estates General and to manage the elections, he replied that this would merely provoke opposition. There was something to be said for this point of view and he may have hoped that if the regenerators could not unite against the government they would be more likely to fall out with each other. What he did do was to persuade the king that the Third Estate should have as many representatives as the other two Orders combined. He believed that public opinion would have settled for nothing less but, quite typically, he left it to the Estates themselves to decide how they should vote. This preserved his popularity for the time being, since the Third Estate assumed that *doublement* logically implied voting by head, without committing Necker to anything in particular. He had to take one or two important decisions. Parish priests were given one vote each, while monasteries and cathedral chapters were limited to one vote for each community. Necker presumably thought the *curés* more dependable allies than their ecclesiastical superiors, but he had overturned the traditional representation of the clergy. He also ordered all elections to be held in judicial districts or *bailliages*. This reassured public opinion that they would not be controlled by the royal intendants, but infuriated the provincial Estates (dominated by members of the first two Orders) who had expected to choose the representatives of their provinces.

During the first months of 1789 the entire country was involved in the business of the elections and in drafting *cahiers* or lists of complaints. These originated at the parish level and it took two or three stages before the merging of local *cahiers* produced the final version that accompanied the deputies to Versailles. Historians have tended to pay much more attention to the *cahiers* than to the elections, which is understandable enough since they seem to offer a remarkable opportunity for discovering the views of the population as a whole. In practice, things are not so simple. Parish *cahiers* were sometimes obsessed with local grievances; some were almost illiterate whilst others echoed the rolling pulpit oratory of the local priest. Some were obsequious towards the local seigneur; others held him up to ridicule. As village *cahiers* were fused into those from wider areas, the lawyers tended to step in, disregarding the question of who was to pay for the repair of the local bridge and substituting demands for a constitutional monarchy. Granted the inevitable special pleading, which was most obvious when the clergy or the nobility tried to look after their corporate interests, the *cahiers* of the three Orders had a good deal in common. They offered the basis for a type of constitutional monarchy that would have been much closer to the *Ancien Régime* than the one that was actually to emerge.

The elections themselves both reflected the political temperature in the different parts of the country and helped to decide how deputies were going to see things when they got to Versailles. In Dauphiné the revived Estates were allowed, as a special favour, to nominate their deputies collectively. To keep the electors from the three Orders united, the commoners guaranteed all forms of property, which included what many people considered to be illegitimate feudal survivals. Even then, the clergy were dissatisfied and some of the nobility sent a deputation to the Estates General pleading that the elections had been irregular.

The elections in Brittany produced further violence. The local Estates met at the end of 1788, with 951 nobles and 54 men officially representing the Third Estate, although some of them were noble too. At Nantes, Rennes and Saint-Malo local meetings voted to boycott both local and national Estates unless granted *doublement*, fiscal equality and the abolition of the road tax. The Breton *curés* were urged on by their opposite numbers in Dauphiné: 'Don't be imposed on by the authority of your bishops . . . In civil matters the bishops are only citizens like you.' Le Chapelier and Lanjuinais, who had supported the noble offensive in the previous summer, were now actively campaigning against their former allies. Denied satisfaction, the Third Estate withdrew from the local Assembly, while the nobility pledged themselves to defend what they saw as the liberties of the province and to boycott any national assembly that seemed likely to interfere with them. They protested against double representation for the Third Estate and even refused to accept fiscal equality. Through their own political machine they mobilized the poor in Rennes and produced a succession of riots in the town. Their opponents appealed for support, a meeting at Nantes swore 'hatred to aristocrats' and despatched 250 men to Rennes. In protest against the rules that Necker enforced for the election, the nobility and upper clergy refused to attend the Estates General at all and the deputies of the Third Estate set off for Versailles in a belligerent mood.

Artois was another province where the survival of local Estates produced animosity.[8] The Estates of Artois consisted of the usual three Orders but most of the nobility were excluded and the representatives of the Third Estate, some of whom were actually nobles, were nominated by the other two Orders. This cosy arrangement seems to have worked reasonably amicably until those who were determined to get themselves elected to the Estates General acquired a new interest in the composition of the local body. The nobility of the Estates tried to defy Necker's ruling about the elections and keep out of the electoral body those who were not allowed to attend meetings of the local Estates. Claiming that Artois was 'absolutely foreign to and independent of the Estates General', they argued that their own constitution could only be modified by themselves and they warned that the province would not consider itself bound by the decisions of irregularly elected representatives. The battle raged for months, both sides making full use of the columns of the local paper, founded in the previous December, which got off to a lively start. When it came to the actual elections, there was a walk-out in each of the three Orders. Maximilien de Robespierre, who just managed to get himself elected, was a member of the local bar, the Arras Academy and the local literary society who had not hitherto played a leading part in the life of the town. He fought an aggressive electoral campaign, in the course of which he published a couple of pamphlets. *To the Artesian nation* combined lyrical tributes to the king and Necker with a more or less ritual denunciation of the 'formidable enterprises of despotism emanating from Versailles'. *The enemies of the nation unmasked*, which came out during the actual election, was a good deal more hysterical. The occasion was 'the combat of prejudice against reason, of humanity, honour and patriotism against pride, vanity and personal interest. What will be the prize of this combat? The safety, glory and happiness of present and future generations or their humiliation, their servitude and eternal misery.' After proclaiming *la patrie en danger*, he ended with an extraordinary elegy on his own martyrdom. This seems to have done the trick, but only just. He was elected fifth out of six.

Where there were no provincial Estates things often went more quietly. In Bordeaux the ambitious archbishop, de Cicé, cultivated the Third Estate so

---

[8] The information concerning Artois is drawn from the *Archives National*, series B^a 15, C 12, C 14, H 38 and from the local newspaper, *Annonces, Nouvelles et Avis divers pour la Province d'Artois, la Boulonnais et le Cambrésis.*

vigorously that he alienated the local nobility, but he won the votes of his *curés*, which was what mattered. In all, fifty-one bishops were elected (three of whom did not sit) out of a total of 303 representatives of the clergy. Some bishops found the going easy; others were rejected by their parish clergy. The First Estate therefore consisted of a majority of parish priests, often of men noted for their political independence. The representatives of the Second Estate included a surprising number of Court nobles, often bitter opponents of the queen, a good proportion of local gentry and few parlementaires. The Parlements had played as active a part as anyone in securing the election of the Estates General but it was already clear that it was not going to do them any good.

One noble who showed himself to be remarkably unambitious, at a time when the Robespierres and Mirabeaus were desperate for election, was the comte de Montlosier. His main interest was in the origin of the extinct volcanoes of his native Auvergne, about which he brought out a book in the spring of 1789. It was not a good time to be publishing books on geology. Elected as a reserve deputy, he decided to go to Versailles to see the opening of the Estates General, but could not resist stopping to examine the terrain round Fontainebleau on his way and arrived too late. When one of the Auvergne deputies wanted to resign, Montlosier tried to dissuade him, so that he could go back to his volcanoes. His failure to do so launched him on a political career that was to last for the next forty years.

A noble whose election raised many eyebrows was the comte de Mirabeau, who had already achieved national notoriety. The son of an irascible economist and leading member of the Physiocrats, Mirabeau had already spent a fair amount of his time in gaol, at his father's request, which had given him an understandable aversion to *lettres de cachet*. A notorious rake, he was a man of few principles and many debts. Attracted to power like a moth to a candle, he had been employed as a hack ministerial pamphleteer, a job he had farmed out to others, since he was as idle as he was intelligent. Shipped off to Berlin by the foreign minister, to get him out of the way, he returned with the manuscript of a scandalous book on the Prussian government, which he was paid to surrender. He then published a duplicate copy. Mirabeau, like a good many other people, but with more justification, saw the Estates General as the theatre for the exercise of his political abilities and, in his own case, for the solution of his financial problems. His first thought was to attach himself to the government, but the foreign minister had had enough of him. He then presented himself for election by the nobility of Provence but was rejected on the ground that he did not own a fief. It was a tribute to his remarkable talent for managing people that he succeeded in getting himself elected by the Third Estate, despite his noble birth – on an anti-aristocratic ticket.

A man of similar convictions but very different character was Malouet, who was elected for the Third Estate at Riom. The head of the naval administration at Toulon, Malouet was immured in his own rectitude. As an important civil servant, he was used to dealing with ministers - which made it easy, later on, for his opponents to denounce him as their puppet. He had personal experience of the anomalies and inefficiency of the *Ancien Régime* administration and was eager for reform, but with the bureaucrat's penchant for improvement from above, and little use for those he called 'the sectaries of Rousseau'. 'I have studied facts rather than theories and found in history rather than in moralists all the precepts and philosophy that governments must follow in order to preserve themselves.' This was a far cry from Sieyès. He admitted, in his memoirs, that he had been too ready to see plots everywhere and too reluctant to associate with potential allies who did not see things exactly in his own way. Despite - or perhaps because of - his long absence from his home town, he was curiously popular in Riom, where he was elected by acclamation and allowed to draft his own *cahier*, which included the guarantee of the 'legitimate' property rights of the first two Orders, which was a nice civil service equivocation. In addition to the usual constitutional provisions, Malouet's *cahier* called for a guarantee of the right to work and for easy access to credit. In an assembly of economic liberals he was to stand out as an advocate of state intervention in the economy in the interest of working people. He almost declined election when he heard 'petit bourgeois, lawyers with no knowledge of public affairs, declaiming vehemently against tyranny and abuses, each one proposing his own constitution and quoting the *Social Contract*'.

This sample of deputies who were to make a name for themselves in the next two years is sufficient to suggest the diversity of the men themselves and the circumstances of their election. There were, of course, no political parties, not even in the loose sense in which these were understood in England. The new deputies did not know each other, even by reputation, except in isolated cases. Some were grandees or princes of the Church, many were parish priests or local lawyers who would never have got into the British House of Commons. Their election had often been attended by a fair amount of snapping and snarling, but if one is not to have a completely false picture of the state of France in the spring of 1789, it is essential to bear in mind the extraordinary wave of hope that engulfed the whole country - literally the whole country, since every parish had drafted its *cahier* and elected its spokesmen. It *was* bliss in that dawn to be alive. The elections had sometimes been rough. The men of Brittany and Artois in particular went to Versailles full of suspicion of their local elites, but equally full of confidence in the king and Necker. There was a readiness to let bygones be bygones: the Breton deputies went to ask the advice of Moleville, the man they had chased out of Rennes in the previous year. Most of them took it for granted that the regeneration of France had already begun and that, under their guidance, everyone could make a new start and their reborn country would become an object-lesson to the rest of humanity. It was in this mood that they all converged on Versailles.

3

The End of the *Ancien Régime*

W HEN the curtain went up on the great national drama for which everyone was waiting so impatiently, the actors did not know their parts and there had been no rehearsals. One or two people had made national reputations for themselves in different ways, but there were no recognized political leaders. The nobility were divided between Court and Country, the clergy between bishops and parish priests. The Third Estate was more homogeneous but its 600 members did not know each other and at first tended to cluster in local groups before separating along more political lines. With no party discipline to keep them in line and no relevant precedents, they had nothing to fall back on but first principles. These were derived, in the great majority of cases, from the Enlightenment in general and from Rousseau in particular. The rationalist cast of the Enlightenment and the divorce of the Philosophes from any contact with government had encouraged abstract speculation and the belief that there were logical answers to all political problems. This tended to bring out the prima donna in those who were convinced that their meditations had led them to the correct conclusions and it did not encourage compromise, especially for the Rousseauists, who identified politics with morals, since one is not supposed to make a coalition with the devil. Where there were no organized political groups there could be no tactical alliances.

These characteristics were not to become apparent until the Estates got down to business. The initial problems were ones of protocol. France was a hierarchical society in which matters of precedence, ceremonial, dress and forms of speech mattered a good deal. This was especially true of the Court but it applied at all levels of society. Those educated in the principles of the Enlightenment were impatient of what seemed to them antiquated trivialities unworthy of citizens, which did not make them any less touchy when they thought they were being treated without proper regard for their own dignity. They were quick to scent insult in what had been intended as traditional decorum. The authorities took it for granted that everyone should wear the appropriate dress for the occasion, which meant that the nobility and the bishops were resplendent in bright costumes while the *curés* and the Third

Estate wore black. The bishops insisted – or perhaps took it for granted – that they should process apart from their parish priests, which was a visual reminder of Sieyès's argument that the latter were part of a 'nation' from which the 'privileged orders' were excluded. Many of the *curés* agreed with him at the time, although some of them were to regret it later. Inevitably, when the deputies had to assemble for a meeting, the Third Estate went in last. They did not appreciate the long wait, especially if it happened to be raining. It was said that the king was reluctant to receive the Third Estate officially because no one knew how he ought to do it. Traditionally, they should have been on their knees in the royal presence. No one expected that any more, but where there were no precedents the Master of Ceremonies was at a loss about when people should stand or sit, when they should wear their hats and take them off. If Louis had been a different man he could have emphasized both his own authority and the exceptional dignity of the situation by imposing whatever conventions he thought appropriate but his pathetic concern to do the right thing, without ever knowing what it was, left him the prisoner of protocol.

The fact that the king had lost control over his Court added to his problems. If one can believe a Court witness, the comtesse d'Adhémar, his own sympathies inclined towards the Third Estate.[1] She included him amongst the 'revolutionaries' and quoted him as saying, 'Are the deputies of the Third Estate not my children too, and the most numerous part of my family? Would I not still be their king if the nobility were to lose some of their privileges and the clergy some scraps of their revenue?' 'Those who pay have a legitimate right to know why and to settle how they should pay.' The queen and Louis's brother, Artois, set about converting him to a different point of view. The comtesse d'Adhémar quoted Artois's friend, Vaudreuil, as urging his fellow-courtiers to isolate the royal family: 'Let us make sure that nothing contrary to us reaches them and leads them to turn towards the nation either from prudence or from weakness.' The Court ladies worked on the deputies. Looking back, the comtesse thought they had gone about it the wrong way. 'Scorn and contempt led us to repel the Third Estate, whose dispositions we could so easily have changed . . . our *merveilleux* spurned them and mystified them; all we did was laugh at their ridiculous costume, their bad taste and lack of elegance.'

The main objective of Court society was the conquest of the noble deputies from the provinces. Even Ferrières, a level-headed man, was at first swept off his feet by their attentions. On 22 May he told his wife that Vaudreuil had become his friend and he had been adopted by the queen's circle. 'Would you ever have thought, my good friend,' he wrote again on 5 June, 'that your poor husband would have found himself on close terms with the Great?' A week later he had begun to smell a rat. 'I have been forced to go less often to the Polignacs, because of a host of petty intrigues in which I don't want to get

[1] *Souvenirs sur Marie Antoinette*. Paris, 1836, 4 vols.

involved. It is said that it is they and the comte d'Artois who are preventing the Estates from functioning.' Court society was playing politics in the only way it knew, vacillating between vague fears of revolution and contempt for the would-be revolutionaries. It reassured itself that, if it came to a trial of strength, these absurd bourgeois would not dare to take on the chivalry of France. This was rather a bad miscalculation but an understandable mistake on the part of people who had cut themselves off from the general life of the nation, at a time when one of the many meanings of 'bourgeois' was 'civilian'. As Vaudreuil put it, 'We were all novices; we had never seen a revolution. It is easy to think about building dykes the day after a flood, but who does anything about it the day before?'

Proceedings opened on 4 May with a procession to church and a Te Deum, at which the bishop of Nancy preached a two-hour sermon on the importance of religion in the national life, during which the king dozed off. On the following day Barentin, the Keeper of the Seals, and Necker addressed the deputies. Both spoke too long and most of what Barentin said was inaudible. He authorized the Estates to discuss freedom of the press and reform of the law and of education, but Necker implied that the role of the assembly would be purely consultative, leaving the king free to implement or disregard its proposals as he chose. It looked like the Notables all over again. Necker gave no instructions about the manner of voting, which was left for the deputies themselves to decide.

On the following day they met in three separate groups. The Third Estate then insisted that the credentials of all those who claimed to have been elected should be verified in a common session. In itself the issue was of minimal importance but it was seen by everyone as implying a decision about whether or not the assembly should then meet as one House or as three. The nobles promptly verified their credentials and declared themselves constituted as a separate Order, by a vote of 188 to 47. The clergy, who showed themselves to be badly split, arrived at a similar decision but by a majority of only 19. The 600 deputies of the Third Estate declared themselves unable to do anything at all in the absence of the other two Orders. For a fortnight nothing happened, apart from the exchange of messages between the different Orders.

These weeks of paralysis had unfortunate effects. As had happened in Dauphiné in the previous year, the mere fact of meeting apart generated a particular *esprit de corps* within the Second and Third Estates and hardened their attitude towards each other. If the Third Estate was ever to obtain joint sessions it had no alternative but to filibuster. The nobility would probably have accepted joint meetings if the king had ordered it - 40 per cent of the nobles's *cahiers* permitted it - but they were not going to be bullied by the Third Estate. As the exchanges between the Orders became more acrimonious, the moderates within each found themselves the prisoners of the hard-liners. Those in the Third Estate, like Malouet, who argued the case for conciliation, were discredited when the nobility failed to respond. The commoners, although they agreed on a few rules of procedure and elected the astronomer, Bailly, as their doyen, since they insisted that they were no more than a collection of individuals with no verified status, could enforce no proper rules of debate and got into the habit of disorderly meetings at which unpopular speakers were shouted down. The public galleries were said to hold 2,000 spectators, who could not be prevented from expressing their opinions at what were officially no more than public meetings. When Malouet demanded the exclusion of this audience, he was challenged by one of his colleagues: 'Are you forgetting that you are only their representatives, their agents?' The presence of the public would 'shame the cowardly and perfidious who have been corrupted by frequenting the Court'. That was one way of looking at it. Malouet could scarcely object since, on one occasion, he also appealed to the public galleries when he mistakenly thought that they were on his side.

Conferences between the three Orders tended to make things worse. After one of them the nobility declared the separate existence of the Orders to be part of the French constitution. At another, the Third Estate appealed to what it called the rights of the nation, while the nobles took their stand on tradition, which one of them took back as far as the constitutional practices of the Germanic tribes, as recorded by Tacitus! As both tempers and suspicions rose, Malouet's repeated appeals for compromise merely discredited him. On 5 June he argued that the nobles were at fault but the Third Estate should respect the king's appeal for harmony. Laws were irresistible when they reflected the general will of the nation; the powers of all the deputies were derived from their constituents and since the *cahiers* of the three Orders were virtually unanimous, the clergy and nobility, even if they debated apart, would eventually be forced by public opinion to accept the will of the nation. If the Third Estate persisted in its attempt to coerce them, the issue would have to be resolved by force, which would mean anarchy if they won and despotism if they lost. A good many of his colleagues probably agreed with him but they were not prepared to capitulate in public.

At a final round of conferences, Necker proposed that credentials should be verified separately, with all contentious cases being referred to the royal council. For the time being the Third Estate was saved from the need to challenge royal authority when this proposal was rejected by the nobility, who had not forgotten that they had started the fight against 'ministerial despotism'. They were still trying to make a revolution of their own and the crown had at least as much to fear from them as from the commoners. Since both clergy and nobility had by now voted to surrender their fiscal privileges (the latter only after a constitution had been drafted by the three Orders acting separately), what divided the Second and Third Estates was not fiscal or constitutional policy but social status. They had been partners in 1788 and the increasingly bitter quarrel between them concerned the choice between traditional society with its institutionalized hierarchy and a commonwealth of citizens. Since the more 'enlightened' nobles were prepared to accept the latter and most of the commoners considered themselves to be gentlemen and men of honour who were not to be confused with working people, there should have been room for compromise. The fact that it did not materialize was at least partially due to Necker's failure to provide effective leadership.

Sooner or later something had to happen and on 10 June the deputies voted almost unanimously a motion by Sieyès to issue a last invitation to the other two Orders and then verify credentials in the name of the Estates General as a whole. As soon as they started to do this a trickle of *curés* began to join them. They then had to make good their claim to represent the entire nation. The checking of electoral returns had been a matter of private business but the next step involved a challenge to the authority of the king. Mirabeau saw where this was likely to lead. He proposed that taxes should be authorized only for the duration of the session and the Debt guaranteed only when the bases of the constitution had been voted, but he warned his colleagues that what they were contemplating was not in accordance with their *cahiers* and that any resolution they passed would need the king's approval. In a melodramatic outburst he said that he would rather live in Constantinople than in an aristocracy where 600 men exercised sovereign power. It was a timely warning, but his past life made Mirabeau suspect. He would have been even more so if his colleagues had known that he had just tried to negotiate an agreement with Necker, who had rebuffed him. Malouet's support did Mirabeau no good since Malouet was actually known to be on good terms with some of the ministerial despots. On 17 June the deputies therefore voted, by 491 to 90, to call themselves the 'National Assembly', after the proposer of the motion had said with more bluntness than was tactful, 'Since when has the constitution of nations depended on kings?'. Two days later, by a rather dubious majority, the clergy voted to join them. The nobility, who had defied the king ten days earlier, over the verification of their credentials, now protested their devotion to him. It did not cost them anything and it probably did not impress him much.

Rather late in the day, Necker woke up to the fact that the situation was getting out of control. He decided at last to do what he ought to have done in the beginning: to have the king take the initiative and announce a programme of reform at a royal session. It worked out as badly as his ideas usually did. In the first place, when the deputies of the Third Estate gathered on 20 June they found their meeting-place locked, on the pretext that it had to be prepared for the royal session. After wandering around for a time, they met in a (royal) tennis court where they took an oath never to separate until France had a constitution; in other words, to deny the king any right to dissolve them. Only one member voted against the motion, on the ground that it challenged the king's authority. Bailly tried to reassure him by saying that everyone recognized that all future legislation and the constitution itself would require the royal assent. It seemed obvious enough at the time.

It was not entirely Necker's fault if the royal session on 23 June misfired. His own draft proclamation, which was somewhat more liberal than the one eventually adopted, had been approved by the ministers when Necker's enemies at Court, led by the queen and Artois, persuaded Louis to amend it. The changes probably did not make much difference, although Necker naturally maintained that they were crucial. In his memoirs, he said that he proposed to resign and was only dissuaded by the fear that his doing so might endanger the royal family. What he did do was to boycott the royal session, when his conspicuously empty chair ensured that his own popularity would not suffer, whatever the result.

The amended royal programme made an extraordinary mixture. It began by setting Louis squarely behind the nobility: 'The king wills that the ancient distinction of the three Orders of the State shall be preserved in its entirety as essentially bound up with the constitution of his kingdom.' He therefore declared void the self-constitution of the Third Estate as the National Assembly, together with all subsequent transactions of that illegal body. He authorized joint sessions in matters of common interest, but specifically excluded from this category anything relating to the rights of the first two Orders, the constitution and matters affecting the clergy. In a second declar-ation he destroyed the basis of royal absolutism. He conceded to the Estates General not merely the control of finance, in the form of both taxation and loans, but even - at least by implication - the control of the budgets of the different government departments. Although feudal and seigneurial rights were guaranteed as property, there was to be complete fiscal equality. The Estates were invited to suggest means of dispensing with *lettres de cachet* and introducing freedom of the press. Internal customs barriers and the hated salt tax, together with the *corvée*, were to be abolished and the legal system reformed. In other words, with the specific exception of his control over the armed forces - which no one, at that time, thought of questioning - the king invited the Estates to discuss a whole range of issues that had hitherto been considered part of the royal prerogative, conceding in advance the control over the budget that would ensure that any opinions expressed were much more than matters of advice. If he had offered as much when the session began, the Third Estate would have found it very difficult to drum up public support for joint sessions and the majority of them might well have been content, like the Dauphinois in 1788, to accept the preservation of social distinctions in return for the concession of all their other demands. Louis never went back on these proposals, which he regarded as his last political action as a free agent. To the extent that the revolution was about political liberty, it can therefore be con-sidered to have prevailed by 23 June.

What had happened was the final triumph of the aristocratic revolt: the king had capitulated to those who wanted to combine a political revolution with the preservation of the social status quo. If he had done so a year earlier the course of French history would have been entirely different. As it was, he contrived to make the worst of all possible worlds. After giving the Third Estate six weeks in which to work itself up into a defiant mood, he made his concessions in the tone of a man dictating an ultimatum. His final remarks included the threat that, if the deputies failed to respond, 'Alone I will pursue the good of my people, alone I will consider myself their true representative.' Duquesnoy, one of the more conservative deputies of the Third Estate, who had been grumbling the day before that it was dominated by a dozen ambitious rogues, was scandalized by the tone of the king's speeches. Ferrières, looking back when he wrote his memoirs by which time his enthusiasm for the revolution had cooled, still said that everyone had been offended.

When the king concluded he ordered the deputies to disperse. The Third Estate, as it had agreed in advance, stayed put. When Mirabeau proposed that it should vote the parliamentary immunity of its members, only thirty-four disagreed. It was typical of the incoherence of royal policy that when it was at last decided to make a stand, no preparations were made to deal with resistance. Nothing happened. On the following day 151 members of the clergy, including two archbishops and three bishops, defied the king and joined the National Assembly. The day after, 47 nobles, led by a prince of the blood (Orléans), three dukes and five marquises, did the same. Louis not merely acquiesced in this violation of his formal orders of the 23rd but actually ordered the union of the remaining clergy and nobles. He may have been alarmed by unrest in Paris and Versailles but he was no coward and the alleged danger to the royal family was probably magnified, if not invented, by Artois as the only way of persuading the more quixotic of his colleagues to comply with the royal order. Possibly Louis was merely trying to gain time. What the public did not know was that, on the 26th, the day before he instructed the deputies to meet in common, Louis had issued the first orders for the concentration of troops between Paris and Versailles. What he intended to do with them when they arrived, he did not know either. It looked as though everything had now been settled. This was the view of Arthur Young, the English traveller, who wrote on 27 June, 'The whole business now seems over and the revolution complete.' On the following day he left Paris to resume his investigation of French agriculture, which meant that he missed some rather exciting times.

The union of the Orders did not please everyone. Some of the clergy and nobles protested and continued to hold separate meetings for another fortnight. The former president of the clergy, cardinal de La Rochefoucauld, was unwise enough to tell the Assembly that the clergy were still entitled to meet apart. This earned him a rebuke from Pétion: 'No one can give orders to the nation.' This was an early indication of the deputies's tendency to equate the Assembly with the general will. Mirabeau, forgetting about his preference for Constantinople, was even more emphatic: 'No power on earth, not even the executive power [that was more tactful than saying 'the king'] has the right to say "I will" to the representatives of the nation.' Louis was discovering that for himself.

Despite the protests of disgruntled minorities, contemporaries were unanimous that the general feeling in the Assembly was one of harmony

restored rather than of victors and vanquished. Barère, a deputy of the Third
Estate and future member of the Committee of Public Safety, went rather too
far when he wrote in his newspaper, 'From the first moment of this reunion,
hatred and rivalry have disappeared.' There was, all the same, a general
readiness to make a new start. Ferrières thought the union of the Orders a good
idea. Alexandre de Lameth, a member of the Court nobility who was becoming
one of the leaders of the Left in the Assembly, wrote in his memoirs of 'general
rejoicing'. Mounier said there was a feeling of reconciliation rather than of
victory and pointed out that, when the Assembly divided into thirty bureaux,
for the detailed discussion of proposed legislation, a clergyman or a noble was
elected to preside over each one of them. From 3 July to 28 September, five of
the six presidents of the Assembly were bishops or members of the Court
nobility. Duquesnoy thought that the presence of the first two Orders did
something for the gravity and order of the Assembly. This rather worried his
more radical colleague Creuzé-Latouche, who feared for the firmness and
cohesion of the commoners in the presence of their social superiors. What had
happened put an end to the wrangling of the first two months, even if it could
not efface the memories of it. Granted the abolition of fiscal privilege, the
general agreement about the constitution, the king's renunciation of his
theoretically absolute power and the universal respect for property rights, there
seemed no reason why the Assembly should not get on with its business as
amicably as most parliaments contrive to do. It looked as though Arthur
Young had been right.

While most of the deputies settled down to the business for which they had
been elected, Mirabeau realized that a trial of strength had been postponed
rather than averted. His first worry was about the threat of disorder in Paris
and he suggested issuing an appeal for calm, which was disregarded during the
excitement caused by the arrival of the nobility and clergy. The capital was
indeed becoming increasingly tense. This was partly due to the high price of
bread, which had risen by 20 per cent since the previous November. In April a
massive riot had resulted in the sacking of the house of Réveillon, a wallpaper
manufacturer who was wrongly rumoured to have suggested a reduction in
wages. The French Guards, who shared in the responsibility for maintaining
order in Paris, had fired on the crowd and many people had been killed. The
origins of the Réveillon riot had been essentially economic but the atmosphere
was politically charged; some of the rioters had shouted '*Vive le Tiers Etat*,
Vive M. Necker!' and even '*Vive le Roi!*' During the weeks of political
deadlock the *habitués* of the cafes, especially those grouped in the Palais Royal,
which its owner, Orléans, had 'developed' as a centre of entertainment,
worked each other up with excited commentaries on current news and
rumour. Danton, a hitherto respectable lawyer, was one of those who saw a
new career opening up as a mob orator. The French Guards were fêted and
flattered and towards the end of June some of them began to declare their
support for the Third Estate.

The Assembly, at Versailles, was not quite sure what to make of all this. The deputies were men of order, with an elevated sense of their own dignity and convinced that they had just won a decisive contest by constitutional means. They appreciated that the maintenance of discipline in the armed forces was none of their business, but the mutineers were potential allies whom it might be dangerous to alienate. On 1 July, when a deputation from Paris pleaded for an amnesty for the rebellious French Guards, one motion after another was defeated, until the Assembly voted what might be described as a composite resolution, appealing for calm in Paris, affirming the king's responsibility for law and order and inviting him to show clemency towards the mutineers. Two days later Louis agreed to pardon them and reminded the Assembly that it shared in the responsibility for the maintenance of order.

The one thing that could be guaranteed to raise the political temperature in Paris was the concentration of troops in the neighbourhood which, amongst other things, was likely to aggravate the shortage of food. It was Mirabeau again who, on 5 July suggested inviting the king to cancel the troop movements and to authorize the raising of *gardes bourgeoises*, or civilian militias, in Paris and Versailles. No one opposed him and the first part of his motion was passed with only four dissentient voices. The king replied that the only purpose of the troops was to preserve order. If the Assembly felt that its freedom of debate was threatened by their presence, he would willingly transfer its sessions to Noyon or Soissons. Louis must have enjoyed the feeling that he was beating the deputies at their own game. By now he had about 30,000 troops in the vicinity and felt free to act. On the same day - 11 July - he dismissed Necker and three other ministers, replacing them with uncompromising royalists. This was more an assertion of will than the signal for a *coup d'état*. Moleville thought that the intention of Breteuil, who was generally thought to be the leading man in the new ministry, did not go beyond attaining the premiership. The new men had no preconcerted policy and the troops were probably intended to form a *cordon sanitaire* to isolate Versailles from the capital. The deputies, however, could scarcely be blamed if they took a more alarmist view of the situation and prepared for a dissolution, if not for the arrest of their leading members.

There was no meeting of the Assembly on Sunday, 12 July. In that respect at least, Necker's dismissal had been well timed. The most significant thing that happened on the 13th was a closing of the ranks and a re-formation of the alliance of 1788. The Dauphiné noble, the comte de Virieu, proposed a reaffirmation by the entire Assembly of the resolutions passed by the Third Estate on 17 and 20 June. Several nobles rose to shout that past divisions must be forgotten and that all must unite *pour sauver la patrie prête à périr*. When the king rejected an invitation to recall the dismissed ministers and send the troops away, the deputies formally reaffirmed the motions of 17, 20 and 23 June. In other words, the united Assembly declared taxation to be legal only for the duration of the session, proclaimed their parliamentary immunity and their intention, if dissolved, to reassemble in any place where they could meet.

To prevent any repetition of the royal lock-out of 20 June, some of them maintained an all-night presence for the next forty-eight hours, nominating Lafayette as acting president, in view of the frailty of their official president, the archbishop of Vienne. Ferrières, not a man given to theatrical gestures, was one of those who joined in the all-night sessions. After taking all the defensive measures they could, the deputies devoted 14 July to debating the constitution.[2] It was an impressive display of confidence. The royal government had the military force to disperse and arrest them, but at the almost certain price of civil war, which the king was determined to avoid. The Assembly was anything but powerless; what it lacked was the means of coercing the king without armed conflict. Paradoxically, this was provided by the revolt of Paris.

News of Necker's dismissal did not reach Paris until 12 July. When the crowds of Sunday picnickers began to make their way back to the capital the first thing they did was to attack and burn some of the customs barriers at which import duties were imposed on goods entering the city.[3] According to one eye-witness, the more respectable citizens had already retired to their homes. It would be futile to speculate about how far the motives of the rioters were political or economic. They regarded Necker as the man who could save them from famine and all factors fused in the general excitement. What is more to the point is that the action of the crowds was spontaneous and undirected and that they were at least believed to be drawn from the poorer sections of the population. The more law-abiding members of the population viewed their activities with alarm and expected them to degenerate into looting. It was less than ten years since the Gordon riots had terrorized London. Bailly noted on the 13th that the news from Paris was of brigands plundering. Duquesnoy confirmed that the first reaction in the Assembly to the alarming rumours was one of consternation.

What turned a riot into a revolution was the reaction of the Paris electors. These were the representatives of the sixty electoral wards who had come together to choose the deputies to the Estates General. Since then they had continued to meet informally and on 13 July they took control of the situation, reinforcing the city council and setting about the immediate organization of 48,000 National Guards, a measure explicitly forbidden by the king. During the next day or two everything was excitement and confusion. The electors had no formal authority, but the enlarged city council had enough influence to guide what was still a basically spontaneous movement and to give it the character of a general insurrection. The defection of the regiment of French Guards provided them with some disciplined troops. To arm the National Guards muskets were recovered from those who had stolen them from gunsmiths's shops on the 12th. An expedition to the Invalides induced the governor

2 For these constitutional debates see the following chapter.
3 The nineteenth-century historian Buchez, quoting the newspaper *L'Ami du Roi*, said that the first of these attacks occurred on 11 July, before news of Necker's dismissal had reached Paris: *Histoire de l'Assemblée Constituante*, Paris, 1846, 2 vols, I/371. This is presumably a mistake.

to part with 28,000 more and to surrender 20 cannon. The urgent need was for powder and it was this that prompted the march on the Bastille, a medieval fortress that dominated the East End of Paris. De Launay, the governor, after some parleying, proved less accommodating than his colleague at the Invalides. The French Guards brought up one or two of the captured pieces of artillery and it was they who enabled the crowd to break in, after a good many had been killed by musketry from the walls. How far the city council approved of all this, even they were probably too bewildered to ask themselves. They certainly did not approve of the murder and decapitation of de Launay and his second-in-command, together with the former head of the municipal government. Gradually, however, they came to realize that they had won. The troops had been withdrawn from the streets of Paris to the Champ de Mars, where they did nothing. The capital was not attacked and the crowds, whether or not they were deterred by the National Guard, did not turn to looting. Control of the city passed into the hands of resolute supporters of what was coming to be called 'the revolution'. It was scarcely noticed at the time and it has not been sufficiently emphasized by historians, that a succession of similar revolts, set off either by Necker's dismissal or by news from Paris, effected a similar transfer of power in many provincial towns. The framework of centralized absolutism collapsed; henceforth the king's orders would only be obeyed if they were endorsed by the Assembly.

From the beginning, the storming of the Bastille, which was no more than the dramatic climax to the Parisian revolt, was seized on as the perfect symbol for what had happened and, like all good symbols, it took on a life of its own. The embodiment of both medieval and royal oppression – it had been used to house the political victims of *lettres de cachet* although there were none there in 1789 – had fallen to the irresistible force of the sovereign people. Those who had affirmed with Rousseau, even if they had scarcely believed it, that national regeneration was essentially a question of will, seemed to have been proved right. All things were possible. A people that had dismissed itself as frivolous and superficial had scaled heights thought to have been the monopoly of Englishmen and Americans. Perhaps it had even surpassed them. There was a general disinclination to worry about the few people who had been massacred. Ferrières, a normally humane man, comforted himself without much difficulty on the 15th with the thought that 'the justice of heaven often makes use of the hands of men'. Barnave, to his later regret, asked on the 23rd if the blood of those murdered had been so pure after all. By the end of the month Ferrières had recovered himself and was denouncing de Launay's murder as 'inhuman'. His initial callousness was perhaps a measure of his alarm. He wrote to his wife on the 15th, 'The capture of the Bastille saved us . . . the night of Tuesday 14th to Wednesday 15th would probably have been our last day. (sic) . . . All goes well in the Assembly. The Orders are in agreement.'

On 15 July the king paid a personal visit to the Assembly. It had been agreed that he was to be received in silence until the deputies heard what he had to say but some burst into '*Vive le Roi!*' as soon as they saw him. Louis, addressing them for the first time as the National Assembly, told them that he was giving orders for the dispersal of the troops. Now the cheers were general and the entire body processed with him back to the palace. It was to be an extraordinarily long time before he finally estranged men who were determined to believe that, at heart, he was on their side. Louis, for that matter, was equally convinced that what seemed best to him was something that they would agree with if they thought about it calmly. On the 17th he paid a state visit to Paris that looked more like a penitential pilgrimage. By now Bailly had been made mayor and Lafayette put in command of the National Guard. The Assembly was still debating whether or not it had the right to denounce the ministers and ask for the recall of Necker, when the king informed it that he had invited Necker back.

There were various way of interpreting what had happened. Artois and his friends had clearly lost and he left France to continue elsewhere a career of political ineptitude that was eventually to lose him the throne in 1830. The leader of a Parisian deputation to the Assembly thought that the victory belonged to the Parisians: 'Messieurs, you are the saviours of the nation but you yourselves have saviours of your own . . . They are the fearless men who have just taken the Bastille.' This was a point of view that naturally commended itself to the Parisians, even if few of them went so far as the journalist, Marat, who was soon arguing that neither the king nor the Assembly did anything right unless they were coerced. The deputies saw things rather differently. They had no quarrel with the view that the insurrection was a demonstration of the irresistible will of the sovereign people. Even Malouet said that 'a national insurrection against despotism has a character superior to the powers of the law'. As they saw it, however, the objective of the revolt had been to come to their rescue and they emerged with a somewhat inflated view of their role. The duc de Liancourt described the Assembly as 'the most august in the whole world' only to be outbid by a Breton lawyer who called it 'the most august that has ever existed in the universe'. Such views of their own importance led the deputies to revise their opinions about the powers of the king. On the 17th they had not been sure whether or not they were entitled to ask him to change his ministers; by the 20th one of them was arguing that, until the constitution had been completed, the royal assent was not needed for any decision of the Assembly to become law. This was heady stuff, but in the general euphoria there was no need to face up to awkward questions. With Paris under the control of the former doyen of the Third Estate and its militia commanded by a man who modelled himself on George Washington rather than on Oliver Cromwell, there was nothing to fear from the capital. One of the most important aspects of the July crisis was the fact that it had not quite resulted in a declaration of war by either side. The royal government had not opted for a fight and the result had been determined - despite the fighting round the Bastille - by a victory of will rather than of armed force. Given both the good intentions and the extraordinary pliability of the king, it was just possible to believe that all that had happened had been due to a misunderstanding. With his evil advisers out of the way – and that included Artois as well as the ministers – the path was clear for the king and the Assembly to proceed with the work of national regeneration to which each, if in different ways, felt committed. Another way of looking at this, of course, was to argue that, having fought and run away, the king lived to fight another day. The lessons of the revolutions of 1848, when the rulers of Austria and Prussia bent before a revolutionary storm and were back in control within a year, are a reminder to us of the recuperative power of monarchy. The men of 1789 did not know about 1848, but they did not under-estimate the king's power to fight back.

By 27 July the Assembly was once more discussing the constitution. On the following day the first reports began to come in about widespread rural revolts.[4] All through the spring there had been food riots up and down the country and these had intensified towards the middle of July. Economic in origin, they also reflected the politicization of the countryside by the drafting of the *cahiers* and the elections to the Estates General. As well as the usual practice of commandeering grain for sale at a reduced price, many of the rioters were refusing to pay tithes and manorial dues. Some broke into châteaux and burned the seigneurial title deeds. At times the leaders claimed to be acting in the king's name, against the agents of an 'aristocratic' plot whose intentions were as sinister as they were mysterious. In mid-July there occurred a new phenomenon, distinct in origin although its consequences tended to become confused with the agrarian revolts. This was the 'great fear' – not so much a panic as an alarm – generated by rumours that 'brigands' were threatening to destroy the vulnerable crops on whose safe harvesting the next year's food supply depended. The source of the different 'fears' that spread across most of the country was imaginary in every case. There were no brigands and no crops were actually damaged. Most people, however, believed the rumours for a longer or shorter time (five days in the case of Arthur Young) and were naturally inclined to look for a political explanation behind the wanton destruc- tion of the harvest. As the reports came in, the deputies were in no position to discriminate between true, if exaggerated news of the agrarian revolt, and the tales of the mythical brigands. They got the impression that much of the country was in revolt and they suspected the brigands of being the agents of counter-revolutionaries.

The insurrection in the towns might have been the work of the sovereign people but neither the deputies nor the urban revolutionaries had any sympathy for the rural revolts. The Parisian press was unanimous in denouncing the peasant rebels as bandits and in demanding their repression.[5]

---

[4] On this subject see G. Lefebvre, *La Grande Peur*. Paris, 1932. (Eng. trans. 1973.)

[5] F. Freddi, 'La Presse parisienne et la nuit du 4 Août', *Annales Historiques de la Révolution française*, 259 (1985), p. 46.

In provincial towns, one of the incentives to form National Guard units was self-defence against the surrounding countryside. Revolutionary municipalities had no inhibitions about organizing punitive forays into the villages and hanging the peasant leaders. Two worlds were in conflict, one of which saw grain as food, the other as property.[6] The enemy of the peasant was as likely to be the seigneur's agent as the seigneur himself, especially if the latter was an absentee; the people who made a profit from the collection of seigneurial dues were the kind of entrepreneurs who often identified themselves with the revolution. Many of the deputies, and not merely those of the nobility, were landowners, if not seigneurs, and the rural revolt posed a direct challenge to their property in a way in which the urban insurrections, once the threat of pillage was averted, did not.

The first reaction of the Assembly, supported by both conservative and radical deputies, was to create a *comité de recherches* to investigate plots, despite the warning of the chevalier de Boufflers that France was not at war, that the Assembly had nothing to fear and that it risked creating its own successor to ministerial despotism. On 3 August the *comité des rapports* signalled widespread revolts and château-burning. The Assembly was in a dilemma: it had no sympathy for brigands and incendiary peasants but it was not disposed to ask the king to order his troops to shoot civilians, in case they forgot when to stop. At the end of an inconclusive debate, Malouet made an extraordinary speech. He began with the inconvenient observation that the abuses that the Assembly was about to abolish provided the livelihood of a substantial section of the population. The first victims of measures against the privileged would be the poor who depended on them. Unemployment, already a serious problem, would get worse. He then came up with the very unorthodox argument that public expenditure which generated employment was only a fictitious burden on public funds. He demanded the creation of bureaux of labour and public assistance in every town, to be financed by existing charities and the raising of a new tax. Chambers of commerce of the manufacturing towns were to be invited to suggest means of stimulating the economy. Those who could not be found any employment were to be drafted into the army or navy and anyone found on the roads without a passport was to be arrested as a vagrant. It was probably not his expeditious way of dealing with the unemployable that led to Malouet's speech being badly received. Anything he said was suspected and those who liked to think of themselves as public benefactors in a rather abstract sort of way did not relish being told that the solution to one problem was the creation of another. It was more pleasant to participate in a world where all problems had conclusive answers. The interventionist role that Malouet wanted to give the state must also have shocked the more rigorous economic liberals. Malouet's proposals were

6 For a very perceptive description of this conflict of values, although it refers to a later date, see C. Lucas, 'Themes in southern violence after 9 thermidor', G. Lewis and C. Lucas, *Beyond the Terror*, Cambridge University Press, 1983.

referred to the bureaux and nothing more was heard of them. They are a useful reminder to the historian not to follow the revolutionaries' own practice of putting people into pigeon-holes and to assume that men who were bound by no party whip were equally radical or conservative on all the different issues that came their way.

The Assembly preferred to deal with rural unrest by more dramatic means than those suggested by Malouet. Its problem was to ease the manorial burden on the peasants without challenging the sanctity of property. Its solution was worked out in private and sprung on the deputies during the evening of 4 August, one of the most remarkable sessions in the history of any parliament. The basic idea was that the nobility should surrender rights that the Assembly was not entitled to abolish. It had been arranged that the duc d'Aiguillon, one of the richest landowners in France, should propose, in the name of the nobility, the commutation of all manorial dues. The vicomte de Noailles, a less impressive benefactor since he had very little to lose himself, being a younger son, got in first with the proposal to abolish without compensation all remaining traces of serfdom and obligations implying personal lordship, while commuting those thought to have originated in former transfers of land. The manoeuvre did not work out as those who had planned it expected, for d'Aiguillon and Noailles set off a torrent of emulation. Beneficiaries of every kind of privilege queued up to sacrifice it on the altar of the *patrie*: manorial justice, hunting rights, the heredity and venality of office and provincial privileges all went by the board. When the Assembly adjourned at 2 o'clock in the morning, after voting Louis to be the 'regenerator of French liberty', the deputies had gone far beyond their original intention to do something for the peasants and committed themselves to a transformation of most French institutions that would take years to complete and would change the whole face of the country. This was largely the product of altruism and enthusiasm. It is not fashionable nowadays to speak of national characteristics, but it is hard to think of anything similar happening in any other country.

It had not all been altruism: one or two deputies had sacrificed each other's privileges. When the marquis de Foucault offered up the sacrifice of Court pensions, he was probably thinking more of Noailles than of himself. It was a bishop who put paid to hunting rights. These were rather untypical examples. Most of the sacrifices were genuine: even the impoverished *curés* offered to give up the payment for their occasional services. The immediate reaction to the unforgettable night was one of universal approval and general enthusiasm. Dumont, a member of Mirabeau's brains trust, who witnessed the debate, said that the deputies were weeping for joy. The conservative Duquesnoy thought their intoxication and delirium entirely appropriate: 'What a nation! What glory, what honour to be French!' Rabaut Saint-Etienne thought it a superb spectacle. Ferrières, who had more to lose, marvelled that the unification of the country, which the most skilful minister could not have achieved in ten years, had been brought about in a single night. 'If the result does anything for the general good I shall easily console myself for what I lose as a *gentilhomme* and the seigneur of a fief.' Mme Elisabeth, the king's naïve and unworldly sister, wrote of the nobility acting with an enthusiasm worthy of their French hearts and added, 'I hope that will stop people burning châteaux.'

When it came to working out the details, the euphoria of the 4th sometimes wore thin. After swallowing a camel, the nobility strained at a pigeon and there was a violent argument about the abolition of seigneurial dovecots. The main discussion, however, concerned the Church. It had been decided on the 4th that tithes should be commuted, which would have allowed the clergy to invest in land the compensation that they received and retain both their wealth and their independence. When this was debated, the issue became one of abolition. It exposed the first fundamental division within the Assembly. Anti-clericalism had already surfaced within the Third Estate, where there was always someone ready with a disobliging remark about the clergy. Much more serious was the fact that many, if not most deputies regarded organized religion not as a divine institution but as a social service. Those who had fewest inhibitions about saying so tended to be nobles and the religious division cut across politics. Conservative nobles could be violent anti-clericals, while the radical Breton deputy Lanjuinais was always ready to come to the defence of religion. What was at issue was one's conception of society. For most of the clergy and laymen like Lanjuinais, whatever one rendered unto Caesar, there remained things that belonged only to God. Their opponents went far beyond the obvious debating point that the upper clergy had tended to include in the latter category the appurtenances of an episcopal life-style that owed nothing to the Scriptures. Classically educated and reared in the traditions of the Enlightenment, and especially of Rousseauist republicanism, for them the claims of civil society were total. Citizens could not serve two masters and the unitary state could not tolerate the existence within itself of a dual allegiance or of autonomous corporations of any kind. That was one of the aspects of French society that the session of 4 August had been intended to destroy.

On 6 August the comte de Custine made a nasty reference to the clergy's 'belated repentence'. Next day the marquis de Blacons suggested that, if a new loan were necessary, it could be guaranteed by the property of the Church. Another marquis – Lacoste – said that in any case this belonged to the state. He suggested abolishing tithe, suppressing the monastic orders and all ecclesiastical functions other than those of bishop and *curé*. The Assembly was not yet ready for that. Alexandre de Lameth argued that the property of individuals was sacred but 'political corporations exist only for society'. When the archbishop of Aix proposed that the clergy retire to discuss how they could best use their wealth to guarantee a loan, Lameth and a deputy of the Third Estate, Dubois-Crancé, replied that that was for the nation to decide. After the Assembly had agreed to the loan the debate swung back to the tithe. Lanjuinais defended tithes as sacred while the bishop of Perpignan conceded that they belonged to the nation. Mirabeau provoked the protests of the clergy when he described ministers of religion as salaried officers of morality and education. Perhaps they thought that where morals were concerned he could scarcely claim to speak with much expertise. What was at issue was not so much tithe itself as the autonomy of the clergy. It was generally recognized that impropriated tithes in the hands of laymen were a legitimate form of property. Sieyès, in a hard-hitting speech, said that he was opposed to tithes but saw no reason to make an annual gift of 70 million livres to landowners, if tithes were replaced by an equivalent tax imposed on the population as a whole. 'I am looking for what is being done for the people in this grand operation and I am not finding it.' Turning the tables on those who reproached the clergy for their unwillingness to make sacrifices, he accused the landowners of being out for a killing while they urged generosity on everyone else. Having decided on 4 August that tithes were to be commuted, the Assembly was not entitled to go back on its decision. In the end the clergy gave way. The Archbishop of Paris and cardinal de La Rochefoucauld surrendered tithes to the nation. The clergy may not have appreciated how much ground they had conceded. Henceforth they would be partially dependent on public funds, wholly dependent if the Assembly were to take up the suggestions for the secularization of all their property. The Assembly would neither tolerate their claim to regulate their own affairs as an autonomous corporation nor finance them in the style of life to which they were accustomed. Implicit in the outcome of the debate was the entire reorganization of the Church and no one could predict how far that would go or what its consequence would be.

Even before it had put the proposals of 4 August into their final form, the Assembly acted on the question of law and order. A decree of 10 August instructed the municipalities, most of which were by now in friendly hands, to keep the peace by the deployment of National Guards, the mounted constabulary (*maréchaussée*) and regular troops. The army was to take an oath to the nation, the king and the law. Its officers were not to employ their men against civilians except at the request of municipal officials. Almost casually and with a minimum of debate, the Assembly deprived the king of his control over the armed forces, at least within France itself. Since the new municipalities were under no one's effective control, the most centralized bureaucracy in Europe had suddenly fallen apart.

When the Assembly celebrated its achievement with a Te Deum on 13 August it knew what it had to do. In addition to drafting a constitution it was committed to reshaping most of the country's institutions. The king was no longer in a position to prevent anything and could only hope to persuade. The fact that he replaced Breteuil and the other royalist ministers by men drawn from the Assembly suggested that he expected to be able to cooperate with it. It also deprived the clergy of one of their more popular spokesmen in the Assembly, de Cicé. Although debates had sometimes been acrimonious and the religious time-bomb had already been primed, the Assembly had recovered its unity during the July crisis. As the chevalier de Boufflers had warned, its main danger lay within itself. Incredulous of the extent of its own success, it was inclined to collective paranoia about imaginary plots by elusive counter-revolutionaries, all the more to be feared since no one could discover who they were. At the same time, its elevated view of its own merit and of its authority as the custodian of the general will, made it impatient of criticism, intolerant of minority views and contemptuous of pragmatists. It had no French precedents to guide it and it was coming to resent suggestions that it should model itself on British practices and experience. The walls of the Bastille had fallen at the sound of its trumpets and nothing was impossible.

At bottom the deputies were in general agreement about political principles and, except in matters of religion, their differences about the reshaping of French government and society did not concern fundamentals. What divided them was means rather than ends, until their quarrels and suspicions became so bitter that means became ends and the goodwill turned sour. There were already hints of this happening. Duquesnoy and Ferrières had both welcomed the memorable session of 4 August. On the 12th the former commented that all the concessions - like everything else in the revolution - had been the product of fear and revenge, and the latter wrote to his wife that all the ties that bound him to his tenants were now broken and he would not be spending much time at his château after the end of the session. Two months later, he told her, 'As long as Marsay belongs to me I will never let anyone go short of food or clothing.' One of the dangers of generalizing about historical processes is that it makes people look consistent and whatever happens seem inevitable. When they listened to the Te Deum, the deputies had much to be thankful for and the future was still their to make or mar.

4

The Victory of the Radicals

THE outcome of the crisis of July 1789 had been a victory for the Third Estate and its allies amongst the clergy and nobility and a defeat both for the king and for those members of the first two Orders who had hoped to perpetuate a society where status was largely determined by birth or religious vocation. What even the king came to refer to as the National Assembly was now free to draft its own constitution without fear of coercion or dissolution by the government. It was the government itself that had disintegrated. During the summer, messages of support for the Assembly poured in from the major towns and the intendants seem to have stopped trying to administer the country in the king's name. Henceforth orders from the government could only be enforced when they were endorsed by the Assembly. This meant that the deputies, whether they liked it or not, became involved in the executive side of government, indeed their participation was solicited by ministers who saw no other way of maintaining order and collecting taxes. The decisions of the night of 4 August enormously expanded the agenda of the Assembly; instead of being limited to drafting a constitution, its work had now to include the reorganization of every aspect of public life. What had been intended as a renunciation of privilege implied the radical reform of local government and of the legal system. Depriving the Church of a substantial part of its revenues meant that means would have to be found to finance the areas of social policy for which it had previously been responsible: education, hospitals and poor relief. On 14 July, in one of the worst prophecies of the revolution, the deputy Barère predicted that, as the result of a century of Enlightenment, everyone knew what sort of form the constitution should take and its actual drafting could perhaps be done in a day. Without going so far as that, most of the deputies had assumed that they would not be at Versailles for more than a month or two. After 4 August they realized that things were going to take a good deal longer.

If a revolution implies the forcible overthrow of an old order and its replacement by the victors in an armed struggle, free to impose their will without any need to negotiate with their defeated opponents, then this was something different. The deputies had always professed their faith in the good intentions of Louis XVI even if, in some cases, this represented hope rather than conviction. The great majority believed that they could go on relying on his acquiescence, if not his positive support. Necker had recovered his ministry and the continuity of government had been preserved. This imposed constraints on the freedom of action of the Assembly. In every other respect it was unanimously agreed, both in France and abroad, that what had happened did amount to a revolution. The past was repudiated *en bloc* and the deputies intended to construct an entirely new regime. It was not long before people invented the expression 'the *ancien régime*' to describe a state of affairs that was believed to have come to an end in 1789 and was comprehensively dismissed as the bad old days. Repudiation of the past involved the repudiation of precedent, which left the Assembly with no alternative but to base its new order on principle. This immediately raised the question of what the principles should be. As Barère had said, there was general agreement about many of the essentials: parliamentary government, equality before the law, religious toleration and freedom of speech. This concealed disagreement between those who defined liberty in a negative way, as freedom of the individual from interference by the state, and those who derived individual liberty from participation in a free society. Even if they were not entirely aware of all the implications, the men on each side knew what they were doing when they invoked the patronage of Montesquieu or Rousseau.

Whatever their convictions, none of them could base their choices on ideology alone. There had been a conflict, even if a relatively bloodless one, and it left behind the reasonable suspicion that those who had lost would look for means of renewing the fight. Even if the deputies believed what they professed about the good intentions of the king, two years of opposition to 'ministerial despotism' as personified by Calonne and Brienne had left them with a pathological mistrust of all ministers, even those drawn from the Assembly itself. It was not long before Necker too was regarded as at best a nuisance. The Third Estate's memories of the struggles of the spring also left it suspicious of nobles as a social group, though a good many of the leaders of the Left were of noble birth. Throughout all ranks of French society there was a widespread fear of an aristocratic plot. 'Aristocrat' was a conveniently vague term for describing one's enemies without having to define them. It could imply noble birth but it was also applied to royalists in general, counter-revolutionaries and eventually to the wealthy. It always implied hostility to the revolution; Lafayette might be a marquis, but he was only an aristocrat to the ultra-radical. The fact that there *was* no aristocratic plot, in any meaningful sense, did not make much difference. Enough people were prepared to try to overthrow the revolution by force to generate the feeling, amongst the more timorous or fanatical, that the miraculous victories of July could be quickly reversed. What was going to happen might well turn on the attitude of the king and the ministers who governed in his name. Virtually all the deputies were committed to the idea of a constitutional monarchy. Some of the more traditionally minded insisted that the Assembly did not have the authority to deprive Louis of rights that had accrued to him over centuries of French history. Even those who saw themselves as the spokesmen of an omnicompetent sovereign people recognized that, if a constitutional monarchy were to be effective, the king would have to be given the power to govern. But if 'the counter-revolution' was indeed a real threat and all ministers were potential despots, the power to govern might provide them with the means to subvert the revolution and restore the old order. Whatever constitutional principle might suggest, when it came to practice, such deputies would take no risks and give no hostages to the unprincipled. Fear of counter-revolution was the hallmark of the radical; it was sometimes the main reason for his radicalism.

All this gave rise to a number of passionate debates in which these intelligent and public-spirited men struggled with the problems of implementing the theories that were to regenerate France and, as the more sanguine believed, turn the country into a New Jerusalem that would be a beacon to the world. Like those who took part in the Putney debates in Cromwell's army, the speakers grappled with ideas as old as political theory itself. The issues that they raised were to last as long as the revolution which, ideologically speaking, can be considered a series of variations on the themes first played in August and September 1789. However theoretical the arguments, what was at issue was both the nature of the good society and the political tactics necessary to attain it. Besides showing what was in men's minds, the debates therefore revealed the strength of the different political groups in the Assembly and helped to set its course for the future.

The first issue of constitutional principle concerned the imperative mandates imposed on some of the clergy and nobility in some constituencies, which prevented them, on oath, from taking part in joint sessions with the Third Estate. When the king ordered all the deputies to meet in common, substantial elements of the first two Orders continued their separate meetings and expressed reservations about the extent to which they were bound by the joint sessions of the Assembly. In political terms, it was inconceivable that the majority, after their victory over the king, should allow themselves to be frustrated by the scruples of their opponents, whether these were genuine or invented. The separate meetings came to a sudden end during the July crisis but before then they had been the subject of a revealing debate. Two issues were involved. The first concerned the personal honour of deputies who, in some cases against their personal inclinations, had pledged themselves not to take part in joint sessions. For some of them at least, this constituted a genuine moral dilemma and the Assembly was always very sensitive to questions of honour. The second aspect of the question concerned nothing less than the location of sovereignty. There was general agreement that this lay with the people as a whole, and Rousseauists were well aware of their hero's gibe about the British only being free on polling day. Sovereignty, according to Rousseau, could never be delegated. In that case, the deputies were the mere mandatories of their constituents, who were free to impose on them whatever restrictions they chose. Extricating themselves from the inconvenient consequences of this theory called for some tactical ingenuity.

This was supplied by Talleyrand, the eldest son of one of the most distinguished families in France. An accident in childhood, which left him a partial cripple, diverted him from his natural career in the army into the Church.[1] He combined a total absence of any religious vocation with a determination to get to the top in whatever career he happened to be pursuing. At the age of twenty-six he was made *Agent-Général* of the clergy, which put him in charge of the administration of its corporate affairs. In this role he was a vigorous advocate of every kind of ecclesiastical interest, for which he was rewarded by the bishopric of Autun in 1788, when he was still only thirty-four. Despite his success in the career that had been forced upon him, he welcomed his election to the Estates General as an opportunity for changing sides and his subsequent career was wholly secular. He resigned his bishopric in 1791 and was eventually to become Napoleon's foreign minister. On 7 July 1789 Talleyrand applied himself to the unravelling of the Gordian knot. He argued that electoral constituencies were only discrete parts of the nation and therefore not so much constituent elements of the general will as subject to it. The deputies they elected were representatives, not mandatories, entrusted with the duty of acting in the national interest when this had emerged as the result of debates in the Assembly. To bind them by imperative mandates was therefore to subject the general will, which could only be formulated in the National Assembly, to the particular wills of isolated sections of the population. Burke said very much the same thing to the electors of Bristol, but locating sovereignty in the British Parliament, in a country where tradition was nine points of the law, had rather less serious consequences than in revolutionary France. Talleyrand claimed to have demonstrated that the Assembly had the right to disregard imperative mandates, but deputies who had sworn to abide by them were still bound by their personal honour, and he was too much a man of the *Ancien Régime* to believe that honour could be eclipsed by *patriotisme*. What the men involved should do was return to their constituents who alone could absolve them from their oaths.

Talleyrand was supported by speakers from different parts of the Assembly. The comte de Lally-Tollendal, a follower of Mounier, in words that he probably regretted later, argued that sovereignty was located within the Assembly. A minority that refused to comply with a majority vote put itself in the position of a rebel subject. He even denied it the right to protest against the decision it had opposed. Barère went further. A former barrister in the Toulouse Parlement, he was a man of elegant and ingratiating manners and flexible principles who was never at a loss when it came to making expediency sound respectable. He was an active member of the Constituent Assembly, edited a rather good

---

[1] See R. Lacour-Gayet, *Talleyrand, 1754-1838* (Paris, 1929), 4 vols.

newspaper, the *Point du Jour*, and was eventually to become a member of the Committee of Public Safety in 1793. Like Talleyrand, Barère argued that the legislative power was created by the coming together of the members of the Assembly. He seemed to regard this as equivalent to the formation of Rousseau's social contract. It was therefore the right and duty of the constituted power – the Assembly – to rectify any 'abuses' in the constituent power, that is, the electors. This could be used – Barère himself was going to use it in later years – to justify almost anything.

The Assembly voted to move on to next business, the more scrupulous of the noble deputies asked their constituents to free them from their oaths, after 14 July everyone had other things to think about and the problem of mandates solved itself. It had nevertheless raised questions of principle that admitted of no easy solutions. The claim of the Assembly to draft a constitution of its own choice, which the king must accept, rested on the assumption of popular sovereignty. This implied that the final source of moral authority rested with the nation. Virtually all the deputies agreed that an oppressed nation had the right to revolt against its ruler. The question at issue was whether or not the nation had transferred its sovereign rights to the Assembly, something that Rousseau had proclaimed to be unthinkable. Those who tried to square Rousseauist principles with the need for representative government in a country as big as France, argued when it suited them that the deputies were mere mandatories, while the more conservative emphasized the autonomy of the Assembly.

Both conservatives and radicals, however, were prepared to exchange principles when it served their tactical convenience. In the case of the imperative mandates the Right used the idea of popular sovereignty to insist that the Assembly was bound by the (relatively moderate) *cahiers*. The Left had somehow to counter this by proclaiming the autonomy of the Assembly, while still interpreting the July revolt as a direct assertion of the will of the sovereign people. When the Left emerged as the majority party in the Assembly, it naturally elevated the status of that body, while still justifying resistance to the king's ministers in the name of popular sovereignty. The Right accepted the concept of popular sovereignty but liked to appeal to the silent majority, so long as it remained silent. This did not prevent it from denouncing any local disorder as proof of anarchy and the need to strengthen the executive.

The brief debate on mandates was no more than the curtain-raiser for the serious business of drafting the constitution. One the same day that Talleyrand displayed his ingenuity, the Assembly elected a constitutional committee of thirty, including all shades of opinion from the Centre to the Left. When it was discovered that no members of the clergy had been included, the offer to add six of them to the committee was declined by the clergy themselves, on the ground that they had complete confidence in their colleagues. Such courtesies were not going to last much longer and the constitutional debates accelerated the growth of suspicion and hostility. Two days later, on 9 July, Mounier made a preliminary report in the name of the committee. His assertion that France did not have a constitution repudiated the old claims of the Parlements and excluded any appeal to history and precedent. There was general agreement when Mounier proposed beginning with a declaration of the rights of man, which would define the principles on which the new constitution would be based. Some weeks later an obscure deputy who knew his Rousseau was to argue that a constitution was an agreement by the people themselves, rather than a contract between ruler and people, and that the declaration *was* the constitution, everything else being merely legislation. Rousseau might have agreed with him.

A declaration of the rights of man was a statement about the political rights of *homo sapiens* that was independent of time and geography. The French declaration therefore gave the revolution an international resonance that was in striking contrast to the goings-on in England in the seventeenth century. The Americans, admittedly, had been the first in the field, and Lafayette was to derive many of his ideas about a declaration from the constitution of Virginia, but that was in a far-off country whose society was very different from that of Europe. The French declaration claimed to be a statement of certain eternal truths, rather than a number of particular political options. It therefore admitted of neither reservation nor dissent. When the deputies got down to the problem of defining these truths, however, it soon became apparent that, whatever the Americans might have said, not all of them were 'self-evident'.

The belief that rights were inherent in individuals and that states were to be judged by the extent to which they upheld them, derived from the school of thought represented by Montesquieu. It implied that the individual was more than a citizen, that he came before political society and that the state was only one of several organizations, such as his family and his church, that helped him to realize his potential for self-development and conferred on him certain obligations. For the Rousseauist, rights had no meaning outside a particular society. It was man's participation in a society that conferred a moral dimension on his actions. Citizenship was all. Rights and duties were therefore indistinguishable; both were determined by society within which, and only within which and on its terms rather than on his, could the individual fulfil his highest aspirations. This was a radical divergence of belief that went back as far as Plato and Aristotle. It is still with us and looks likely to remain so for the foreseeable future. It was not the fault of the Constituent Assembly if it failed to harmonize opposites as old as political theory itself. One cannot even argue, as Burke did, that the deputies were presumptuous to try. In the situation in which they found themselves, there was not much else they could do. If they had decided not to draft a declaration, which some proposed on pragmatic grounds, its unspoken principles would still have determined the way in which they approached the business of constitution-making. Taking either theory to its logical conclusion was likely to produce anarchy or totalitarianism. The kind of liberal regime to which almost all of them aspired required some kind of compromise, but one theory was the logical antithesis of the other and the deputies were driven back on logic since they could not appeal to precedent.

An additional problem was the fact that the rights of man in society were not the same as those he might be presumed to have had in a state of nature: freedom of speech did not authorize slander. Some deputies thought it meaningless and dangerous to define the rights of man in advance of a constitution that would prescribe limits to their exercise. This was not merely to invite revolt but to legitimize it in advance.

As always, theory had to be adjusted to the demands of politics. For the more radical deputies, the declaration was a repudiation of absolutism and a guarantee of the equality of rights (although not of what they called *jouissances*) against the pretensions of the 'privileged Orders'. This made them libertarians in politics, when their Rousseauist principles otherwise pointed in a collectivist direction. The more conservative, especially the clergy, like Rousseau, thought in more corporate terms and stressed duties as much as rights, but were suspicious of the power of the state, especially when that meant the majority in the Assembly rather than the king. Although both sides were in general agreement about the kind of society they wanted, they held all kinds of views about how to define it: fifty-six of them put their names down to speak in a debate on whether or not to have any declaration. This is a reminder of the Assembly's practical problem in working out its rules of procedure by a painful process of trial and error. It is a truism that committees are bad at drafting and there were times when the Assembly behaved like a committee of 1,200. Constitutional debates were also interrupted by the need to discuss more urgent matters: for a week, the argument about what had been decided on the night of 4 August took precedence over everything else.

On 27 July Mounier, in the name of his committee, produced a draft document, which was referred to the bureaux. These met in private and their conclusions were often a good deal more conservative than the views expressed on the floor of the House. The Left disliked them and soon managed to have them superseded by specialist committees, on which it was able to place a high proportion of its own supporters. Some of the bureaux accepted Mounier's draft almost verbatim; others rejected it outright. In the meantime, deputies were coming forward with drafts of their own. Lafayette had produced a version with an American accent as early as 11 July. Sieyès, who could not miss an occasion like this, read to the committee a draft that began with a twenty-page discussion of somewhat abstruse political theory. Evidently feeling the need to counter the argument that this might not be regarded as exactly the right thing for the enlightenment of the peasantry, he argued defiantly that everything was called metaphysical until people got used to it. It was perhaps with Sieyès in mind that Mirabeau urged the need to put philosophy aside and produce something practical. What he himself produced was a draft that included: 'Every political body derives its existence from an explicit or tacit contract by which all individuals unite their persons and faculties under the supreme direction of the general will.' If this was being practical, one can imagine the heights to which Sieyès soared.

The issue was debated at length during the first three days of August, when the most perceptive speech was made by Malouet. He took the conservative position that men in an unequal society were more in need of lessons on the limitations of their rights than on the extent of primitive rights in a state of nature. Preoccupied as always with the need to achieve economic growth and relieve unemployment, he went on to argue that the most pressing need was for a positive social policy. If the constitution was to be the effect, rather than the cause, of a regenerated society, the first need was to create the economic and social basis for it. Robespierre was still struggling with that problem three years later. The debate was marked by the first signs of apprehension amongst the clergy, several of whom demanded the inclusion of a statement on the duties of man. After three days of continuous theorizing, tempers were understandably frayed and, if the *Moniteur* is to be believed, every speech on 4 August was interrupted. By a majority of 570 to 433 the Assembly eventually decided not to include any statement about men's duties.

The debate on the declaration was then suspended until the 12th. Since the bureaux were at loggerheads, the Assembly set up a new drafting committee of five. When this reported on the 18th its proposal was immediately rejected and the bureaux instructed to select one of their own drafts for discussion by the Assembly. On the following day the draft of the sixth bureau was chosen, only to be rejected a day later, when the Assembly went back to the committee's text. The rights of man might be inalienable and imprescriptible but they did not seem to be uncontroversial. During these discussions the clergy found new grounds for concern in the omission of any reference to God. One of those who challenged this was the abbé Grégoire, who was usually to be found amongst the radicals. Grégoire was the son of a poor tailor from Lorraine. He had won the prize given by the Metz Academy in 1788 for an essay on the integration of Jews into French society. The fact that a clergyman from one of the more anti-Semitic areas of France should have championed such a cause says a good deal about Grégoire. He more than anyone else saw the revolution as Christianity in action. Something of a Jansenist, he wanted to restore the Church to its primitive simplicity. He was an egalitarian and a democrat in matters temporal and spiritual. The fact that such a man should have expressed alarm at the secular-mindedness of his colleagues was an early warning that the defence of the Church was not just about the selfishness of wealthy bishops. The declaration was eventually issued 'in the presence and under the auspices of the Supreme Being'. Both the clergy and the deists could live with that.

Once the Assembly had settled on a text, the final drafting was relatively speedy, the most acrimonious argument concerning whether to guarantee religious equality or merely the toleration of dissent. When the Catholics, rather oddly, invoked the example of England, which had an established Church, even if it was the wrong one, the Protestant Rabaut Saint-Etienne urged his colleagues not to pay any attention to foreigners. 'French nation, you are not made to receive examples but to give them.' The final text was approved on 26 August.

The preamble optimistically proclaimed that 'ignorance, forgetfulness or contempt of the rights of man' were the *only* causes of political misfortune and the corruption of governments. To discourage people from drawing the wrong conclusions, the declaration ended by claiming that the demands of the citizens, being henceforth based on these 'simple and unchallengeable principles', would always be conducive to the maintenance of the constitution and to the public good. The sovereign people, in other words, had no right to want what the Assembly had decided would be bad for it. The first clause, proclaiming that all men were born free and equal in rights, was a repudiation of divine right monarchy and of the *Ancien Régime* with its privileges of birth, status and geography. The second defined man's natural rights as liberty, property, safety and resistance to oppression. Taken in conjunction with the final clause, which guaranteed everyone against expropriation, except in cases of public need and in return for fair compensation, this meant that the existing distribution of property was included within the guarantee, and could be interpreted as prohibiting the redistribution of wealth by taxation. Resistance to oppression was perhaps inserted to legitimize the July revolt, but since resistance to the law was explicitly condemned, this raised nice questions of definition. Article 3 declared the principle of all sovereignty to reside in the nation. Its intention was to ensure that public officials of every kind should be elected and liable to punishment for misbehaviour, but this intrusion of Rousseauist principles was in potential conflict with the rest of the declaration: what was to happen if the sovereign people opted for the redistribution of wealth, the communal ownership of land or religious uniformity? Articles 4 and 5 defined liberty as freedom to do whatever did not harm others and was not specifically prohibited by law. Article 6 defined law as the expression of the general will and said that all citizens were entitled to participate directly or through their representatives, in its formulation. They were to be eligible for all dignities and offices, *selon leur capacité*. Once again, the reference to the general will was at odds with the concept of natural rights, since it centred these on society rather than on the individual. The article was also intentionally ambiguous. Political rights belonged, not to men, but to citizens. Those who knew anything about Rousseau's Geneva were well aware that citizenship could be defined so narrowly as to exclude the majority of the population. 'Capacity' was another slippery word. Its most obvious meaning was that people were eligible for any employment for which they were competent, but it had a more restricted legal meaning. This could be invoked to justify limiting jobs, or the vote, or the right to be elected, to certain people 'in their capacity' as landowners or substantial taxpayers. Most of those who voted for this clause had no intention of gratifying the democratic aspirations that it seemed to encourage.

Several articles then guaranteed the principles of habeas corpus, freedom of the press and the right of the accused to the presumption of his innocence, besides banning retroactive legislation. The religious clause was expressed in minimalist terms, as a concession to the clergy: no one was to be troubled on account of his opinions, 'even religious ones', provided that their expression did not trouble public order. Article 12, which justified the existence of a *force publique* without any reference to the defence of the realm, reflected the assumption of most of the deputies that peace would be one of the benefits conferred by the new order. Article 13, which promised fiscal equality, was another repudiation of *Ancien Régime* practices. The following article asserted the right of all citizens to consent to taxation and to supervise the expenditure of public funds. This was liable to involve the legislature in encroachments on the executive and it certainly suggested that all taxpayers were entitled to the vote. Article 15 made all public officials responsible to 'society' rather than to the king. Article 16 said that any society in which the rights of man were not guaranteed and the separation of powers established had no constitution. This was a bow in the direction of Montesquieu and his conception of government as a balance of competing forces, which might conflict with the earlier assertion of popular sovereignty. Nothing was said about who was to decide whether or not the rights of man had been violated; the Assembly was in a dilemma here, since it had to justify the July insurrection while denying the legitimacy of any popular revolt against itself.

The declaration as a whole came as near to expressing the general feeling of the Assembly as one could reasonably expect. If one compares its principles with contemporary British practices, its only revolutionary features were the assertion of popular sovereignty and the apparent endorsement of democracy, but it was a revolutionary document so far as the rest of Europe was concerned. It marked the point at which France broke away from the continental tradition of absolutism and opted for self-government. Henceforth the country was never to be without a constitution of one kind or another, except between 1940 and 1944, and the basic principle that power came from below rather than from above, however qualified in practice, was rarely denied in theory. As a timeless statement of essential truths, the declaration left a good deal to be desired. It embodied immediate concerns and awkward compromises. Much of it consisted of the more or less explicit repudiation of the practices of the *Ancien Régime*. It inevitably reflected current ideas about the nature of the state and of society. The role of government was seen as basically negative: nothing was said of any right to education or employment. In the eyes of the Assembly, man emphatically did not embrace woman. In theoretical terms the document revealed a basic incoherence, with the separation of the powers coexisting uneasily with popular sovereignty. This was apparent to at least one of the deputies: Robespierre tried unsuccessfully to get any mention of the separation of the powers deleted, on the ground that it contradicted other articles. Some of the clauses, such as habeas corpus, were quite specific but the majority were elastic enough to admit of very varied interpretations. Putting flesh on these bones would reveal further disagreement. There would then arise the question of whether or not some particular action of the government or the Assembly violated the terms of the declaration and nothing was said about how this was to be decided. The American solution of a Supreme Court was not open to the Assembly, which had heard quite enough about Parlements and Plenary Courts. Since one could scarcely trust the executive to judge complaints against itself, that left only the legislature, which was in flat contradiction of Montesquieu's principle that 'There is no liberty at all if the power of judging is not separated from the legislative and executive powers'. He had, admittedly, been thinking of criminal courts, but his objection applied even more forcibly to constitutional cases. It was inevitable that the Assembly, which considered itself to be the embodiment of the general will, would claim the right to interpret its declaration and it was unlikely to concede that its own actions were illegitimate. 'The Assembly' meant in practice the opinion of the majority, and the defeated minority was going to object that tyranny was still tyranny, even if a few hundred people declared it to be the general will. It is difficult to see any practicable way in which this could have been avoided. Whatever Sieyès might think, there was no magic formula for squaring circles.

With the declaration out of the way, at some cost in bad temper and growing suspicion, the deputies were free to tackle the basic issues of the constitution, defined, as far back as 27 July, by Mounier's ally, the comte de Clermont-Tonnerre. Speaking on behalf of the constitutional committee, he presented the Assembly with a digest of the *cahiers*. These had been virtually unanimous about many things, most of which were embodied in the declaration of the rights of man. One that was not was the need for the king's assent to all laws. Questions where opinion was divided included the precise nature of the king's legislative powers, his right to dissolve future assemblies and whether those bodies should consist of one House or two. There matters rested for the following month. When they came up for debate, at the end of August, the argument polarized around the nature of the king's veto and the structure of the Assembly; only the purest of royalists believed that the king was entitled to annul the constitutional proposals of the Constituent Assembly itself. To concede that would have been to throw away everything that had been won since the royal session and the July revolts. In effect, even if it was reluctant to claim as much until later, the Assembly was asserting that it was a sovereign body and that the king would have to take what he was given. That might still amount to a good deal.

Those deputies who were beginning to cohere as a moderate or conservative group accepted the principle of popular sovereignty. For them, the clearest expression of the general will was to be found in the *cahiers*, which had taken the existence of the monarchy for granted and been in general agreement that the king was involved in the business of legislation. The deputies had been elected to reform the monarchy, not to create a new constitution for a nascent society. To will the end meant willing the means: for a monarchy to function properly, the king would have to be given complete control of the executive and a veto over legislation. Adoption of this way of seeing things was partly a matter of temperament. It appealed to those who mistrusted theory, had their doubts about the moral regeneration of the nation and were more worried about anarchy than about a return to absolutism. Their pragmatic approach to politics led them to look abroad for systems of government that seemed to work reasonably satisfactorily. In practice that meant England, two Houses and a royal veto, and they were somewhat tactless in holding up the national rival as a model of every kind of political virtue which France would do well to imitate and could not reasonably hope to surpass.

The Left was both more and less realistic. Less ready to forget the events of the previous month, it tended to substitute for some abstract 'prince' the old bogey of ministerial despotism, and it had no intention of giving the executive enough power to reverse the achievements of that miraculous summer. Belief in an aristocratic plot made it suspicious of the idea of an Upper House. Rather less plausibly, it declared French society to be already regenerated, in the sense that it had renounced the vices of its past and had nothing to learn from foreigners. The British constitution might have shone like a relatively good deed in a very naughty world before 1789; it was now to be left far behind and the radicals took an understandable enjoyment in dwelling on its imperfections. A single Chamber and a merely suspensive veto for the king offered no threat of majority tyranny and both were necessary to safeguard the victory of a revolution that was still threatened by aristocrats and royalists.

There was a good deal of right - and wrong - on both sides. Neither was disposed to carry its principles to their logical conclusion but each suspected the other of doing so. If the Right had really been serious about the powers of the Assembly being defined by the terms of its convocation, it would have opted for a merely advisory role. Only a handful of cavaliers were prepared to go so far. It was, after all, the conservative leader, Mounier, who had proposed the Tennis Court Oath. If the Left really believed that the executive power was the sworn enemy of the revolution, it should have pressed for a republic. From its point of view, the king and his ministers would not reconcile themselves to a limited monarchy and their continued humiliation would merely intensify their inevitable hostility. The Right was in too much of a hurry to bury the recent past and pretend that there had been no revolution; the Left was liable to create the very situation that it hoped to prevent. What was needed was careful weighing of the odds and nice tactical judgement: the Assembly had to decide one way or another, the debate was bound to polarize opinion and exacerbate suspicions and, whichever way the vote went, the defeated minority would find the result hard to accept.

The Left maintained, even after its opponents had rather reluctantly agreed to substitute an elected Senate for a House of Peers, that an Upper House would revive the old distinction of the Orders. If all citizens were equal and there was only one general will, there was no need to imitate British practices that had originated in a hierarchical society and owed more to tradition than to principle. If the general will was expressed in future assemblies, as the Left assumed it to be embodied in the Constituent Assembly, to give the king an absolute veto would be to allow ambitious ministers to subordinate the general good to their own ambition. To this the Right replied that an assembly of representatives was inevitably something of an aristocracy, with sectional interests of its own. Two Houses were necessary, as even the egalitarian Americans had realized, not to represent competing social interests, but as a safeguard against the ambitions of a single sovereign body. Whatever the virtues of this argument, it was unrealistic to expect the Assembly, which was certainly not lacking a sense of its own dignity and rectitude, to concede the fallibility of itself or its successors. The conservatives justified the absolute veto on the ground that the king, like the deputies, was a representative of the general will. Unlike them, he represented the nation as a whole, whereas each of them had been chosen by only a fraction of the population, which might well have sectional interests of its own. They weakened their case, when they thought that they were strengthening it, by arguing that a nominally absolute veto would in practice be merely suspensive, since a determined Assembly with public opinion behind it could enforce its will by its control over taxation.

On 14 July the Assembly had replaced its unwieldy constitutional committee of thirty with a new body consisting of only eight members, one of whom, de Cicé, the archbishop of Bordeaux, left to become a minister in early August. That left the majority with Mounier and his allies, Lally-Tollendal, Clermont-Tonnerre and the Parisian lawyer Bergasse. Of the remaining members, Sieyès, Talleyrand and Le Chapelier, only Sieyès held radical views about the constitution. The strength of the conservatives seemed to be confirmed when Clermont-Tonnerre was elected president of the Assembly in mid-August. Mounier set the ball rolling with the publication of his *Considérations sur les gouvernements*. Although he argued that it would be a mistake to pay too much attention to philosophes, what this contained was essentially a para-phrase of Montesquieu. The so-called classical democracies had, in fact, been aristocracies, 'the worst of all governments'. Power derived ultimately from the nation but it could be expressed only through the election of represent-atives. Ordinary people, although unfit to govern, were good at making this kind of choice and 'despite the sophistry of the admirers of Greece and Rome', representative government was the most successful kind. The Assembly was not a convention but had been mandated to respect royal authority. The king was the representative of the nation as a whole and the sectional interests of the Assembly were at least as dangerous as his personal ambition. The best example of the working of a successful constitution was to be found in England.

'One cannot pretend to do better than that nation. Not long ago, on the credit of several writers, people professed the most exaggerated admiration for the British constitution. Today they affect to despise it, following the opinion of an American writer [Paine?] who is full of contradictions.' He therefore advocated two Houses and an absolute veto, adding that there was no need for a referendum on the constitution since public opinion was clearly on the side of the Assembly.

On 19 August Lally-Tollendal, speaking on behalf of the committee, gave the Assembly what was essentially a summary of Mounier's pamphlet. He was rather too fulsome about the British, 'The people who, throughout the whole world, has the best understanding of the science of government.' Serious debate did not begin until the end of the month, after the completion of the declaration of the rights of man. By this time the political temperature in Paris has risen alarmingly and the cafe radicals had become incensed about the idea of giving the king a veto. How far this was in response to prompting from their allies in the Assembly, it is impossible to tell, but the conservative deputies naturally put two and two together and made four and a half. The question of an Upper House excited fewer passions, but the veto lent itself to every kind of over-simplification. Some of the Parisian districts were talking of recalling their deputies and even of putting on trial those who favoured an absolute veto: popular sovereignty could prove a dangerous weapon to unsheath. The 'patriotic assembly of the Palais Royal' threatened to burn the châteaux of those who voted for a veto and Lafayette had to call out the National Guard to disperse a crowd that was preparing to march on Versailles.[2] For the first time, popular pressure was directed against one wing of the Assembly, rather than against the government. A meeting between Mounier's group, who were beginning to be known as 'Monarchiens', and the royalists, urged the king to move the Assembly further away from Paris but he refused, either because it would interfere with his hunting or because he was not averse to seeing the deputies themselves exposed to threats from the street. Rumours that he was planning to leave Versailles then helped to fuel the agitation in the capital. None of this helped to cool tempers in the Assembly or to incline the deputies towards compromise.

When the debate started the case for the Right was put by Mirabeau and Malouet, whose arguments followed the general lines of Mounier's *Considérations*, which Mounier himself summarized on the floor of the House. A lawyer from Bourges, professed himself alarmed by the 'frightening progression in people's ideas' and argued that a suspensive veto, which its advocates defended as an appeal to the people, would, in practice, leave all power in the hands of the Assembly, whose pretensions were more dangerous than the ambitions of the king. Treilhard, a Parisian lawyer, said that the

---

[2] See A. Mathiez, 'Etude critique sur les Journées des 5 et 6 octobre, 1789', *Revue Historique*, 67 (1898), 68 (1899).

nation was free to give itself any constitution it liked, but if it wanted a monarchy it must allow the king the power to govern. The recent past should be forgotten and the present dangers arose mainly from the readiness of the Assembly to sacrifice the present good in pursuit of something better. He favoured a single Chamber and an absolute veto. Bergasse contributed a ninety-page pamphlet to the discussion. 'I know you don't like members quoting the experience of other peoples. I know we already think ourselves wise enough to pass ourselves off as models.' If England was suspect, he suggested looking at the example of America. Bergasse thought an absolute veto and two Houses necessary to counter-balance the alarming power of a single Chamber. 'The proof of what I am arguing is happening before our eyes. Who, today, dare complain publicly about the actions of the legislature, when you see the licence with which people talk about the king and queen?' As further evidence of the threat of mob rule he quoted his own difficulty in finding a printer prepared to bring out his pamphlet. 'Show me how this constitution of yours is going to last when your way of drafting it is to excite men's passions instead of ordering their habits, when, carried away by the maxims of a futile philosophy, you spread uneasiness in all hearts, exaltation in all heads and sow mistrust in all spirits.' He believed that the majority would make life so unpleasant for the king that they would drive him to try to overthrow the constitution.

As is customary in parliamentary debates, few of those present admitted to changing their minds as a result of the speeches they heard. One who did was the duc de La Rochefoucauld, who commented significantly on his conversion to a single Chamber and a suspensive veto, 'Montesquieu will be opposed by Rousseau'. La Revellière-Lépaux, an Angevin landowner, made the valid point that plenty of Englishmen were demanding the reform of a constitution that contained enormous abuses and did not conform to any logical plan. When the French people had drafted their *cahiers*, public opinion had not had time to develop and the *cahiers* were therefore to be taken in the spirit rather than in the letter. That was true too, but the argument could be used to justify almost anything and La Revellière let the cat out of the bag when he went on to say that the only difference between a monarchy and a republic consisted in the government being in the hands of one man rather than vested in a collective body. Barère described Montesquieu's belief that political liberty depended on the balancing of rival powers as 'an old error'. He wanted all laws to be provisional until they had been ratified by the voters at the next election, which would have made things rather difficult when it came to drawing up a budget. Rabaut Saint-Etienne, forgetting about the Americans, described the existence of two Houses in England as a historical accident rather than a matter of principle. Since the general will was infallible, it must not be subject to the will of the king, who could make mistakes. The same point was made rather more aggressively by a notary from Poitou, Goupilleau: the king was more likely than the Assembly to subvert the constitution and ministers were 'vile flatterers for whom the general good is only an empty word'. Two months before, the Assembly had been threatened by 'intrigues, cabals and abominable projects' and France had only been saved from civil war by the *patriotisme* of the army and popular devotion to liberty. The fact that so many of the speakers for the Left were subsequently to play active political parts in the republic suggests that this debate exposed some kind of basic political division.

One of the most cogent statements of the case for the Left came from Robespierre, although he was unable to make it to the Assembly and had to print it.[3] He brushed aside as unworthy of consideration the awkward argument that no one had authorized the Assembly to act as the voice of the nation. Governments were established by and for the people, and the king, that 'powerful adversary', was the man entrusted by the nation with the execution of its will. When it had decided to disregard imperative mandates, the Assembly had already shown that it did not consider itself to be bound by the *cahiers*. 'Don't quote me the example of England . . . the representatives of the French nation . . . are not made for the servile imitation of an institution born in days of ignorance, out of necessity and the strife of opposing factions.' He went on to explain very sensibly why England was not relevant: it had 'admirable civil laws' which compensated for the defects of its constitution, no standing army of any size and the national spirit had been tempered in long and terrible struggles with its kings. He disposed of the argument that humiliating the king would turn him against the revolution by saying that the surest way of depriving him of the power to do any harm was to deny him any veto at all. This, he said, was the secret view of many who only advocated a suspensive veto because they despaired of winning a majority for the solution they really wanted. Robespierre was strong on rhetoric and logic – up to a point. The cardinal weakness of his argument was that, by assuming the hostility of the king to be inevitable, it pointed towards a republic. His own reasoning could be turned against him: if it was dangerous to entrust the 'powerful adversary' with even a suspensive veto, why have a king at all? The answer was that Robespierre knew that a republic would be unacceptable both to the Assembly and to the public opinion whose sovereignty he claimed to accept. If one had to live with the king it might be unwise to insult him, and Robespierre could be accused of provoking the conflict that he feared, by taking its inevitability for granted.

Sieyès was not to be left out of an argument of this kind. As usual he had a solution of his own that would resolve all the problems. The king had no part in the formulation of law and any kind of veto was 'a *lettre de cachet* against the national will', which could only mean the will of the Assembly. It therefore followed that an appeal to the verdict of the people – the argument used to justify a suspensive veto – meant an appeal to the Assembly itself. Once the right constitution had been adopted, conflict between the executive and the legislature would be impossible. If the impossible were to happen, someone

[3] For the text see *Oeuvres de Maximilien Robespierre*, ed. M. Bouloiseau, G. Lefebvre and A. Soboul (Paris, 1950), VI/86-95.

would have to summon a convention. To guard against impulsive legislation, the Assembly should be divided into three sections, each with a veto over the other two. Clermont-Tonnerre tore this argument to pieces: since any future legislature would be bound by the terms of the constitution, it could not embody the sovereign will of the people; to summon a convention whenever there was a disagreement between the two branches of government was asking for trouble; dividing the Assembly was pointless if one of the sections could merely postpone action and the worst form of veto imaginable if it could prevent it.

The battle raged for more than a week and these few extracts are merely a tiny sample of the debate. On the whole the Right had the better of the argument since few members of the Left were prepared to follow the logic of their case to the point of denying the king any veto at all and no one went so far as to suggest a republic. Leadership of the Left was being assumed by a triumvirate composed of Barnave, Duport, who had been one of the Young Turks in the Paris Parlement, and comte Alexandre de Lameth, a member of the Court nobility and a cavalry officer who had fought in the American war. Lameth was the only one of the three to intervene in the constitutional debate and the triumvirate was so pessimistic about its prospects that if offered Mounier a compromise that would have given him most of what he wanted. Confident of complete success, Mounier rejected any bargain. Necker let him down by offering to accept a suspensive veto, but the Monarchiens prevented his letter being read to the Assembly until a vote had been taken. The result of the voting, on 10 and 11 September, probably surprised everyone. The motion for the creation of an Upper House was rejected by 499 to 89 with 122 present but abstaining. On the following day a majority of 733 to 143 agreed to a veto and this was made suspensive rather than absolute by 673 votes to 329. The difference between the numbers voting on the two days – 588 or less than half the Assembly on the 10th and more than 1,000 on the following day – is hard to explain. It is unlikely to have been due to intimidation since popular hostility was directed towards the veto rather than towards an Upper House. The fact that 143 deputies opposed any veto at all is more surprising than the majority for a suspensive one. On the day after the second vote, Mounier, Lally, Clermont-Tonnerre and Bergasse, treating the result as a vote of no confidence, resigned from the constitutional committee.

One can argue that the defeat of the Monarchiens did not mark a decisive turning-point in the revolution. It related to a constitution that was not to come into force for two more years and the Assembly showed its personal regard for Mounier by electing him president on 28 September. The debates had, however, created a permanent division within the revolutionaries and shown that the majority were inclined towards Rousseau, the emulation of the classical republics and the pursuit of a political idea, rather than towards Montesquieu, England and pragmatism. As La Rochefoucauld had said, Montesquieu had been opposed by Rousseau and Rousseau had won. From now onwards it was he who was quoted most of the time. The Monarchiens might have been able to retrieve the situation if they could have relied on the support of those further to their right. To the genuine royalists, however, Mounier and his friends were merely former radicals who had got what all radicals deserved. There could be no question of joining forces with them, of accepting that what had been done could not be undone and combining forces to preserve what was left of royal power. Henceforth the two groups could accept neither the revolution nor each other.

The Monarchiens had warned the Assembly of the danger of alienating the king by treating him as a potential enemy and the immediate question was how Louis would react. The events of the summer had deprived the king of the power to dismiss the Assembly and the government could not maintain order or collect taxes without its support. Louis had neither the power nor, in all probability, the will to reverse the revolution by force but this did not mean that he had to sign anything that the deputies chose to put in front of him. Only a minority of the Assembly followed Robespierre in taking the hostility of the king for granted. Most of them were looking for some sort of cooperation with him, although their exalted sense of their own mission and virtues did not dispose them to compromise. The result of all this was a situation that could have evolved in various ways and there was nothing inevitable about the actual outcome.

The day after the vote on the suspensive veto, on 12 September, rumours reached the Assembly that the king did not intend to promulgate the decisions of the night of 4 August. Even Malouet insisted that this would be intolerable, although others argued that the resolutions were incomplete and needed revision, especially where tithes were concerned. The Assembly voted to request the immediate promulgation of the decrees of the 4th. When the question was raised again, on 14 September, the debate became acrimonious, with both sides appealing to the kind of principles that made compromise impossible. This time the Monarchiens came to the support of the Right and argued that the king was free to raise objections to the proposals. Barnave proposed that the deputies should go on strike until the king gave way, but the Assembly contented itself with repeating its demand for promulgation. The royal answer was read out on the 19th. Louis professed his general support for the proposals but expressed doubts about those relating to the seigneurial dues owed to foreigners, the payment by the clergy of annates to Rome and the gift of between 60 to 80 million livres a year to landowners as a result of the suppression of tithes. He invited the Assembly to reflect that the abolition of the manorial dues owed by small tenant farmers might encourage their seigneurial landlords to foreclose their leases and take over their holdings. The king's objections related to the honouring of international obligations and the defence of the general interest against encroachment by the wealthy. He also indicated his acceptance of a Bill for free trade in grain, adding the warning that to enforce this too rigidly would create hardship. This was something that

Necker had been saying for a long time and he may have been responsible for drafting the king's message, the tone of which was extremely conciliatory. 'I will modify my opinions and even give them up without difficulty if the observations of the National Assembly should impel me, since I will never depart from its way of thinking without regret.'

The Assembly did not know what to make of this. Le Chapelier delivered the automatic response that the king must promulgate and not negotiate. Mirabeau was rather more constructive: although the Assembly had tactfully abstained from proclaiming the extent of its own authority, its members were tacitly agreed on its sovereignty. Old habits, however, died hard and allowances had to be made for them. The decisions of 4 August were maxims that the king had to accept but the Assembly could take account of his warnings and reservations when it came to converting them into positive laws. Robespierre wanted to make no concessions to the king but Pétion, who was usually on his side, deserted him to support Mirabeau. Duport eventually persuaded the Assembly to request immediate promulgation while promising the king to consider his reservations when decisions of principle had to be turned into laws. On this relatively amicable note, the Assembly turned to other business.

By the time the question of the royal sanction came up again, on 4 October, the entire atmosphere had changed. When it had heard, on 21 September, that the royal bodyguard at Versailles was to be reinforced by the thousand men of the Flanders Regiment, the Assembly had decided to take no action. Even when it received a letter from the mayor of Paris, Bailly, to the minister of war, requesting that the troops be sent back, it still did nothing. On 1 October the officers of the bodyguard gave a banquet to welcome the new arrivals. This degenerated into a rather wild affair. The unwise appearance of the royal family led to some alcoholic professions of devotion, the band played '*O Richard, O mon roi, l'univers t'abandonne*' and there were reports that court ladies distributed the black cockade of Marie Antoinette's Habsburg family, while the *tricolore* was trampled underfoot. The whole business did not pose any sort of threat to the Assembly – there were too few troops for that – but it certainly indicated where the sympathies of the officers lay and appeared to lend credibility to the aristocratic plot. Before the banquet, the sensible and sceptical Ferrières had written to his wife that there had always been, and still was, a conspiracy against what he referred to as the 'Estates'.

On the day after the banquet the Assembly submitted the declaration of the rights of man to the king. He replied on the 5th in less accommodating language than he had previously used, accepting some laws and agreeing to the bases of the constitution, 'but only on the positive condition, from which I will never depart, that the general result of your deliberations is to leave executive power entirely within the hands of the monarch'. He requested the help of the Assembly in assuring the collection of taxes, the freedom of circulation of grain and the protection of individual liberty. He had no comment to make about the declaration of the rights of man until its principles had been incorporated in positive laws. What the king was claiming did not amount to much more than what the majority of deputies might have been prepared to concede, but his tone was peremptory and their tempers had been soured by the banquet. Only the extreme royalists supported him and there was a more vigorous parade than usual of what were, in effect, republican principles. Robespierre told the king that he was merely an emanation of the constituent power, which he had no right to criticize; Pétion argued that he had to rule in accordance with whatever laws the nation chose and Barère said much the same thing. Mirabeau again suggested asking the king what he had in mind but this time the Assembly was not looking for conciliatory formulae and it requested the immediate confirmation of the rights of man.

All this might not have led to anything decisive if the initiative had not been passing out of the hands of both king and Assembly. Opinion in Paris had been simmering ever since the debates on the veto and the rumours at the end of August of the king's intention to leave Versailles. The Palais Royal was in a state of continual ferment and Marat was demanding a purge of the Paris Commune and the Assembly, which he said was dominated by traitors. Rumours that the food supply was about to give out, while Versailles lived in plenty, added to the panic and anger. The well-publicized 'orgy' of the banquet for the Flanders Regiment was a double insult to both hunger and revolutionary principles. What followed has never been fully explained and the participation of politicians remains a matter of conjecture. It is the sort of problem that never can be explained to everyone's satisfaction, but the outline of events is reasonably clear. On the morning of 5 October a crowd composed mostly of women demanding bread stormed the Hôtel de Ville in Paris. They were persuaded to march to Versailles to put their complaints before the king and the Assembly. Later in the day a substantial body of the Parisian National Guard insisted on following them, under the more or less willing command of Lafayette. They would have gone in any case and he may have believed that his influence over them would allow him to maintain some sort of order.

When the women reached Versailles they invaded the Assembly, sat amongst the deputies and interrupted the debate. They sent a deputation to the palace where the king apparently managed to persuade them that something would be done about the shortage of food. Louis, who had hurriedly been recalled from the hunt, is said to have agreed to leave Versailles under military escort, but changed his mind after his success with the women's deputation. What he did do was to offer his unconditional acceptance of the declaration of the rights of man. Lafayette and the National Guards reached Versailles about midnight. He deployed his men in the palace courtyards, leaving the closer protection of the royal family to the bodyguard. The Assembly suspended its session about 3 o'clock in the morning and after satisfying himself that all was quiet, Lafayette went to bed, which was to earn him the royalist taunt of having *'dormi contre son roi'*. Early in the morning of the 6th, unidentified members of the crowd, who had been passing the night in the streets, broke into the palace, murdering some of the bodyguard, and made for the queen's apartment, presumably intending to kill her. Marie Antoinette managed to escape and after some confusion Lafayette and the Parisian National Guard were able to restore some sort of order. At the request of the crowd, the king and queen appeared at a balcony and were met with cries of '*À Paris!*', to which they acceded. Whether or not this was the object of the whole enterprise is perhaps a meaningless question. It was presumably some people's objective and the king's acceptance suggests that it was more than an impromptu shout from a handful of demonstrators. That afternoon the royal family left for the Tuileries, the Parisian palace that Louis XIV had abandoned a century earlier, the victims in a triumphal procession where the heads of their murdered bodyguards accompanied them on pikes.

This was a turning-point in the revolution in more ways than one. Understandably enough, Marie Antoinette never forgot the experience of that terrifying night, for which she blamed Lafayette. Once in Paris, she and the king considered themselves the prisoners of the revolution and Louis made no more attempts to bargain about the constitution. For people like Robespierre, who believed that kings could be restrained only by force, that might look like an advantage. Since Louis regarded himself henceforth as not bound by whatever he had to accept under duress, it was a defeat for those who had hoped to base the new order on consent. What was true of the king applied equally to the royalists in the Assembly and the knowledge that they denied its legitimacy when, as usually happened, they were in a minority, while expecting their opponents to abide by any vote that the Right happened to win, gave the Left some ground for denouncing them as factious and hypocritical. Things had changed for the majority too. When Paris had revolted in July it had been thinking primarily of its own defence but it had seen the Assembly as its ally in the fight. This time the Assembly had been ignored and humiliated. When it followed the king to Paris some of its members felt as much prisoners as he did. For Mounier and his friends it was the end of the road. So far as they were concerned, the Assembly had ceased to exist as an independent body and they tried to organize a mass exodus that would bring it to an end. They claimed to have persuaded several hundred deputies to ask for their passports, with a view to returning home. The radicals frustrated this tactic by persuading the Assembly to vote that any deputy who wanted a passport must justify his request on the floor of the House. This was enough to discourage all but a handful of leaders. Mounier, Lally and Bergasse left and Mounier even tried, without any success, to persuade the Estates of his native Dauphiné to disown the Assembly. The Left, faced with the divided opposition of Monarchiens and royalists, could now generally rely on winning a majority in the Assembly. Its problem was to secure the acceptance of the revolution by the powerful forces it had alienated and by the nation at large, less politicized than Paris and still attached to the king. Only a few deputies regarded the indefinite coercion of the king and the parliamentary opposition as acceptable and most of them were still thinking of an eventual accommodation, although one on their own terms. The attempt to base the making of the constitution on consent had failed. What remained to be seen was whether or not the minority would consent to it when it had been made.

5

The Ambiguities of Class Conflict

T HERE is an obvious sense in which the revolution had something to do with the tensions within French society and the government's failure to resolve them. These tensions were of many kinds and some of them were economic. Economic relationships, like political and ideological ones, involve both cooperation and competition and developments within the economy produced new forms of both. Some of those who were alive at the time attached a good deal of importance to this and two members of the Constituent Assembly produced interesting ideas about the place of the revolution in the long-term development of French and European society.

Barnave, a Grenoble lawyer, had been Mounier's right-hand man in 1788 before becoming one of the leaders of the Left in the Constituent Assembly. After the session was over he wrote an *Introduction to the French Revolution*.[1] This was a conscious attempt to translate into dynamic terms Montesquieu's rather static account of the inter-relationships between the different aspects of a society. Barnave's emphasis was rather more determinist than Montesquieu's, in the sense that he attributed more importance to the conditioning pressures of the environment and less to human actions: 'The will of men . . . has little or no effect on the form of governments. It is the nature of things . . . the social stage that a people has reached, the land it inhabits, its wealth, needs, habits and customs, which regulate the distribution of power.' Where Montesquieu had been inclined to see a variety of forces – economic, ideological, religious and political – influencing each other, Barnave believed that the economic basis of a society determined its legal and ideological options. He began with the widespread eighteenth-century belief that all human society had evolved from hunter–gatherers, through agriculture, to commerce and industry, each stage in this process having its appropriate form of government.[2] Demographic pressures and the automatic improvement of productive techniques led irresistibly from one form of society to another. The

---

[1] *Oeuvres*, ed. Beranger de la Drôme (Paris, 1843), 4 vols. For a useful, though much abridged translation, with a good commentary, see E. Chill, *Power, Property and History: Joseph Barnave's Introduction to the French Revolution and other writings* (New York, 1971).

[2] See R. L. Meek, *Social Science and the Ignoble Savage* (Cambridge, 1976).

first type generated primitive democracy and the second feudalism and decentralized aristocratic government. The third stage gave him problems since it could apparently lead either to centralized absolutism or to a more advanced form of democracy based on commercial wealth. Intellectual inquiry, of which the Enlightenment was the most recent example, arose from the self-confidence that stemmed from wealth and economic independence.

Much of this was orthodox doctrine, on which Marx was to draw fifty years later, and it did not prove very helpful to Barnave when he tried to relate his general theory to the specific causes of the French revolution. In the first place, he saw the process of modernization as European, or at least affecting all the maritime states, and Spain, Great Britain, France and the Netherlands had little in common with respect to their political evolution. The general theory was too general and when it came to explaining the actual course of events, Barnave was inclined to allow plenty of room for contingency: if the king had opted for the Third Estate in 1789, the result would probably have been 'some sort of a compromise between the different parties and a rearrangement of what existed rather than a total revolution'. What actually happened was therefore the result of a political choice. Once the revolution had begun, Barnave saw it as the exact opposite of a process of class conflict. His revolution, like that of Marx, was the political consecration of an economic order in which exploitation had ceased and human relationships were based on harmonious cooperation. His 'industrial and commercial society' corresponded to Marx's socialist one. 'Industry, commerce and luxury . . . bring the classes together by wealth, knowledge, education and life-style.' A modern economy rested on a *classe laborieuse* that embraced both capital and labour. Its political institutions should therefore be based on a 'leisured and enlightened class' which would have to 'defend the interests and respect the dignity of the most numerous class' if its members were to get themselves elected.

Where Barnave attempted in a very general way to combine a universal history of mankind with an account of the Constituent Assembly, Roederer was much more down to earth. The man himself - he sat on the extreme Left of the Assembly, with Robespierre and Pétion - was an exception to most of the norms of eighteenth-century French society.[3] Born in 1754, he acquired noble status at the age of twenty-five by buying an office in the Parlement of Metz. That was conventional enough, but seven years later he invested half a million livres in a glassworks that employed 700-800 men. (Glass-making was one of the few industrial occupations open to the nobility.) He then adjusted his opinions to suit his change of status. He had previously sided with local merchants who wanted to retain the economic attachment of Lorraine to Germany. Henceforth, as an industrialist, he wanted access to French markets

[3] See K. Margerison, 'P. L. Roederer: the industrial capitalist as revolutionary', *Eighteenth-century Studies*, II (1978), and 'P. L. Roederer: political thought and practice during the French Revolution', *Transactions of the American Philosophical Society*, 73 (1983), pt 1.

and advocated the economic integration of Lorraine within France. He was to get his way, despite local protests, in 1790.

As a practical businessman, Roederer realized that the 'industrial and commercial bourgeoisie' consisted of two separate classes whose interests often conflicted. Industry was on the whole located in the country, commerce in the towns. Roederer was inclined to regard both industry and agriculture as productive forces, in opposition to rentiers, office holders, professional men and merchants. One of the few radicals to survive the revolution, it was not until 1815 that he wrote his *Spirit of the Revolution of 1789*. This began by adopting a point of view that seems at first sight to have much in common with Marx: industrial and commercial capital in France had grown until it became greater than the sum of landed wealth. Then, however, the bourgeois consolidated their fortunes and status by investing in land and manors. By this time nobility and bourgeoisie were indistinguishable in life-style and sources of income. The revolution could therefore not be explained as some sort of an economic conflict between Tweedledum and Tweedledee. In one sense its origins went back to the days when townsmen had defied feudal barons in the eleventh century. Since then there had been a continuous struggle to recover the lost rights of freeborn Frenchmen. This was very similar to radical mythology on the opposite side of the Channel. Things had got worse under Louis XVI when a weak and easily influenced king had reserved his favours for the nobles who surrounded him. The antiquated constitutional form of the Estates General had *created* a conflict between nobles and wealthy bourgeois. If the king had had his way at the royal session of 23 June 1789 this would have become institutionalized and the Third Estate would have had to 'strip itself of that familiarity which it had acquired in its relationships with the nobility'. Reaction to the royal diktat set off a vigorous movement for social equality. 'The revolution was not so much about improving men's fortunes and increasing individual rights as about the triumph of national pride.' This was also the view of the maverick royalist Montlosier, speaking from the opposite wing of the Assembly. 'In a country like France, one is almost certain to be mistaken in giving first place to what are commonly called interests.' *Amour propre* was much more important.

The two members of the Constituent Assembly whose writings seem at first sight to suggest that they saw the revolution as some sort of class conflict between landed and mercantile or industrial interests, therefore turn out, on closer examination, to have been saying the opposite, and their impressions have been confirmed by modern scholarship.[4] In economic terms, the men who opposed each other so fiercely belonged to the same class. If their material interests conflicted, this was usually due to tensions within the Orders, which estranged bishops from *curés*. Court from provincial nobles and merchants

---

[4] For example, by G. V. Taylor in 'Types of capitalism in eighteenth-century France', *English Historical Review*, 79 (1964), and 'Non-capitalist wealth and the origins of the French Revolution', *American Historical Review*, 72 (1967).

from manufacturers. Most of the early leaders of the revolution – Mirabeau, Lafayette, Mounier, the Lameths and Duport – were nobles, some of them Court nobles, and Ferrières testifies to the initial enthusiasm of some of the provincial gentry. It was, after all, the Parlements, the provincial Estates and the bishops who had sounded the charge against 'ministerial despotism'.

From the start, however, there *were* signs of a profound social division that the revolution was to politicize and eventually inflame into bitter and bloody conflict in some parts of the country. This was something of which contemporaries had only a confused awareness. Frenchmen were divided into those who understood and shared the enthusiasm for the creation of a new kind of society and those to whom the whole business was an incomprehensible threat to their traditional values and way of life. To regard the former as 'bourgeois' is only true in the etymological sense that most of them lived in towns. They included 'liberal' nobles, members of the professional classes and some of the more politically conscious artisans. It is quite true that most of this 'revolutionary bourgeoisie' had not much in common with working people; they were worried about mob violence and tended to be apprehensive of threats to property. Few of them, however, were employers – except of servants – they were not personally concerned about wage rates and what really isolated them from the majority was their fear and suspicion of the countrymen who made up four-fifths of the population. Their adversaries consisted of about half the clergy, many conservative gentry and large sections of the peasantry.

The division of the country had become apparent as early as July 1789, when the new municipalities had distinguished sharply between the urban masses whom they accepted, however uneasily, as allies, and the rural rebels for whom they had no sympathy at all.[5] This attitude was to continue. On 22 February 1790 Mirabeau, while insisting that, in the towns, the forces of order (troops or National Guards) should be strictly subordinated to the municipal authorities, was prepared to give them a free hand against riotous peasants.

The deputies, almost all of them from towns, had ambivalent feelings about the peasantry. Many shared the tendency of that other townsman, Rousseau, to romanticize a way of life about which they had no personal experience, seeing the smallholder as typifying economic independence and a way of life close to nature. Both sensibility and suspicion of seigneurial landlords inclined the Left to dream of a country of peasant proprietors, despite the insistence of economic theorists that big farms were more efficient than small ones. This rather abstract respect for the personifications of rural virtue was superimposed on a more ancient suspicion of the peasant as an uncouth semi-barbarian, prone to incomprehensible acts of violence that were liable to take the form of indiscriminate attacks on towns and the representatives of urban society who operated in the countryside, such as millers and grain merchants. The revolution accentuated this fear of the peasant, who was seen as the gullible victim of the 'aristocratic plot' and, somewhat later, as the credulous

[5] See above, p. 54

tool of a fanatical priesthood. The transformation of local government offered those townsmen who chose to participate the heady feeling that the revolution had given them new dignity and responsibility. From the viewpoint of the Assembly, the revolutionary municipalities were its natural allies and it was generally disposed to accept their view of local conflicts about which it had no other sources of information. In many parts of France the relationship between town and country was amicable enough and regional loyalties could embrace both. Local administrators spoke up for their fellow-countrymen in the villages, explaining as ignorance or a harmless attachment to the old ways, what Paris might have seen as disobedience. Elsewhere the new authorities saw themselves as beleaguered outposts of revolutionary civilization in hostile territory and their officious self-importance and sense of their own superiority tended to provoke the hostility that they took for granted.[6]

As the revolutionary transformation of French institutions progressed, it substituted for an order based on tradition, connections and an authority that could be paternal as well as arbitrary, a system of formal law, based on abstract concepts of civic virtue. Those who understood the new ideas and had the means and education to defend their interests in courts of law, saw the revolution as the beginning of a new and better world for everyone. To many peasants things looked very different. Landowners may have gained more from the abolition of the tithe than they lost from increased direct taxation, but tenant farmers often found that the revolution had done them little good.[7] When the property of the Church was sold, they frequently saw the land that they coveted snapped up under their noses by urban speculators. Accustomed in the past to policing themselves and running their own affairs in their own way, they became subject to much closer scrutiny and control by the new revolutionary authorities – all based in the towns – whose National Guards were a more effective, and sometimes more brutal, instrument of repression than the old *maréchaussée* had ever been. The religious policy of the Assembly added insult to injury when it deprived villagers of their familiar priests and replaced them by outsiders.[8] Revolutionary ideas of efficiency and integrity could be incomprehensible to people brought up in old-fashioned societies where kin counted for more than contract.[9] The very changes that some Frenchmen celebrated as constituting a leap forward to a better world could appear to peasants as an outrage to their beliefs, interests and practices, against which they had to defend themselves by force since all the constitutional weapons were in the hands of their enemies.

[6] See the illuminating article by Alison Patrick, 'The approach of French revolutionary officials to social problems', *Australian Journal of French Studies*, 18 (1981), no. 1.

[7] See D. M. G. Sutherland, *The Chouans*, Oxford University Press, 1982.

[8] On the religious settlement, which is discussed in chapter 9, see T. Tackett, *Religion, Revolution and Regional Culture in Eighteenth-century France* (Princeton, NJ, 1986).

[9] See the very perceptive study of peasant attitudes by C. Lucas, 'Themes in southern violence after 9 thermidor', in G. Lewis and C. Lucas (eds), *Beyond the Terror* (Cambridge, 1983).

This was a clash of cultures rather than of classes. It arose from an incompatibility of attitudes rather than from a conflict of economic interests, although the latter was not entirely absent. Immured in their self-esteem as the torch-bearers of the Enlightenment, the deputies for a long time could not see that they were splitting the country in two. When the occasional country gentleman sounded a warning, he was easily dismissed as a reactionary who was hoping to profit from peasant ignorance. The Assembly as a whole only became aware of what it had done when it was too late to repair the damage inflicted by its religious settlement. The revolution did indeed eventually split the country, but for reasons that did not divide the Constituent Assembly. So far as the deputies were concerned, antagonisms due to class conflict, although not entirely insignificant, were of secondary importance.

The reshaping of French society by the Assembly was conducted on principles that, intentionally or otherwise, would benefit some sections of society more than others. This was bound to be the case, whatever principles were adopted, and the fact that they were shared by almost all the deputies, while it eliminates class conflict as a major source of dissension within the Assembly itself, does not absolve it from the charge of promoting the interests of one section of society at the expense of the community as a whole. Almost all of the deputies were economic liberals. They believed, that is to say, that the 'economic laws' of the Physiocrats and Adam Smith were laws of nature, like those of physics, and not social arrangements that rested on political choice. According to the new theories, respect for the 'natural order' would lead to the indefinite expansion of wealth. The more austere economists believed that those with nothing to contribute to this process but their labour were condemned to subsistence wages, while the more fortunate, with capital to invest, could look forward to continuous enrichment. What is easily forgotten is that, for a substantial section of the population, subsistence wages would have meant an improvement in their standard of living. The Assembly's *comité de mendicité* was to estimate, on the basis of a remarkable national survey in 1791, that nearly two million people could only support themselves by begging. Lack of employment was a more serious problem than low wages and the liberals had a plausible case when they argued that the way to deal with it was by free competition rather than by the traditional state controls.

The starting-point for the liberals was their belief in the sanctity of private property and the right of property-owners to use it as they thought fit. With this went the assumption that it was no part of the state's duty to redistribute wealth. If one regards this as a political option, rather than the recognition of economic law, it was one that would have appeared self-evident to almost everyone in 1789, although men of widely varying opinions – Necker and Robespierre for example – favoured limited state intervention to keep down grain prices in times of scarcity. True Physiocrats believed that new wealth was created only by agriculture; commerce and industry merely transformed things or moved them around. If taxation was not to limit the amount of wealth in circulation, it should therefore be imposed exclusively on land. This may have been mistaken, but it can scarcely be described as class selfishness when most of the deputies were landowners of one kind or another. They were compensated by what they gained from the abolition of the tithe. Seigneurs lost, although whether or not they lost more as seigneurs than they gained as landowners would vary from one individual to another. There were probably few whose losses were so serious as to transform their way of life. Office-holders - and there were plenty of them amongst the deputies - were compensated when their offices were suppressed, but at a rather parsimonious rate. Granted its commitment to property and liberal principles, the Assembly cannot be accused of tipping the balance deliberately in the direction of its members' interests.

The consequences of the economic policies adopted were largely unintended. The introduction of the new principles in the countryside substituted cash relationships for what had been partially social ones. What this meant in practice must have been infinitely variable. Ferrières, as we have seen, despite his grumbling about the 'abolition of feudalism' on 4 August, went on regarding himself as responsible for the welfare of 'his' peasants. He was that kind of endearing man. Others were no doubt more logical and the gap in understanding between town and country widened at an alarming rate. The peasants could be logical too. If the Assembly condemned a tax or manorial payment as unjustified, they stopped paying it at once, without concerning themselves about the effect on the current year's budget. What the effects of the Assembly's economic policies would have been if other things had been equal is impossible to calculate. Other things never are. Emigration increased unemployment in the towns. The uncontrollable deficit led to the sale of the property of the Church, which created new discontents when townsmen outbid local peasants in the competition for land. The paper money for which Church wealth was supposed to provide the backing began to depreciate almost immediately. When, in 1792, France began a general European war that was to last for more than twenty years, every aspect of the economy was distorted and the revolution itself driven to unimaginable extremes. It would therefore be absurd to infer the intentions of the legislators from what actually happened. All that one can do is to examine how they saw their problems and tried to resolve them.

One of the most obvious ways in which the Constituent Assembly revealed its views about how the affairs of the country should be managed concerned the future franchise. The Assembly's constitutional committee proposed that the number of deputies to be allocated to each département should be determined both by the size of the population and by the value of the taxes that it paid. This was approved, despite protests from the Extreme Left, the Left and the Right, in the persons of Pétion, Barnave and Montlosier, all of whom wanted representation to depend on population alone. The committee then went on to divide Frenchmen into 'active' citizens, who paid a minimum of three days' wages a year in direct taxation, and 'passive' citizens who did not. Only the former were to be entitled to vote. Once again Montlosier, who wanted to enfranchise all married men, joined in the protest from the Left. The acceptance of the committee's proposal was certainly contrary to the spirit of the declaration of the rights of man, but it meant less than might appear at first sight. The *comité de mendicité* classed those who paid only two or three days' wages in taxation in the last social category but one and considered them to be automatically eligible for poor relief in the event of accident or misfortune. It was not unreasonable for the committee to argue that, since voting was public, to enfranchise such people was to invite them to sell their votes. The proportion of active citizens varied with the wealth of the local population but in the country as a whole it included over half the adult male population. The sight of high-minded deputies trying to prove that the doctrine of popular sovereignty required them to disenfranchise some of the people who had elected them to the Estates General had its ironical side, but the Assembly was certainly not restricting the franchise to the wealthy. If one remembers that, even in Paris, the poll rarely exceeded 10 per cent, it is very unlikely that many of the *passifs* would have voted unless they had been paid to do so.

Voters chose electors and electors chose deputies. To be eligible as an elector, the committee proposed that a man must pay ten days' wages in taxation, with a *marc d'argent*, or 54 livres, as the qualification for a deputy. This was challenged by democrats like Robespierre, who wanted everyone to be eligible for everything. Pétion agreed with this in principle but recognized the need to take account of the vulnerability to temptation of an 'ancient and corrupt people'. The nearest the Assembly got to the expression of what might be considered class interests was when one or two members of the Right wanted to insist that deputies must be landed proprietors, although even they suggested only a minimal qualification. Malouet explained – not necessarily disingenuously – that the intention was not to exclude peasants, who were very unlikely to be elected in any case, but impecunious adventurers who were trying to get elected in order to sell their votes in the Assembly. The constitutional committee itself proposed that anyone who secured 75 per cent of the votes at the first poll should be exempt from the landed qualification and the Assembly rejected this by a mere ten votes. The *marc d'argent* involved the payment of rather less than £3 in direct taxation. This was not likely to exclude many people who stood any serious chance of election.

A more deliberate attempt to restrict the franchise, and also to counter the argument that Rousseau would have been ineligible for election as a deputy, came at the end of the session when most of the former leaders of the Left had turned conservative. The committee charged with the revision of the constitution saw that the vital point was the social composition of the electors. They therefore persuaded the Assembly to transfer the *marc d'argent* qualification from deputies to electors and accepted a proposal by Roederer that any active citizen could become a deputy. The Extreme Left protested that the new franchise was even worse than the old, but since it was too late to apply it to the 1791 elections and universal male suffrage was introduced a year later, it did not have any practical consequences. There was therefore an attempt to restrict the franchise in August 1791, but one has to retain a sense of proportion. Active citizens were not necessarily 'bourgeois'; many were on the poverty line. By contemporary British standards the French franchise was democracy run mad and an 'aristocracy' of men paying £3 a year in taxation was not exactly exclusive.

Where social policy was concerned the Assembly did not divide along class lines.[10] In England, pure economic liberals like Burke were inclined to comfort themselves with the thought that there was nothing that governments could do to alleviate shortages imposed by Providence, but the French revolutionaries took a more humane view of the situation. This was expounded in the Assembly by the duc de Liancourt, who became chairman of the *comité de mendicité* which was created in January 1790. From the traditional outlook of Catholic society the poor were part of the divine dispensation. Sturdy beggars should be made to work and the charitable relief of the deserving poor conferred merit on the more fortunate members of society and formed one of the obligations of the Church. Liancourt and his committee took a different view. Poverty was a problem to be solved and the dynamism of a liberal economy would provide the wealth to solve it. There would always be some who could not support themselves, such as orphans, the sick and the aged, who were entitled to state help. Economic change would itself generate temporary unemployment, for which the solution was labour exchanges. The relief of the poor was not to be seen as the exercise of charity by the benevolent but as the discharge of a duty by the state. This meant the transfer of assistance, hitherto inadequate and haphazard in its distribution, from the Church and individuals to a national organization, financed by taxation and guided by an accurate knowledge of local needs and resources. Rational *bienfaisance* was to replace old-time charity.

The committee set to work with a will and its impressive social surveys revealed for the first time the appalling extent of the problem. The Assembly, despite the desperate state of the national finances, voted 15 million livres to set up *bureaux de charité* at the end of 1790. There were, inevitably, one or two people who complained that too much was being lavished on the undeserving. One ingenious deputy advocated more vigorous methods of dealing with the work-shy who should be locked in cellars that flooded unless they manned the pumps for 24 hours a day. This was a tribute to his own imagination rather than an indication of what any sensible deputies thought. The committee's intentions were irreproachable and the Assembly gave it what support it could, but the problem was insoluble. If the number of those

---

[10] See A. Forrest, *The French Revolution and the Poor* (Oxford, 1981) and C. Jones, *Charity and Bienfaisance: the treatment of the poor in the Montpellier region, 1740-1815* (Cambridge, 1982).

dependent on relief was in the region of two million it would be many years before the expansion of the economy could generate the wealth to provide for them. A pre-industrial society, by an extraordinary effort of will, could evaluate the extent of the problem but it simply did not have the resources to solve it. The public workshops that were set up in Paris were a disaster. The unemployed streamed in from neighbouring areas and by July 1791 31,000 men were costing almost a million livres a month. It was impossible to supervise such numbers and many of them were said to be drawing their allowance and going off to work elsewhere. When the Assembly voted to close the workshops it had certainly entered a more conservative phase, but it would be unrealistic to regard the decision as provocative or retrogressive. Paris was consuming two-thirds of the resources allocated to the whole country and the situation had become impossible.

In actual fact, the revolution proved to be a disaster for the poor, but this was no one's fault and no one's intention. The sale of Church property drastically reduced the funds available for charity and the care of the sick. Private benevolence shrank as some of the wealthy left the country and the state's assumption of responsibility gave the impression that everything could be left to the government. Economic recession multiplied the demands on the social services. Eventually, war was the most crushing blow of all, turning the sick out of the hospitals to make way for the wounded, wrecking the economy and devouring public money. All this was the exact reverse of what the Constituent Assembly had intended in the happier days of 1790 and whatever it proves, it says nothing about their intentions.

A more plausible example of class bias on the part of the deputies was the *Loi Chapelier* of 14 June 1791, which prohibited what would now be regarded as trade union activity. When Le Chapelier explained the issues to his colleagues, he put them in political rather than economic terms. Recent attempts at collective action by journeymen were in contravention of the principles of the constitution, which had abolished all the old corporations. 'There are no more corporations within the state; there is only the particular interest of each individual and the general interest.' This was the old Rousseauist argument against anything that stood in the way of the general will. The journeymen claimed that all they were doing was to set up benefit societies, but this was now the responsibility of the state and their real intention, according to Le Chapelier, was to create unrest. By his own admission, his Bill was therefore directed, in part, against collective agitation, but the reaction of the Assembly suggests that it was not seen as class legislation. Robespierre and Pétion, those self-constituted watchdogs of the people, failed to bark. The only criticism that Le Chapelier encountered arose from his expression of the personal opinion that wages were rather too low. The economic interests of the deputies were not directly involved, since few of them were employers of labour and none was a master craftsman. This is not to deny that Le Chapelier's law was to be used in the future to obstruct trade union activity, or that the deputies may, almost instinctively, have identified themselves with employers, however humble, rather than with their employees. It would, however, be wildly anachronistic to see the law in nineteenth-century terms as indicative of a major preoccupation of the Assembly and a decisive intervention on the side of capital against labour. To the extent that there may have been an element of class conflict in the *Loi Chapelier*, it was barely conscious and it failed to attract the attention of any of the deputies who were usually so quick to scent slights against the 'people'.

Where the peasants and their manorial obligations were concerned, the Assembly was largely responsible for its own difficulties. In February 1790 there were reports of widespread rioting, refusal of payments and château-burning over much of south-west France. One of the main reasons for this was probably the fact that the Assembly had done nothing to implement its 'anti-feudal' decisions of 4 August, beyond ordering all payments to continue for the time being. No one was in a position to know what was going to be abolished and what was regarded as legitimate. The Assembly therefore ordered its feudal committee to produce draft legislation as quickly as possible. When it did so, its interpretation of the decisions of principle taken on that famous night was somewhat conservative. *Triages*, the compulsory division of common lands at the request of the seigneur, who took a substantial part, were declared to be an abuse of his authority, but this was to have no retroactive effect. To universal applause, the chairman of the committee reassured those whose manorial records had been burned, or who had not dared to try to collect their dues, that their rights would be maintained. Where the seigneur could not produce his title, two recognizances would be an acceptable substitute. To the deputies, this was merely to go about things in a law-abiding manner. To the peasants it looked rather different.

The members of the Assembly saw the riots as essentially a question of law and order, which they interpreted in terms that corresponded to their political alignment. The Right stressed the need to restore to the king and the ministers the power to maintain order. The abbé Maury, who saw the disturbances as the beginning of civil war, wanted the ministers to be authorized to use troops without consulting the local civil authorities. Cazalès, another leader of the Right, spoke of a war between the have-nots and the haves, taking it for granted that his audience would sympathize with the latter. He and one or two others proposed giving the king dictatorial powers for three months. The Left replied predictably that the reports of disorder were exaggerated and that 'aristocrats' were to blame. Lanjuinais blamed troubles in Brittany on the seigneurs; Robespierre denounced those who slandered the 'people' and his main concern was to deny power to unspecified 'enemies of the revolution'. Charles Lameth, despite the fact that both he and d'Aiguillon had had châteaux burned, referred to the arsonists as 'misled and wretched rather than guilty'. Malouet, looking as usual for a compromise and earning the hostility of the Left without winning any effective support from the Right, said that a dictatorship was unnecessary but that there was no danger in placing municipal authorities under royal control since the Assembly could make sure that this was not abused, a proposal that Pétion promptly denounced as 'servitude'. Mirabeau's assumption that peasants were potential enemies of the revolution was shared by a member of the *comité des rapports* who complained that counter-revolutionaries were stirring up the countryside against the towns. What emerged from the debate was not so much a manifestation of class bias as a parade of political loyalties and a search for tactical advantage. The deputies of the Left did not challenge the legislation proposed by the feudal committee and they had no intention of attacking the sanctity of property. They interpreted the riots as a manifestation of the sovereign people, whose intentions were beyond question, even when they were misled. The Right was inclined to hail every brickbat as proof that the country would collapse into anarchy if the authority of the king were not immediately restored.

By the end of 1790 every rural disturbance was being attributed – often very plausibly – to resentment against the religious policy of the Assembly, which was cited as further proof that peasants were easily misled by counter-revolutionaries. Very few questions were seen as arising from a conflict of economic interests. One that was, was the future of French trade with Senegal and especially the Far East. This was controlled by two monopolistic trading companies, of which the more important, the East India Company, was obliged to land all its cargoes at Lorient. This might have seemed a good subject for the deployment of economic theory but the deputies treated it almost entirely in terms of local self-interest. On 25 February 1790 a deputation of Bordeaux merchants requested the abolition of the two chartered companies. When the question was debated on 31 March the air was soon thick with special pleading. True to his cloth, the abbé Maury saw the issue in moral terms: the India trade was a curse since it not merely deprived France of specie but corrupted the nation with the taste for luxury. The merchants who profited from it were 'the real enemies of the nation'. This would have delighted Rousseau, who had once referred to shipwrecks as *vrais avantages*. Most of those who took part in the debate were thinking more prosaically of their constituents and it was soon obvious, as Roederer had realized before the revolution began, that the 'industrial and commercial bourgeoisie' consisted of two conflicting groups. The merchants naturally wanted as much trade as possible. Alexandre Lameth explained in his history of the Constituent Assembly that they feared that competition would force up the cost of their purchases in India and depress selling prices in France. On the whole they were content with the status quo. Nairac of Bordeaux, who claimed to have invested over a million livres in a single expedition to India, insisted that 'the nation cannot lose when the merchant gains', which was an early version of 'What's good for General Motors is good for the USA'. For the industrialists, the India trade in printed cottons was a source of imports with which they could not compete. De Cretot, who introduced himself as a cotton spinner from

Normandy, said bluntly that he was in favour of free competition in the hope that it would kill the India trade. A deputy from Languedoc declared himself commissioned by local manufacturers to support free trade, presumably on the same grounds. The textile interest got some support from southern merchants, resentful of the monopoly of far away Lorient. To confuse the issues, Bégouen, a prominent merchant from Le Havre, favoured free competition as good for trade. There is certainly plenty of evidence here to delight the economic determinists, but it scarcely points towards an assault on a feudal aristocracy by the united forces of the bourgeoisie. When the Assembly eventually voted for free trade, it is impossible to know whether this was a victory for the manufacturers or whether it thought it was defending economic principle against sectional interests.

In July 1790, when a free trade Bill was submitted, the question of Lorient's monopoly set off another battle of local interests. Bégouen had now changed sides and advocated restricting trade in the interests of French industry, a rare case of personal disinterestedness for which he was congratulated by Malouet. Those who wanted to harm the trade as much as possible were inclined to favour keeping the Lorient monopoly. This was the view of Roederer and of a deputy from Amiens who may have been thinking of the local textile industry. Le Chapelier also favoured Lorient, which was not surprising since he came from Brittany. The Lorient interest won the backing of the southerners – on condition that they were given a port too. They tried to discredit the advocates of unrestricted import by insinuating that their real intention was to multiply the ports of entry in order to avoid paying import duty by smuggling. A more sophisticated argument was introduced by a deputy who thought that, now that merchants were less likely to retire from business and invest their profits in the purchase of noble status, France could develop a thriving re-export trade. Malouet seized on this. Preoccupied, as always, with unemployment, he was in favour of restricting imports from India into France, but thought they might well be re-exported to Italy and the Levant. This would mean allowing them to be landed at Toulon, a secure naval base where it would be comparatively easy to prevent smuggling. It was also the place where he had been *intendant maritime* in 1789. When a deputy from Nantes, perhaps thinking that the Atlantic ports were on the defensive, suggested consulting the chambers of commerce, a *curé* countered by proposing to find out what the manufacturers thought. After all the vested interests had had their say, the Assembly finally voted to restrict imports to Lorient and Toulon. If any side could claim to have won, it was the Mediterranean lobby.

During both debates, what was remarkable was the participation of many deputies, usually introducing themselves as speaking on behalf of Lorient, Nantes, Languedoc etc., who rarely opened their mouths on any other subject. Equally striking was the silence of the habitual spokesmen of the Left and Extreme Left. When the Assembly was confronted by a genuinely economic issue its behaviour was thoroughly untypical. Those who have been credited with leading a bourgeois revolution said virtually nothing and those who actually represented commercial and manufacturing interests were at sixes and sevens.

The complexity of the issues raised by the India trade was simplicity itself when compared with the problems posed by France's relations with her very valuable colonies in the West Indies, of which the most important was Saint Domingue.[11] The royal government hoped to preserve its control over the internal politics of the colonies and also keep them in total subjection to the mother country. French merchants in the Atlantic ports, to whom the colonists were heavily in debt, were in complete agreement with the ministers about French control of colonial trade but were less concerned about colonial self-government, unless this would threaten the French trading monopoly. Within the colonies, the free population tended to divide into three antagonistic groups: planters, *petits blancs* and coloureds. All of them shared a commitment to the preservation of slavery and the slave trade. In Saint Domingue itself there were three regional assemblies which did not see eye to eye with each other but shared a suspicion of the general assembly of the colony as a whole. The overwhelming majority of the colonial population consisted of slaves. Colonists and French merchants, committed to slavery, were on their guard against the abolitionist theories of the Enlightenment, which found concrete expression in the activities of the *Amis des Noirs*, an anti-slavery society supported by Mirabeau and Lafayette. Some of the members of the Assembly, including the Lameths, who saw themselves as leaders of the Left, owned substantial estates in the colonies. This made for rather complicated politics, from most of which the reader may be spared, since our immediate concern is with the way in which the economic interests involved affected the behaviour of the Assembly.

When the Estates General first met, the outlook for the planters was not promising. Necker, in his opening address, spoke of the abolition of slavery, which many of the deputies seem to have regarded as part of the regeneration of French society. The first move of the planters, who had not been invited by the king to send representatives to Versailles, was to nominate their own. While the Third Estate was refusing to verify its members' credentials, it was difficult for it to exclude anyone. The unofficial representatives of Saint Domingue insisted on swearing the Tennis Court Oath, which subsequently allowed them to claim that they had vindicated their right to membership of the Assembly by sharing the dangers of its heroic days. When the Assembly constituted itself, the question had become one of how many deputies Saint Domingue should have. The colonists claimed twenty-five, on the basis of a population count that included all the slaves. This was over-playing their hand. Lanjuinais and others said that their *cahiers* demanded the abolition of slavery and La Rochefoucauld demanded that this be decreed before the end of the

11 On slavery, the slave trade and the French West Indies, see the writings of G. Debien, especially *Les Colons de Saint Domingue et la Révolution. Essai sur le Club Massiac* (Paris, 1953).

session. Mirabeau drew attention to the fact that the seventeenth-century colonial code, under which the colonies were governed, did not recognize colour. When the planters had chosen their deputies they had therefore had no right to disfranchise the free coloureds. The marquis de Montesquiou wanted to give the colonists merely consultative status. The representatives of the ports were not much more helpful, Nairac of Bordeaux insisting that the colonies did not form part of France. The planters had to make do with a somewhat grudging six deputies. It was to prove enough. At the end of the year another deputy from Nantes opposed the creation of a colonial committee, which earned him a denunciation by the leader of the Saint Domingue deputation as the tool of the foreign minister. Royalists, merchants and abolitionists united to prevent the appointment of the committee, for the time being. A petition for voting rights, from the coloureds, was sympathetically received.

The anti-colonial coalition was broken by the question of the slave trade, which contributed a good deal to the prosperity of the Atlantic ports. Nairac raised the issue towards the end of 1789 and two months later a deputation from Bordeaux claimed that slaves were property and talk of abolition was liable to provoke revolts in the colonies and was perhaps a perfidious British manoeuvre to take over the French trade and colonies. On the following day a well-calculated speech to the Jacobin Club, by a Nantes merchant, offered a bargain: a free hand for the planters in return for continued French control over colonial trade. In the debate that followed, Mirabeau, who had already denounced the slave trade in his newspaper, attacked it again. Soon afterwards the colonial minister complained to the Assembly that the colonists of Saint Domingue were claiming internal self-government. This brought the royalist Cazalès to his support – and made it difficult for the Left to take a stand against representative government. The deputies then reversed their earlier decision against creating a colonial committee. The committee, dominated by the planters, was able to present its case as the voice of expert opinion and soon became a powerful lobby. On 8 March 1790 Barnave, the friend and ally of the Lameths, won an important vote to the effect that no innovations in colonial policy were to be made without the colonists being consulted. According to Duquesnoy, the Assembly was divided fairly evenly and the colonial lobby managed to precipitate a vote in order to prevent Mirabeau from denouncing the slave trade once again.

The colonial lobby organized its own political club at the Hôtel Massiac, which coordinated policy, looked after public relations and waged a press war against Brissot, the editor of the *Patriote Français* and a leading member of the *Amis des Noirs*. In a diatribe against Brissot, the leader of the Saint Domingue deputies, the marquis Gouy d'Arcy, wrote that 'The planters have assumed the responsibility for the happiness of a million Africans. Blacks in the colonies have never known wretchedness or need.' Abolition, in other words, would be cruel to the slaves. It would also ruin six million Frenchmen and destroy the constitution. This was unlikely to have convinced anyone who was not already determined to believe it, but the work of the Club Massiac may have been responsible for the fact that a second coloured deputation, in March 1791, received a less friendly reception than the first.

By this time there was no question of abolishing either slavery or the slave trade. The question had narrowed down to the granting of political rights to the free coloureds, which turned on the question of whether or not the colonists were to be allowed to regulate their internal affairs for themselves. This was already a major victory for the colonial lobby. If it persisted in its rather risky opposition to the claim of the coloureds, it was presumably because it saw this as the thin end of the wedge of French intervention. Malouet, whose wife owned property in the West Indies, acknowledged the sincerity of his opponents, which was rather a contrast to the Club Massiac, but argued that granting political rights to the coloureds would mean conceding that the declaration of the rights of man applied in the colonies, which would logically imply the end of slavery itself.

In May 1791 colonial policy was the subject of several debates. The colonial committee proposed on the 7th that all questions concerning personal status should be left to the colonial assemblies. This time the deputies divided on Left-Right lines and the Left, believing itself in a minority, got the debate adjourned. When it resumed four days later, everyone was inclined to sacrifice plausibility to the need to win support. The Left insisted, against all the evidence, that opinion in Bordeaux and Lorient favoured the emancipation of the coloureds. Barnave replied that if the colonies were left alone they would gradually emancipate their slaves; if not, the settlers would revolt. Robespierre, although he made plain his passionate objection to slavery, did not disdain the contradictory argument that contenting the coloureds would enlist their support in keeping the slaves quiet. On the 13th the Assembly voted to leave all matters relating to slaves to the initiative of the colonists and the president closed the session before a vote could be taken on the coloureds. When the debate resumed, the latter were granted political rights, but since any further concessions were to be dependent on the agreement of the colonists, this was a partial victory for the planters. Even so, the colonial deputies announced that they would boycott the Assembly.

They were not beaten yet. The question was revived at the end of the session, when one senses some campaigning behind the scenes. On 25 August a petition from 300 Nantes merchants complained that the vote of 15 May would lead to civil war, counter-revolution and the loss of the West Indies. Three days later, five new members were added to the colonial committee, three of whom resigned within 24 hours, complaining that the committee was under the thumb of planters and merchants. Early in September implausible petitions from the ports were produced by both sides. Lanjuinais attacked Barnave who complained that the trouble in the colonies was all Brissot's work. Alexandre Lameth and Barnave both demanded the re-examination of the decision taken on 15 May. On 24 September they got their way and the fate of the coloureds was abandoned to the colonial assemblies. It was a complete victory for the colonial lobby but it did not do them any good. Massive slave revolts had already destroyed many of the Saint Domingue plantations; within three years slavery itself was to be abolished and the colony was on the road to independence. The colonial policy of the Assembly, despite its final verdict in favour of the white settlers, is scarcely proof that the attitudes of the deputies were determined by class interests. It is a rather specialized example of the triumph of a political lobby in support of a particular vested interest. As such, it cut across normal party lines and the 'commercial bourgeoisie' of the ports allied with the conservatives in the colonies and won the support of individual deputies who regarded themselves as leaders of the Left. The cause of the coloureds was defended by genuine abolitionists like Lanjuinais and Robespierre, but it also won some support from royalists whose main concern was to frustrate the autonomist pretensions of the colonists. In the summer of 1791 the colonial issue certainly helped to embitter the quarrel between Left and Extreme Left but it had not done much to cause it. Things would have gone on in much the same way if the West Indies had never existed.

The deputies in the Constituent Assembly, like the members of any other parliament, had an eye for their individual and collective economic interests. They shared the general human tendency to assume that what suited them was based on principles that were in everyone's interest. On one or two occasions, such as the fate of the East India Company, they were quite open in defence of the sectional interests they represented. This was small beer. It did not happen often and the particular issues involved took up only a tiny fraction of the Assembly's time. More generally, one could argue with greater or lesser plausibility that the economic liberalism embraced by the great majority would benefit the haves rather than the have-nots. It is by no means certain, however, that the poor would have done better if the Assembly had persevered in the old ways of the monarchy. In any case, what is at issue here is not class conflict amongst the deputies but the relationship between the Assembly as a whole and the rest of the population. The great majority of the deputies came from a single economic class; many, if not most, derived part of their income from land - which did not prevent them from taxing it more heavily than in the past - and they were not aware of any basic conflict between the landed and the commercial or manufacturing interests, for the excellent reason that none existed. If economic issues had been their central preoccupation they would have had few occasions for quarrelling. In fact, the Assembly split into antagonistic groups that eventually came to reject all possibilities of compromise or cooperation. These conflicts may have been exacerbated, from time to time and in a minor way, by economic issues, but their origin and intensity had to be explained in some different manner.

6

The Unhelpfulness of Ideology

A T first sight it might appear that the members of the Constituent Assembly resorted to political theory merely to give an air of respectability to whatever happened to suit their political convenience. Those who wanted to stress caution, moderation and compromise could usually quote Montesquieu in their support, while the radicals turned to Rousseau, but each side was prepared to abandon its standard-bearer in pursuit of political advantage. In the debate on the constitution, in September 1789, Mounier taunted his Rousseauist opponents for claiming that an elected assembly could be the custodian of the general will, when this was something that Rousseau himself had vehemently denied. In May 1790, when opposing the appointment of judges by the king, Barnave and Roederer quoted in their support Montesquieu, 'the favourite authority of the Right', 'a writer who is always being opposed to popular opinion', and Cazalès replied that Rousseau, 'a philosophe who is not suspect to this Assembly', had described kings as natural judges. This did not amount to much more than the scoring of clever debating points.

Sniping of this kind was incidental to the main battle, which was fought over the location of the general will. Even here, the demands of politics could impose some striking contortions on ideology. Once it had obtained a majority, the Left usually maintained that the people had entrusted the exercise of sovereignty to its deputies. Their adversaries denounced this as Rousseauist heresy and claimed that the expression of the general will was to be found only in the *cahiers*. What this meant, in political terms, was that the *cahiers* had taken a conventional view of the extensive powers of the king, which the Right wanted to safeguard. The Left, in order to justify their curtailment, argued that the nation-wide revolt of July 1789 had created a new situation and relegated the *cahiers* to the pre-history of the revolution. Claiming that they had the support of public opinion, which was plausible in a general sort of way but unverifiable where specific issues were concerned, they gradually came to locate popular sovereignty within the Assembly itself. Whenever it suited their purpose, however, both sides reversed their theoretical arguments. When, in 1791, the citizens of Arnay-le-Duc tried to prevent the king's aunts from going to Rome, the Right proclaimed itself shocked by the insult to the sovereignty of the Assembly, while the Left applauded this particular example of the resumption of its sovereignty by the people.

Such incidents were incidental examples of the fundamental ambiguities that bedevilled the entire work of the Assembly. In both theoretical and practical terms, it was impossible for the deputies to define with any clarity the situation in which they found themselves. Summoned to Versailles to advise the king, as a result of the July revolt and the collapse of royal authority they found themselves responsible for running the country. After he had been brought to Paris, the king, whatever his actual feelings, appeared to accept his situation and even declared his support for the Assembly. At the same time the deputies were intensely aware that they were making a revolution. As revolutionaries, they were the victors in a - mercifully almost bloodless - conflict, with no obligations towards the defeated party and with an authority that rested, in the last resort, on force. This was not something that many of them were prepared to admit. They preferred to argue that the July crisis had been due to a mis-understanding and there had been no interruption to the continuity of government. France remained a monarchy, as it had been for centuries; the king was still on his throne; the nation was united, the Assembly spoke in its name and whatever the deputies did had to be justified by some sort of constitutional process. As the session drew towards its close and the former leaders of the Left began to think it time to strike some kind of a bargain with the king, this ambivalence took on a different shape. There *had* been a revolution, in which it had been necessary at times to resort to insurrectionary means in order to overcome the resistance of counter-revolutionaries, but the revolution was now over and henceforth the need was for order, and the protection of the rights of all. The dangerous maxim of *salus populi suprema lex*, whatever its justification in the past, no longer applied. In political situations so complex, ambiguous and mutable, decisions had to be based on the tactical assessment of what was practicable at any particular time. Theory was too crude and inflexible to be of much use and the pursuit of strategic consistency implied a good deal of tactical versatility. Looking back on it all, Mounier said that the *Social Contract* was the most frequently and favourably cited of all political treatises but that the French people would still have proclaimed their sovereignty if it had never been written. This may be true, but it is not the whole truth. Political situations contain their own imperatives and constraints, but the situations themselves derive in part from how men think about politics. Options only become options when they are seen to exist and imperatives are necessary means to the attainment of what people choose to perceive as ends. Political theory was more than a coded language for talking about something else. It was the language in which the revolutionaries thought, and if one neglects it one will never understand what they were trying to do.[1]

[1] For a discussion of the role of ideology, especially Rousseauist ideology, on the revolution as a whole, see F. Furet, *Understanding the French Revolution* (Eng. trans.) (Cambridge, 1981),

Almost all of them believed in some form of popular sovereignty. This was taken as axiomatic by the Left and it was also accepted by the constitutional monarchists and by many of the royalists. In a letter to his constituents, Malouet wrote, 'The will of an entire society, or of the majority of its members, is and always will be an act of sovereignty.' Mounier described as an 'undeniable truth' the view that the principle of sovereignty was located in the nation. Royalists like Montlosier, who said that 'all rights derive from the people', were of the same opinion and the comte d'Antraigues proclaimed this to be the unanimous view of the Assembly. He was not quite right: a few cavaliers like d'Eprémesnil were still arguing that the people were not entitled to change their government, and the abbé Maury, the most pugnacious spokesman of the Extreme Right, was ambivalent. When he claimed, in a speech that included two references to Rousseau, that the rights of the clergy were based on the will of the people, he was probably merely trying to offer his fellow-clerics the most waterproof umbrella at his disposal. At the end of 1789 he forgot himself so thoroughly as to say that 'all powers derive from the people and belong to the people'. He took a very different line in his *Opinion sur le Souveraineté du Peuple*, which he wrote up after the session and which was not published until after his death. Here he denounced popular sovereignty as a 'disastrous and illusory principle' which was derived from 'the words rather than the reasoning of a Genevan visionary, most of whose followers do not understand him . . . who did not always understand himself'.

Belief in popular sovereignty could mean anything or nothing. In its specifically Rousseauist form it implied belief in the sovereignty of the general will, an expression that occurs over and over again in the reports of debates. This in turn implied several things. In the first place, it postulated the existence of a single national interest. Once this had been established, it was morally incumbent upon everyone to prefer it to his own personal or sectional advantage. If the concept of the general will meant no more than that, it was neither very dangerous nor very helpful, amounting to nothing much more than an exhortation to put the community first. The trouble began when one tried to locate this moral will in political terms. The deputies, like Rousseau when he forgot himself, transferred to the majority in the Assembly obligations and rights that had originally been associated with a metaphysical concept. This was virtually bound to happen if one tried to apply the ideas of the *Social Contract* to real political situations. The marquis de Castellane was only one deputy amongst many to run the two concepts of popular sovereignty and the general will together: 'The people has invested us with its power. The general will is always wise and prudent.' The Assembly, in other words, was infallible and the sole judge of what was good for the country as a whole. What further complicated the situation was the fact that the deputies, like Rousseau, thought that any major revolution was as much concerned with morals as with politics.

and N. Hampson, *Will and Circumstance: Montesquieu, Rousseau and the French Revolution* (London, 1983).

In order to succeed it had to regenerate society. The sovereignty of the general will therefore implied a new moral order in which universal concern for the common interest would replace calculations of sectional advantage. It was this, more than anything else, that inspired the deputies with the belief that they were working for the redemption of France, and by France's example, of humanity at large, and conferred on their revolution a heroic dimension that it has never entirely lost. Malouet had already felt something of the new spirit as far back as the end of 1788. 'A power of reflection and feeling, unlike anything else, has been created in our midst. It is coordinated with the general will.' Once the revolution was under way this spirit developed into something that was both an exalted sense of mission and an expression of collective pride and national self-satisfaction. In virtually identical terms, Duport and Robespierre said that the liberty and happiness of the world rested on the fate of 'the first assembly of the universe'. Men who genuinely saw things in this way were unlikely to be tolerant of contradiction or opposition.

Their sense of a unique destiny reinforced their impatience with those who rejected Sieyès's advice that France should think only of 'the beautiful and the good' and believed that she should learn from the experience of other countries. In the Europe of 1789, that meant Great Britain, Montesquieu's model and the only constitutional monarchy of much importance. As Necker put it, looking back after the event, 'The British government was there to serve as an example to the Constituent Assembly, but it aspired to the honour of being a convention. It wanted to consign to oblivion the Numas, Solons and Lycurguses and smother with its own glory all other legislators, past, present and future.' This dedication of the majority of the deputies to what their critics called 'chimerical perfection' was both a cause and an effect of their preference for Rousseau, who had never had much time for the British. They were understandably irritated when men like Mounier kept harping on the virtues of their neighbours: 'I am speaking here merely in Montesquieu's terms. The British constitution is the natural constitution of any monarchy that has passed from feudal obscurity to political liberty.' Some of them knew enough about the ways of 'Old Corruption' to argue that, whatever the civil liberties enjoyed by the British, their political system was not much of an advertisement for *vertu*. Generations of war and commercial rivalry were not easily forgotten and the persistent French ambivalence towards England was already visible. On the whole the deputies were well disposed and Le Chapelier was criticized for referring to the British as 'our rival and enemy' – he was a Breton and his countrymen had suffered more than most from all the naval warfare – but there was much applause when another deputy threatened England with invasion in the event of war.

Belief in popular sovereignty and the omnipotence of the general will made, it very difficult to decide what to do about the king. Rabaut Saint-Etienne thought that 'The national assembly suffered from the terrible disadvantage, which held it back for a long time, of constituting a monarchy when the monarch was already there.' Divine right was rejected from the start. Maury, who seems to have derived many of his ideas from Bossuet, defended it in his *Opinion sur la souveraineté populaire* but not in the Assembly itself, and his fellow-royalist, Cazalès, dismissed it as a 'ridiculous fairy-tale'. Prescription and tradition were also eliminated as legitimizing factors, since anything contrary to the general will was automatically invalid. Mirabeau was particularly emphatic about this. 'There is no legislative act that a nation cannot revoke; whenever it wants it can change its laws, its constitution, its organization, its mechanism . . . whatever is merely an effect of the general will must stop as soon as that will changes.' At the same time, virtually all were convinced – it was one of the few points where Montesquieu and Rousseau were in agreement – that a country of the size of France could only be a monarchy. When they looked back in 1791 some of the deputies thought that they would have done better to suspend the monarchy as it existed, in order to reconstitute it on their own terms. That was being wise after the event. Few would have wanted, or been prepared to risk going so far in 1789 when they believed, or at least hoped, that they could carry the king with them.

This left them in an impossible situation. The *cahiers* had taken the continuance of the monarchy for granted and it took a long time for the personal popularity of Louis XVI to evaporate. For both practical and theoretical reasons, the Assembly was anxious to present itself as the voice of a united country, working in concert with the king, rather than as the victor in a fight for power. At the same time it regarded all ministers, even those drawn from its own ranks, as yearning to restore royal absolutism. No one, including in all probability the unfortunate Louis XVI himself, could be quite sure where the king stood. Malouet argued that the electorate had charged the Assembly to respect royal authority but that the king, after having called his subjects to liberty, was not entitled to say that he did not want them to be free. This was not very helpful. It was often said that both the king and the deputies, in their different ways, represented the sovereign will of the people. That did not help very much either. If the king was free to reject the proposals of the Assembly, including its draft constitution, France was still an absolute monarchy. If he had to accept whatever the Assembly wanted, it was effectively a republic. If the declaration of the rights of man was what it claimed to be, it was a statement about inalienable rights that were enjoyed by all members of any political society. It did not make much sense to say that, in the France of 1789, such rights depended on the goodwill of Louis XVI.

The transfer of the king to Paris deprived him of his freedom of manoeuvre without expressly curtailing his authority. From then onwards he signed what was required of him, but this merely meant that the conflict went underground. His position was henceforth the main subject of conflict between Left and Right, and perhaps the main cause of the division between them. On one issue after another the Right claimed that since France, by the will of its people, was a monarchy, acts of the Assembly that deprived the king of the means of governing were illegitimate, because contrary to the general will. The Left denounced this as a refusal to accept the democratic decision of the majority and a rejection of the revolution, of which they were the custodians. Monarchists then accused them of covert republicanism. There was some truth on both sides, although less than either believed. The Right had the better logical case but the Left did not trust the king, or at least his ministers, and they were not prepared to allow the executive enough power to reverse changes to which all deputies, or almost all, were committed. The more they deprived the king of the authority that should theoretically have belonged to the executive, the more they alienated him and incited him to resist them. As the arguments of both sides became more shrill and intemperate and suspicions mounted, they appeared to confirm the mistrust of which they were the product.

Leaving aside the insoluble problem of royal authority, the doctrine of the sovereignty of the general will left the status of the Assembly fundamentally ambiguous. If the people were sovereign, how were they to express their will? On specific issues they could theoretically have been consulted by referendum, but this had few advocates. The problems involved in organizing such consultations, with the means available to an eighteenth-century society, were virtually insoluble and even the proposal to hold a referendum on the constitution itself won little support. Infrequent consultations of this kind would not have been of much use to the Assembly in its conduct of everyday affairs. Its main business was to draft a constitution but events had thrust upon it a substantial share in the government of the country; ministerial orders that did not have its endorsement were likely to be disregarded. The exercise of a parliamentary role required constant decisions on points of detail, about which it was impossible to seek the opinion of the electorate.

True to the Rousseauist doctrine that sovereignty was inalienable and the general will could not be represented, the Right insisted that the powers of the Assembly were restricted to implementing the national will as it had been revealed in the *cahiers*. This conveniently ignored the fact that the *cahiers* themselves were far from unanimous. According to the Right, whatever went beyond the initial mandates imposed on the deputies by those who had elected them was a usurpation of power by the Assembly, whose only constitutional status was to advise the king. D'Eprémesnil, who was an embarrassing ally for anyone, claimed that monarchy had been endorsed by the national will for the past 1,500 years, which would have made the later Roman emperors the first kings of France. Cazalès was content with 800 years, which made more historical sense. From the Extreme Right to Malouet, and as far as Mirabeau, when he was on his royalist tack, deputies reminded the Assembly that it was not the nation. This was a useful stick with which to beat the Rousseauists on the other side, but few of those who wielded it were prepared to give the king the last word on the constitution. They had, after all, begun the challenge to royal authority in 1787, when d'Eprémesnil had been one of their more intemperate leaders. Mounier was even prepared to admit that the Assembly might be considered a convention, where the constitution was concerned. The Left could not forget that its power derived from its victories over the king. Unwilling to say this outright, and even to admit it to themselves, the deputies looked for ways of legitimizing their position. Sieyès had foreseen the problem in his famous pamphlet *What is the Third Estate?*, where he had conceded that a meeting of the Estates General had merely advisory powers. His own solution, which he repeated in the summer of 1789, was that the Assembly should order the election of a constitutional convention. According to British and American precedents, a convention was a sovereign body, entrusted with the task of preparing or changing the constitution of a country. As such, its powers exceeded those of an ordinary parliament but, as the Right was quick to point out, they were confined to strictly constitutional business.

Force of circumstances drove the Assembly as a whole to act on the assumption that it was entitled to draw up a constitution that the king was not free to modify or reject. The Left went much further than that, claiming that the Assembly was a convention, a body to which the nation had transferred its sovereign rights. Its therefore enjoyed supreme power in any sphere where it chose to exercise it. Mirabeau, in 1790, argued that the Estates General had become a convention when the deputies of the Third Estate swore the Tennis Court Oath, since this had been necessary for the salvation of the country. This was a blunt appeal to the dangerous doctrine of *salus populi suprema lex*, that could be used to justify whatever the majority regarded as necessary. The Assembly, according to Mirabeau, was responsible only to itself and could be judged only by posterity. This eventually became orthodox doctrine on the Left. Towards the end of 1790 a deputy from Toulon proclaimed: 'It is time for the Assembly, elevated to a constituent power by the unanimous wish of all Frenchmen, to make known by a positive law what are the rights of those to whom the executive power is entrusted.' That was perhaps an accurate assessment of the distribution of power; as a historical account of the source of the Assembly's authority, it was wholly fictitious.

For Rousseauists, there could be only one general will. Since this expressed what was actually in the interest of the community as a whole, it was, by definition, all that it ought to be, and it applied to every aspect of social and political life. From this starting point the Left went on to make the thoroughly unRousseauist assumption that, as one deputy put it, 'Whatever the people themselves do in a [direct] democracy, they must do [in France] by their representatives.' It followed, as Mirabeau said, that the deputies spoke in the name of the nation and expressed the general will. The Assembly therefore enjoyed all the powers that had belonged to 'the first individuals who created the French nation'. During the debates on the reorganization of the Church it was even argued that the deputies were entitled, if they wished, to change French religion, since this was something that the people themselves were free to do if they wished. One can, of course, argue that, since the Assembly had no intention of doing anything of the kind, this was so much hot air, a mere rhetorical flourish added to policies that were adopted on thoroughly pragmatic grounds. This would be to deprive the revolution of the Messianic dimension that constitutes its uniqueness. From one point of view the deputies were hard-headed men trying to find practical solutions to practical problems, but unless one appreciates that most of them were also convinced that they were at the same time building a new heaven and a new earth, one cannot even begin to understand them. It was not their fault if they failed to find satisfactory theoretical answers to questions that more stable societies can allow to lie safely unasked. All of them contradicted themselves rather than cut their own throats when theory pointed in the direction of political suicide. It was circum-stances as well as beliefs that gave the Right the appearance of pragmatists and made the Left seem unworldly enthusiasts. In their different ways, both were dedicated to the achievement of something like an ideal society. This was their glory and one of the main reasons for the ferocity of their hatred for each other.

The deputies of the Left therefore equated the general will with the opinion of the Assembly and, to quote Mirabeau again, so long as they remained true to the general will [and they were the sole judges of that] they enjoyed 'what was almost a veritable dictatorship'. 'Almost' was a concession to modesty rather than an admission of limits; in the Roman sense, in which a dictatorship implied the suspension of normal constitutional safeguards, there was no 'almost' about the authority of the Assembly. As Mirabeau himself said on another occasion, 'No one can impose any reserves on the nation. No power on earth, not even the executive power [i.e. the king] has the right to say "this is my will" to the representatives of the nation.' It took only two sentences to reduce the nation to 1,200 deputies.

In fact, of course, the Assembly was never unanimous. Like any other parliament, it took majority decisions. If those decisions were automatically equated with the general will, then that will could only be the will of the majority. Alexandre Lameth spelled things out in precisely these terms. 'The will of the Assembly is the expression of the general will. Whatever a handful of people may say, the opinion of the majority of the representatives of the nation is the expression of the general will.' Sieyès expressed the same idea in his more abstract way. 'Any society can have only one general interest . . . the social order necessarily implies unity of aim and agreement as to means.' Those who came together to form a society were therefore presumed to have willed the means, as well as the end, and this implied majority voting. 'The general will is constituted by the will of the majority.' This had been denied by Rousseau, but if his theories were to be applied to the actual government of a country, it is difficult to see what else the deputies could have done. If one accepted the fatal ambivalence in the definition of the general will between an actual parliamentary majority (obtained, as the deputies knew well enough, by rhetoric, lobbying and, on occasion, by intimidation) and what was genuinely conducive to the welfare of society as a whole, it followed that any majority vote was not merely the expression of a political preference, but an indication of what the minority itself ought to have wanted, if it was really concerned about the common good. The minority were therefore free to debate a law but, once it was passed, it was not enough for them merely to obey it. They were not entitled to criticize it or to campaign for its repeal. The deputies – and subsequent historians – tended to lump together the result of all the Assembly's decisions into a kind of metaphysical entity called 'the revolution'. Any opposition or criticism of any aspect of the Assembly's policy was therefore opposition to 'the revolution' and since the revolution was the work of the sovereign people, which had transferred its powers to the Assembly, to oppose any aspect of it was to confess one's self an enemy of the people. A deputy who protested against any policy was 'a subject who is trying to bind the sovereign'. Expressions of protest, opposition, or even reserve, were 'a conspiracy against the legislative power'. This denial to the minority of the right to persevere in its convictions was not the product of a particular political situation but the consequence of a specific ideology. It played a very important part in convincing both Right and Left that what was at issue was a conflict between two wholly irreconcilable points of view. Each was convinced that the other had no right to think the way it did. Mirabeau expressed it all very clearly: 'If it is immoral to act against one's conscience, it is no less immoral to base one's conscience on false and arbitrary principles. The obligation to compose one's conscience precedes the obligation to follow it.' The Inquisition could scarcely have put it better. Since, for Rousseauists, morals and politics were two aspects of the same thing, opposition was not merely illegitimate but wicked and any compromise was a pact with the devil.

The minority was therefore not entitled to protest about anything at all since, strictly speaking, it had no right to exist, once it had been revealed as a minority. Mirabeau said that those who interrupted him were insulting 'the sovereign majority of the nation'. This was more than a political fiction that suited the purposes of the Left. It was implicit in the Rousseauist atmosphere that everyone breathed, and the deputies of the Right were just as convinced that their opponents were not entitled to think as they did and should be forced to be free. In 1789 moderates like the archbishop of Aix and Lally-Tollendal had located the general will in the majority and denied the opposition any right to protest. That was when the political situation was still fluid and no one thought of himself as being permanently in the minority. By the end of 1790 the Left hoped that it constituted a permanent majority and Alexandre Lameth provided the clearest definition of the new orthodoxy. Opposition was legitimate only when it took the form of resistance to despotism.

A party which opposes only the general will, which resists only the laws of the state, which tries all the time to retard the work of the Assembly and prevent the execution of its decrees, in other words, to prolong as far as it can the state of uncertainty inseparable from a revolution, such opposition is disastrous, it is sacrilegious.

He had a point – by this time some of his opponents were committed to reversing the revolution by any means they could command, and even those who would not resort to violence themselves would have been prepared to profit from its exercise by others. Some of the Right had now opted for the *politique du pire*. They had given up trying to limit the damage and welcomed extreme measures that they hoped would discredit the Assembly and accelerate the counter-revolution that they had come to regard as necessary. Their sense of isolation, outrage and alienation was only partially derived from the defence of interests that had been damaged by the actions of the majority. It was also a protest against the assumption of moral superiority by their opponents, which denied them the right to their own opinions.

Since the sovereign people were not given any opportunity to say what they thought of their representatives – when the Corsican electors tried to do so, deputies of both Right and Left were scandalized – it was normally easy enough to assert that whatever the Assembly did had popular support. On occasions when it became clear that it did not, the theory of the general will made it comparatively easy to demonstrate that it was the electorate that was in the wrong. This had first emerged in the debate on imperative mandates, which was a fairly typical example of the Assembly adopting a common sense solution to a particular problem and justifying it by means of a theory that entitled it to do whatever it liked.[2] On another occasion Barère said that it was for the Assembly to preserve the people from the excesses of its own enthusiasm and Duport argued that a representative constitution was protected from the impulsive movements of public opinion. That may have been good political sense – which was why Montesquieu had said it before him – but when allied to a Rousseauist belief in total sovereignty, it led to dangerous conclusions. Duport went on to say that the *cahiers* were merely an expression of the opinion of isolated groups of people. It was the Assembly that embodied the nation as a whole and was authorized to *faire vouloir le peuple*. 'It's will lies here.' On the same tack, Charles Lameth thought that there might be times when the Assembly had to 'rectify public opinion when it was mistaken and rule it in order to return to it the benefits that we derive from it'. He may not have put it very clearly but the consequences of his argument were obvious. Another deputy explained that requests from the people had always to be considered, although it might be necessary to reject them in the people's own interest. The wheel had come full circle and popular sovereignty now meant that it was for the elected to tell the electors what they ought to think. When Robespierre, for his own tactical purposes, persuaded the Assembly that its members should not be re-eligible at the next elections, he justified this interference with the right of the electors to vote for whomever they chose, on the ground that the Assembly was entitled to do anything that was for the public good.

---

2 See above, pp. 62-4.

The Right was on firmer ground when it argued that, as a matter of historical fact, the sovereign people had never voted to transfer its powers to the Estates General, but it had problems of its own. It had no answer to the question of who was responsible for defining the powers of the king and no grounds for its assertions that the silent majority was on its side. Maury put the Right's point of view with his usual pungency.

It is too easy to enthrone the general will in the place of legitimate authority and soon afterwards to substitute one's self for this pretended general will, while claiming to be its agent. No one can define popular sovereignty for us precisely since no one dares to admit that this pretended sovereignty is merely the right of the strongest. Remember that we are, in actual fact, representatives of the French nation and not Jean-Jacques Rousseau's plenipotentiaries; we have not submitted the *Social Contract* to the verdict of the electorate, as the measure of our power and the title of our mission.

The Devil could quote scripture and Maury enjoyed himself by recalling that Rousseau had said that long debates were a sign of the ascendancy of sectional interests, that he had rejected democracy as too perfect for human society, asserted that large states needed to be monarchies and proclaimed representative government to be the negation of popular sovereignty.

It was unrealistic of the Right to go on insisting that the general will was to be found in the *cahiers* and to ignore the transformation of the political situation that had taken place since July 1789. The supporters of the monarchy were on firmer ground when they accused their opponents of continually encroaching in fact on the powers that, in theory, they admitted belonged to the executive, and creating a republican constitution while pretending to respect the rights of the monarchy. It was impossible for the Left to give them an honest answer to this, which would have involved admitting that the 'best of kings' was not to be trusted and that he might be tempted to use the powers to which he was logically entitled in order to subvert the revolution and restore absolutist government.

The Right was therefore able to argue that the assumption of sovereign power by the Assembly was a usurpation of the rights of both king and people. Cazalès claimed what he called the Englishman's right to campaign against the majority, and even to denounce it. 'We want the nation to know that, subject to your laws in our capacity as citizens, we have voted against them as legislators . . . whatever opinion it professes, the party of the opposition is always the party of the people.' It is not clear whether this actually reflected a liberal assertion of the right to dissent, or whether Cazalès was merely claiming that the people were on his side, The Right shared more common ground with the Left than either side would have cared to admit. It was they who had first defied the king and some of them were still prepared to concede that he was the nation's servant and not its master, but, as Montlosier reminded his fellow-deputies, 'He is the nation's servant and not yours.' They insisted that Rousseau's prescriptions for direct democracy in small republics could not be transferred to the representative government of a monarchy. Any assembly of representatives was, in the nature of things, a kind of aristocracy, as liable as the monarch to aspire to extend its own powers and to encroach on those of everyone else. The main danger of despotism came not from the king, whose intentions, at least according to Montlosier, were irreproachable and whose power had already been tamed, but from the pretensions of the Assembly. What was at issue was partly an assessment of the intentions and resources of Louis XVI and partly the resentment of the Right at finding itself almost always in a minority and the target for popular abuse and intimidation, which the Left tolerated and to some extent encouraged by denouncing its opponents as bad citizens.

The seriousness of the threat of a restoration of absolutism - which neither side wanted - was a matter of political judgement, on which it might have been possible to arrive at some kind of a *modus vivendi*. What made compromise impossible was ideology. The Left presented its opponents as the selfish defenders of sectional interests against the common good and the Right retaliated by denying the legitimacy of anything that the Assembly did. This put it in a false position since the great majority of its members continued to participate in debates, in the hope of salvaging what they could, without considering themselves under any moral obligation, despite what Cazalès had said, to abide by the results when these were unfavourable. This was an inevitable response to the assertion of the Left that the minority was not entitled to hold the views it did, and the result was a complete breakdown in any sense of national solidarity. Civil war began in the minds of the deputies before it actually broke out on the ground. As Montlosier wrote in 1796, 'We insisted on believing that all the decency was on our own side. We could never believe that others might be mistaken and that we might be mistaken ourselves.'

One or two deputies realized, especially in retrospect, that popular sovereignty was ultimately an assertion that might was right, and that its logical consequence was civil war. Within the Assembly the proof that one particular party embodied the general will was its ability to outvote the other. More generally, a nation was entitled to resist oppression and to overthrow its government, but for one section of the population to defy the general will was factious. Since all parties to a quarrel were going to assert - and believe - the purity of their intentions, whether or not a vote or an insurrection reflected the general will would depend, in theory and in practice, on who won. Success was proof that one actually reflected, indeed embodied, the will of the nation; failure was a sign of faction. Roederer wrote, long after the revolution, that sovereignty was essentially a question of power. Rights existed only when there was the will and the means to enforce them. Mounier said that belief in popular sovereignty rested ultimately on a confusion between sovereignty and what he rather oddly described as 'the right of force'. Rousseau had said that Hobbes had been criticized for the wrong reasons and the Hobbesian chickens were coming home to roost.

7

The Failure of Politics

I F one had asked the members of the Constituent Assembly for their views about the kind of society they were hoping to create, the great majority would have been in closer agreement than the members of most British parliaments. With the exception of some of the clergy, such as Maury, and a handful of cavaliers, they saw themselves as heirs of the Enlightenment, which might have provided the basis for political agreement. The majority, including a good many of the *curés*, took a secular view of political questions. They believed that human nature was essentially the product of environment and that society was regulated by natural laws, concerning which they were in general agreement. Politics was therefore a matter of finding rational solutions to rational problems. The result would be to eliminate conflict, stimulate the production of wealth and, by putting an end to cruelty, superstition and pauperism, lead to the regeneration of human nature itself. From Montlosier to Robespierre, they saw themselves as inaugurating a new and better era in human history. It was the Convention, in 1793, that adopted a new system of dating to replace the Christian calendar, but the proposal was first made in the Constituent Assembly.

Talleyrand might regret the demise of the *douceur de vivre*, but there were surprisingly few regrets for the passing of the *Ancien Régime*. Malouet, despite his own successful career, was very critical of the old royal administration. The fact that their mother had been in receipt of a royal pension did not deter the Lameths from trying to promote a social revolution. Members of the court nobility such as Lafayette, d'Aiguillon and Noailles were more conscious of their grudges against the queen than of their former advantages.[1] It was they and their peers who took the initiative in attacking 'feudalism' on 4 August 1789 and they were mainly responsible for the abolition of noble titles in 1790. Ferrières spoke for a whole social group when he said that 'People were so weary of the court that most of the nobles were what was subsequently known as democrats.' 'It was without regret that the majority, even of the

---

[1] D. Wick, 'The court nobility and the French Revolution', *Eighteenth-century Studies*, 10 (1980).

provincial nobility, saw the new constitution establishing itself.' Where secular matters were concerned, most of the clergy concurred.

This agreement extended to the kind of regime that the deputies hoped to substitute for the old order. Malouet had been so popular at Riom in 1789 that he had been allowed to draft his own *cahier*. The reform programme that he prescribed for himself included the control of all taxation by an elected assembly and its approval of all legislation, the abolition of fiscal privilege, freedom of the press and habeas corpus, ministerial responsibility and reform of the law. This was virtually the same as the terms on which Lafayette and Mirabeau, in 1790, told the king that they were prepared to work for the stabilization of the revolution. Montlosier, whom most people regarded as an extreme royalist, wrote in a pamphlet that he published in 1790,

Everyone asked from the king the restoration of the imprescriptible right of men living in society to obey only such laws they had made for themselves, to pay only taxes to which they had consented; to make laws and vote taxes, that was the revolution that all citizens demanded and all honourable people had in mind.

That revolution has happened, the nation has recovered possession of all these rights . . . which was what had been agreed by all the Orders and classes of citizens. There can be no doubt that the sum of all these articles constitutes one of the greatest and one of the finest revolutions in the history of nations.[2]

The following year, in another pamphlet, with the incendiary title *De la nécessité d'une contre-révolution en France*, he still repeated the same message: 'This was the revolution that the king gave you, the nobility desired, the Parlements requested and the entire nation wanted.'

The successful establishment of a regime along these lines would have satisfied most of the deputies of the Left. They were constitutional monarchists, which implied – in theory at least – leaving the king and his ministers responsible for the execution of policy. By modern standards, they held very restrictive views about the extent to which the state should intervene in the economy and very emphatic ones about the sanctity of private property. They were not economic levellers and they even shared with the nobility a conception of honour that Montesquieu had regarded as the activating principle of monarchy.[3] There were occasions when the majority conceded that their personal honour entitled deputies to disregard the will of the Assembly.

Granted this basic similarity of aims and outlook, the inevitable question is why the deputies found themselves unable to cooperate in order to implement them. As Necker put it in 1795, 'We should have today the English government, and an improved version of the English government, if the king,

[2] *Essai sur l'art de constituer les peuples* (Paris, 1790), pp. 15-16.
[3] See N. Hampson, 'The French Revolution and the nationalization of honour', in *War and Society: historical essays in honour of the memory of J. R. Western, 1928-1971*, ed. M. D. R. Foot (London, 1973).

the nobility and the Third Estate, who each desired it at one time or another, could all have wanted it at the same time.' This was to re-state the problem, rather than to suggest a solution to it. Some historians have been content to accept the verdict of the contemporary journalist Mallet du Pan, that it was all a matter of defective leadership: 'Agreement would have saved them all and France as well, but there was no leader, no one active, skilful and farsighted enough to tighten up the joints. Instead, people took a pride in widening them.' This reduces the explanation to a tautology: the proof that leadership was defective was its failure to reach agreement and this failure was the proof that the leadership was defective. This does not get us very far.

One must never forget the deputies's lack of political experience. The effects of this were reinforced by a climate of opinion that regarded politics as the pursuit of *vertu*, collective political action as faction or intrigue and compromise as a concession to sin. The members of the Constituent Assembly were often men distinguished by their successful careers in administration or law, by the breath of their education and their capacity for abstract thought. In all these respects they compare very favourably with the members of modern parliaments. What they lacked - although they themselves would have considered it a positive virtue - were rules and precedents and the habit of subordinating individual perceptions to the pursuit of collective goals. They had been chosen as outstanding people in their own right, rather than as the men who would implement a programme that their electors believed, on balance, to be preferable to that of an alternative team. This tended to reinforce their *amour propre* and their reluctance to compromise even with those whose views were very close to their own.

Montlosier admitted that he was always in a temper and spoiling for a fight. He admired Cazalès, who kept him at arm's length, and was courted by Maury, whom he disliked. He thought Maury was jealous of Cazalès and too preoccupied with his personal oratorical triumphs and their likely effect in Rome. It was a common belief that Maury's real objective was a cardinal's hat, in which case he was one of the very few revolutionary leaders to end up with what he wanted. Cazalès, in Montlosier's view, was mainly concerned to put Maury in the shade. This may be no more than the kind of personal gossip to which politicians are prone when reminiscing about their 'friends', but Montlosier knew both men well and the evidence of the debates suggests that they took little trouble to concert their policies. In his opinion, most conflicts in the Assembly were concerned less with opinions, 'where people could have arrived at an understanding and rapprochement' than with the pursuit of popularity, personal ambition and vengeance.

Malouet admitted that he had been too prickly and censorious - Ferrières somewhat uncharitably described him as 'puffed up with his empty conceit' - and he came to regret having suspected the motives of those who disagreed with him. In the beginning he found even Mounier, who shared almost all his political views, too extreme. Malouet's assumption of moral superiority exasperated his colleagues and he was the kind of man who could get a popular motion defeated by the way in which he supported it. Mounier was less stand-offish but equally reluctant to compromise: 'When I thought a principle was true I felt obliged to defend it.' Barnave, his colleague from the Dauphiné, tried to bring together Mounier and Sieyès but 'these imperious men' refused to cooperate.

Further to the Left, the Lameths were jealous of Lafayette's power as commander-in-chief of the Parisian National Guard and suspected that his quixotic chivalry would lead him to make too many concessions to the king. Mirabeau was understandably suspected by everyone since he regarded everyone as a potential rival and, when he wrote to enlist one man's support, almost invariably disparaged someone else. Lafayette did little to conceal his dislike of Mirabeau and his passion for all things American made it difficult for him to work with those who adopted the British constitution as their model As he wrote to George Washington, 'The rage of party, even between the different nuances of the *patriotes*, has gone to every length short of bloodshed.' On the whole, though, the Left was rather better than the Right at concerting policy, thanks to the Jacobin Club. This was the most successful of the many political associations. It was the home of the more radical deputies and of aspiring politicians of every kind. Its meetings were public, which allowed its members to concert their policies without incurring the charge of faction. It developed the habit of debating in advance measures that were about to come before the Assembly, which allowed the Jacobin deputies to evolve a party line to which they then gave collective support. Even so, there were no means of enforcing any kind of party discipline, of which the very idea was anathema, and the club was the scene of some memorable battles between rival deputies.

The absence of organized parties made it very difficult, especially in the early days, to predict the outcome of a vote. The deputies, each jealous of his personal independence, voted in accordance with their reactions to the speeches, and a skilful intervention or a blunder could swing the whole outcome of a session. It was perhaps this that led Mounier to make a disastrous mistake in August 1789. Whether from conviction or from pessimism about the strength of their support, the triumvirate of Lameth, Barnave and Duport offered him an absolute veto for the king and a bicameral legislature provided that the Upper House had only a suspensive veto and the king had no right of dissolution. Confident that he could get everything he wanted, Mounier turned the offer down. Perhaps he would have lost in any case, since the triumvirate could not guaranteee to deliver a majority, but his defeat produced the first lasting division within the revolutionaries.

The difficulty of concerting policy was revealed again when the Assembly moved to Paris in October 1789. The Left decided that the time had come for a change of ministry. Lafayette had just exerted his influence to pack the duc d'Orléans off to England, since he was suspected of complicity in the march on Versailles. Although favouring a change of ministers, Lafayette wanted to retain Necker. Mirabeau, furious at the exile of Orléans, with whom his own name was linked, hoped to get rid of Necker and take his place. The Lameths also regretted the departure of Orléans but were determined to keep Mirabeau out of the ministry. The result was that they all failed and the Assembly's vote that no deputy should become a minister not merely frustrated Mirabeau's personal ambition but deprived the country of a possible channel of communication and understanding.

Cooperation proved no easier outside the Assembly. Malouet and his allies tried to create a club which – with characteristic insensitivity – they proposed to call the 'Impartials'. They invited Lafayette to become its leader but he refused when he got the impression that he was to be made the mere figurehead of an organization over which he would have no control. Soon afterwards he himself helped to set up the '89' club. The 89 and the Jacobins then joined forces to destroy the Impartials, after which they quarrelled between themselves. According to Lafayette their objectives were very similar and the disagreement was mainly a question of *amour propre*.

Things were no better on the other side. The king and queen conducted separate policies through their personal advisers, without informing the ministers and perhaps without fully informing each other. When they added Mirabeau to their team they ordered him not to reveal the fact to the ministers. The ministers, appointed to placate the Assembly, did not have the confidence of the king and were frequently at loggerheads with each other. Different groups of advisers were kept apart from each other. If one takes into account Louis XVI's lethargy, self-distrust and habit of agreeing with the man to whom he had spoken last, the Court policy of encouraging approaches from all-comers was bound to result in incoherence and inaction. When Lafayette offered his support for a partial restoration of royal authority in return for the king's acceptance of the revolution, Louis appeared to agree, but on terms so vague that he could escape from them without loss of honour, and Marie Antoinette continued to treat Lafayette as an enemy. In the short run there was perhaps something to be said for a policy of buying off possible opposition with money or fine words but it made any firm agreement between the king and the Assembly impossible and fed the suspicion that was the main cause of political instability.

Throughout the revolution the main motive for political action was fear. This could take many forms and, in one way or another, it applied to everyone. At its simplest it was fear of attack on one's person or property, if one voted for unpopular motions. The deputies were exposed to continual threats, both from the public galleries in the Assembly, which held several hundred people, and in the press. No deputy was actually killed or seriously injured but some had narrow escapes. This allowed the Left to dismiss talk of intimidation as propaganda by the minority, although some who said this were inclined to change their minds when they became unpopular in their turn. Some were not above using the threat of mob violence as a political weapon. Mirabeau, on one occasion, threatened unnamed 'conspirators' with popular vengeance and told them it was just as well for them that fear of popular movements should have deterred them from putting their plans into action.

It is impossible to know how far intimidation affected speeches and votes. The Right exaggerated its influence and the Left denied it. Mounier claimed that not more than 150 deputies genuinely supported the majority, which obtained most of its votes through fear. That looks highly unlikely, but there were probably many occasions when close votes were determined by those who thought conformity the better part of valour. The usual practice of the Assembly was to ascertain the majority by sitting or standing, which preserved the anonymity of those whose faces were not known to the public. Doubtful cases and decisions on matters of exceptional importance were resolved by an *appel nominal*, in which each deputy recorded his vote. The comte de La Marck, a deputy of the nobility, reported in October 1790, almost as a matter of course, 'The *appel nominal*, always a dangerous trial for the weak, led over a hundred deputies to leave the chamber and the decree was rejected by a majority of sixty-three votes.' In this particular case the issue was a vote of no confidence in the ministers, which the Left hoped to win. Fear of identifying one's self could cut both ways. When Barnave said that fear was the dominant sentiment of most of those who took part in the revolution, he seems to have meant fear of 'aristocrats'. Fear probably contributed something to the chronic absenteeism that plagued the Right in particular. The Assembly changed its president and secretaries every fortnight and these elections were by secret ballot, which tended to produce rather more conservative verdicts than public votes on matters of policy. There were swings and roundabouts, but where personal safety was concerned, the Right had obviously more cause for anxiety than the Left.

Fear of a less personal kind also influenced political behaviour. The king and queen were apprehensive of the power that his command of the National Guard conferred on Lafayette. He in turn described them as 'great children who only swallow their beneficial medicine when one mentions were-wolves'. The ministers, for whom no one had a good word, were inclined to avoid taking action for fear of denunciation in the Assembly and the press, with the result that they were condemned for not trying to make the new constitution work. Necker was thought to have accepted a merely suspensive veto for the king because he feared that the Parisian radicals would march on Versailles. Even the abbé Grégoire, personally popular as a *curé* of the Left, was reluctant for the Assembly to move to Paris because of threats to the clergy.

More generally still, it would scarcely be an exaggeration to say that the course of the revolution was determined by people voting not for what they thought most desirable, but for what they believed to be necessary, as a result of counter-balancing fears of counter-revolution on the one hand and anarchy on the other. Fear of counter-revolution had initially very little foundation and was something of a turnip-ghost with which nervous deputies like Robespierre frightened each other. The Left could not believe in the decisiveness of its victory over absolutism and was sceptical of the readiness of the nobility and upper clergy to accept an egalitarian new order when they had so stubbornly resisted voting in common. When the Parlements had been such a thorn in the flesh of the monarchy, it seemed too good to be true that the Assembly could simply brush aside their opposition. As time went on, the deputies became understandably concerned about the noisy clamour of the increasing number of *émigrés* and their boasts about the counter-revolution that they would enforce by civil war. Artois, the nominal leader of the *émigrés*, tried to enlist the armed support of the Habsburg emperor (Marie Antoinette's brother) and the king of Savoy for the insurrection that he hoped to start in southern France. It is easy for historians to argue that Artois was an incompetent bungler who could be relied on to make a mess of whatever he attempted. We know that his hopes of foreign help were illusory and that his irresponsible posturing infuriated the king and queen. Whatever their intentions with regard to the revolution, Artois was a nuisance to them. Contemporaries could not be so sure and they could not afford to take any chances. The king's failure to make a public repudiation of Artois in forthright terms was bound to arouse suspicion and the more fervently one believed the revolution to be the beginning of a new European order, the more likely it seemed that the beneficiaries of the old one would try to suppress it.

Within France itself, resistance to change became more militant, especially when the Assembly involved itself in an unnecessary and divisive religious policy. The abolition of noble titles incensed many of the provincial gentry, some of whom felt that honour demanded some kind of defiance. In the event of serious trouble, the deputies were far from confident that they could rely on an army whose officers were joining the *émigrés* in droves, often because of chronic indiscipline within the regiments, which the Assembly did not dare to punish. If one leaves out the religious question, the threat to the revolution from 'aristocrats' was real enough to be taken seriously, without constituting a mortal danger, but its limited potential is more apparent now than it was at the time. The Left was aware that, if it came to a fight, some of those who claimed to form a loyal opposition within the Assembly would join the revolt against it. Montlosier advocated armed resistance and even constitutional monarchists like Malouet would put the safety of the king before their political principles. This naturally led the radicals to treat as rebels those whom they suspected of merely waiting for a suitable opportunity to declare themselves. This in turn strengthened the conviction of the royalists that there was no place for themselves within the new France.

Disregarding the contribution of their own ambivalent attitude to the disruption of national unity, the deputies of the Right accused their opponents of tolerating, if they did not actually encourage, disorder and social subversion. Ferrières, who was better than most at seeing both sides to a question, thought that the majority had the means of restoring order but was too frightened of the king and queen to do so. Both Right and Left were reluctant to take decisive action against embarrassing allies on whose support they might come to depend. The Assembly therefore never made any serious attempt to restrain journalists like Marat who incited their readers to lynch and revolt. They admonished mutineers in the army and navy but never punished them severely enough to deter others from imitating them. To some extent, this may have been due to their revulsion against the barbarity of the *Ancien Régime*, which had broken violent criminals on the wheel, and their determination that the new order should be one of humanity. To their opponents, the humanity seemed all one-sided: the Assembly was quick to act against parlementaires or army officers but content to wag a cautionary finger against popular violence. As examples of this double standard multiplied, the royalists accused their adversaries of bad faith, of preaching principle and practising the rule of force. They came to see themselves as victims of the revolution, mistrusted, denounced and humiliated, even when they had accepted the sacrifices demanded of them.

'Left' and 'Right' were, of course, relative terms and they meant different things at different times. Initially at least, there was a good deal of agreement about the goals; what was at issue was the means necessary to achieve them. The first step, whether or not it was publicly admitted, was to extort from the 'executive' more concessions than the king and his ministers were willing to make of their own accord. This was apparent after the dismissal of Necker in July 1789, when the Assembly had presented a relatively united front in opposition to the new ministry. It had been saved from whatever Breteuil and the new ministers intended to do to it, only by popular insurrection. After the king had climbed down and recalled Necker, the nature and extent of royal authority was the touchstone that separated Left from Right. The latter argued that tradition and public opinion, as expressed in the *cahiers*, made the king a participant in the general will. More prosaically, a constitutional monarchy implied a monarch with the power to rule. If the king were to be persuaded to reconcile himself to his new constitutional role, he would have to be treated with respect and provided with the means to play his part. The Left was more inclined to emphasize the fact that it was insurrectionary action that had actually saved the Assembly. Whatever the intentions of the vacillating Louis, ministers were not to be trusted. The only way to safeguard the revolution was therefore to deprive the executive of the means of subverting it, which inhibited the deputies from taking forceful repressive measures against outbreaks of the kind of mob violence that had saved it in July. Eventually, it was hoped, the king, and perhaps even the ministers, would concede defeat and abandon all thought of counter-revolution. Only then would it be safe to allow the executive the powers that it needed in order to function properly. Each point of view had a good deal to be said for it, but the pursuit of either excluded the other.

The intention of almost everyone was to arrive at a new *modus vivendi* with the king. Where the deputies disagreed was in their assessment of the balance to be struck between reliance on his professions of sympathy for the revolution and their fear of anarchy. At any time, the Right consisted of those who believed that the revolution was now safe and the Left of those who thought that the counter-revolutionaries had not yet conceded defeat. The former insisted that the revolution was over and that normal constitutional rules should henceforth apply; the latter justified the continuance of exceptional measures which they agreed would eventually have to be discarded. The Right therefore demanded that their opponents should practise the constitutional principles they preached and the Left accused them of having sold themselves to the Court and of hypocritically pretending to accept the revolution when their real aim was to subvert it by a treacherous legality. Both sides were sincere about their own intentions and mistaken about those of their opponents. As one group after another judged that the time had come for an agreement with the king, the point at issue remained the same but the actors changed their parts. This process might have been expected to lead to a continual reinforcement of the Right, if present policies had been all that mattered. What actually happened was that former opponents could not forget the suspicions they had entertained about each other and the insults in which they had indulged. New divisions were added to old and the final result was to destroy them all.

In one sense, the first people to try to withdraw their chestnuts from the fire they had helped to kindle were the parlementaires. They had stoked the political crisis in 1787-8 and joined in the clamour for the Estates General. They had scarcely won their point when they realized that, in the political climate of 1789, the Estates General would put paid to their own political pretensions. By the spring of that year the Paris Parlement was said to be violently hostile to Necker and prepared to offer the king almost any terms if he would get rid of the rival body. This, however, is rather a special case since the parlementaires were prepared to accept a modified form of the old absolutism and very few of their members sat in the Constituent Assembly.

Within the Assembly itself, the first group to declare that the revolution had gone far enough consisted of the men round Mounier; from August 1789 onwards, that included Malouet. Mounier had come to Versailles with a national reputation for radicalism that he had won in Dauphiné.[4] It was he who proposed the Tennis Court Oath and on 13 July he had called for a vote of no confidence in the ministers who had succeeded Necker. Mounier changed his ground during the constitutional debates of August and September, when his group came to be denounced as '*monarchiens*'. As always, motives were

---

[4] On Mounier, see J. Egret, *La Révolution des Notables: Mounier et les Monarchiens* (Paris, 1950).

mixed and what was at issue was not merely the amount of power to be entrusted to the king. For Mounier and his *Anglomanes* the adoption of a British type of constitution was a matter of *amour propre* as well as of principle. Whatever the reason, he now thought that the revolution had gone too far and, according to his parliamentary colleague and biographer, Lally-Tollendal, regretted the Tennis Court Oath since it had deprived the king of the power of dissolution. He was probably the first of the genuine revolutionaries to be prepared to give back some of the ground that he had won. The breaking point for Mounier was the march to Versailles in October 1789. He was presiding the Assembly when it was invaded by the crowd of women, which cannot have been a pleasant experience. After the decision to move to Paris he tried to organize a mass exodus from the Assembly. This was the first of the boycotts of the Right. When it failed, he himself withdrew to Dauphiné and eventually to Switzerland. Malouet, like most of the Monarchiens, remained in the Assembly while denying its legitimacy. One does not need to have exalted ideas about the sovereignty of the general will to think that this put him in a false position.

Lafayette saw himself as a paladin rather than a politician.[5] In a typical gesture, in August 1789, he proclaimed that 'If the king were to refuse the constitution, I will fight him. If he accepts it, I will defend him, and the day when he declared himself my prisoner [?] did more to devote me to his service than if he had offered me half his kingdom.' Lafayette was inclined to protest too much; he meant what he said but fine words of this order were unlikely to butter many constitutional parsnips. Initially he worked very closely with the Lameths, but he began to drift away from them when he refused to support their campaign to bring down Necker. As the man responsible for maintaining order in Paris, he was part of the establishment, even if it was a revolutionary establishment. This put him in close contact with the king and gave him more realistic ideas about the sovereign people than those entertained by some of his more visionary colleagues. He saw himself as the guarantor of a revolutionary settlement, rather than as a participant in a revolutionary struggle. In April 1790 he offered Louis XVI his support in return for a commitment to accept and maintain the constitutional status quo. The king's acceptance in principle and his promise of 'complete confidence' committed him to rather less than Lafayette probably imagined. Marie Antoinette hated him as much as ever and within a month the court had bought the services of a new adviser - Mirabeau - who immediately tried to discredit Lafayette. The latter knew enough of what was going on to be on his guard, but his situation and his quixotic sense of loyalty to a king whom he could not trust alienated him from his former friends of the Left. He was too honourable, where Mirabeau was not honourable

[5] The fullest account of Lafayette's activities is to be found in the works of L. Gottschalk, all published in Chicago: *Lafayette between the American and French Revolutions* (1950); (with M. Maddox) *Lafayette in the French Revolution, through the October Days* (1969); *Lafayette in the French Revolution: from the October Days through the Federation* (1973).

enough, for either to be the effective leader of a party. No one trusted Mirabeau, and Lafayette was too trustworthy to consider using his control over Paris to dictate terms to both the Assembly and the king. It was Washington rather than Cromwell every time.

By the end of 1790, when the constitution was nearly finished, the triumvirate, the effective leaders of the Left, were beginning to think of the future. The next assembly would not inherit the sovereign powers of its predecessor and would be merely a parliament with circumscribed authority. If there was to be any constitutional settlement, it would have to be reached before the elections. That meant offering to give back to the king some of the ground that the triumvirate had fought so hard to win.[6] According to Mounier, Barnave wrote to him expressing his regret at former hostilities and promising to try to repair some of the damage. The triumvirate failed to conciliate the Right and the change of policy that they tried unsuccessfully to conceal from the Assembly alienated many of their backbench supporters. Robespierre, Pétion and the handful of deputies on the extreme Left won more support than usually came their way when they raised the ever-popular cry that the leaders were betraying the revolution. Barnave and the Lameths had used it in their time; Robespierre was later to employ it against Pétion.

It was generally conceded, even by those who disliked and distrusted him, that Mirabeau was the outstanding politician in the Assembly. He owed this reputation to his intelligence, his sense of political tactics, his virtuosity in debate – when many of his colleagues could do no more than plough through their rehearsed scripts – the quality of his team of advisers and the power of his lungs. Both then and subsequently, it has been argued that he alone could have provided the Assembly with effective leadership. A glance at his political role is therefore appropriate, if only to demonstrate that politics had its own sphere of action that could be quite independent of ideology.[7]

Mirabeau's first objective was to make sure of his election to the Estates General at almost any cost. His rejection by the nobility of Provence ensured that this would have to be on an anti-aristocratic ticket; he himself said that his attitude would have been very different if he had sat as a member of the Second Estate. Despite having cheated him in the matter of the Berlin correspondence, he tried to enlist the support of Montmorin, the foreign minister, in December 1788.[8] 'Without at least the secret support of the government, I cannot be elected to the Estates General.' True to what was to become his form, he threw in a disparaging reference to Necker. He told his friend, La Marck, whom he knew to be more or less in the queen's confidence, 'The day when the king's ministers agree to negotiate with me, I shall be found devoted to the royal

---

[6] See G. Michon, *Essai sur l'histoire du parti feuillant: Adrien Duport* (Paris, 1924). See below, chs 10 and 11, for the attempt to compromise with the king.

[7] In default of any good biography, the best source on Mirabeau is still *Correspondance entre le comte de Mirabeau et le comte de La Marck*, ed. A. de Bacourt (Paris, 1851), 3 vols.

[8] See above p. 40 for the publication of the Berlin correspondence.

cause and to the salvation of the monarchy.' Montmorin, an honourable nonentity, refused to join in the criticism of his colleague, Necker, and viewed the prospect of Mirabeau's absence from the Estates General with exasperating equanimity. Mirabeau waited until he had been elected and then sent Montmorin a letter that was as offensive as eighteenth-century *bienséance* permitted. His next move – towards the end of May – was to approach Necker, who more or less asked him his price. That was no way to treat Mirabeau. During June and July 1789 he distinguished himself in opposition to the royal government. This was probably a matter of conviction, at a time when the Assembly seemed in danger, though it may also have been an attempt to raise his price. As he said afterwards, 'I am the man for the re-establishment of order, but not of the old order.'

During the summer of 1789 Mirabeau was widely suspected of being involved in what were rumoured to be the intrigues of an Orléanist faction. Orléans himself was too idle and timid to constitute much of a threat to his royal cousin, Louis XVI, but the ambitious politicians who surrounded him were trying to make him *lieutenant-général du royaume*, which would have relegated the king to a nominal political role. Orléans and Mirabeau were said to have been behind the march on Versailles in October, with this end in view, although a judicial inquiry failed to produce any conclusive evidence against them. When Orléans lost his nerve and allowed Lafayette to bundle him off to England, Mirabeau dropped him. With the help of Lafayette and the triumvirate, he then tried to unseat Necker and take his place. On 19 October he wrote two letters. One was to Lafayette, promising that 'whatever happens, I shall be yours to the end, because I am strongly attracted by your great qualities'. The other was to La Marck, attacking Lafayette as a dictator. This scheme collapsed and the vote of 7 November that banned deputies from becoming ministers put paid to Mirabeau's ambitions in that direction. He then transferred his attentions to the king's brother, Provence, who was involved in plans for some kind of a *coup d'état*. In a memoir to Provence, Mirabeau said that everything was going wrong. The Court party must repudiate the nobility and the Parlements in order to popularize itself. To regain his independence, the king should escape to Rouen and order the Assembly to join him. He should then dissolve it and summon a convention that would revise the constitution in such a way as to restore his authority. Mirabeau's objective may have been a revised form of constitutional monarchy but he was far too wily not to have realized that the means he proposed were likely to produce a very different end. News of a 'royalist plot' leaked out, a scapegoat was executed and Provence hastened to cover himself by disclaiming any knowledge of the business. Mirabeau was back where he had started.

He seems to have been fairly subdued during the first months of 1790. In April he made another approach to Lafayette, congratulating him on having distanced himself from the triumvirate, 'worthy neither of you nor of me'. He wrote again on 13 May, urging the need for the two of them to concert their policies. In the meantime he had struck a bargain with the Court, through the mediation of La Marck.[9] Louis paid Mirabeau's debts, made him a monthly allowance and deposited a million livres with La Marck that were to be given to Mirabeau at the end of the session if his conduct was judged satisfactory. Mirabeau argued that it was necessary to liberate him from his creditors in order to give him freedom of action but the conditional million was scarcely an inducement to independence and La Marck himself was rather disconcerted by the extent of Mirabeau's delight with the financial terms. The king and queen presumably thought that they had brought his support, or at least his neutrality, without any need to pay attention to his advice. Marie Antoinette had said to La Marck in October 1789, 'I don't think we shall ever be so wretched as to be reduced to the painful extremity of turning to Mirabeau.' What had changed since then was her view of the political situation rather than of Mirabeau. He, on the other hand, liked to think that he had become a kind of secret prime minister. Like everyone else when they thought that things had gone far enough, he now proclaimed the revolution to be over. 'The agitation that was necessary to allow us to escape from our nullity must give way to ideas suited to our long-term organization . . . it is time to move from a state of legitimate insurrection to the lasting peace of a true social state . . . one does not preserve liberty by the means that won it.' Mirabeau's first suggestions to the court included the need to destroy the political power of Lafayette. Creating a new ministry would make it possible to blackmail him by threatening to reveal his links with the old one.

What followed was not very satisfactory to either side. Mirabeau argued, reasonably enough, that it would do the Court no good if he discredited himself by advocating policies of ostentatious moderation in the Assembly. He said that he defended royal authority over issues that mattered and preserved his radical reputation by violent outbursts over such trivialities as the form of the naval ensign. The king and queen took his protestations with a grain of salt. They did not share his concern for his political reputation and suspected him of making the best of both worlds, so that he could eventually opt for the side that looked more likely to win. This was probably a mistake: it would have taken a good deal to make Mirabeau forget that a million livres depended on his appearing to give satisfaction.

Mirabeau was certainly not deficient in political dexterity and he alone had the power, on occasion, to impose his personal authority on the Assembly. His total failure probably owed something to the deviousness of the man and to the well-earned reputation for venality that he had brought with him in 1789, but it also reflected the intractability of revolutionary politics. It was beyond the wit

[9] It has been argued (by P. and P. Guirault de Coursac, in *Enquête sur le procès du Roi Louis XVI*, Paris, 1982, pp. 202-5) that Mirabeau's contact was with the queen alone, although she deceived him into thinking that the king was also involved. This would involve rather a lot of people having lied for a long time for no obvious reason, and they do not explain how Marie Antoinette raised the money to pay Mirabeau.

of anyone to construct a stable majority in the Assembly for any policy that involved cooperation with the government. The ministers were divided and mistrusted as the agents of rulers who, in fact, kept them in ignorance of their intentions. Suspicions fed on themselves until they came to justify themselves. There was a purely political dimension to the revolution, as well as an ideological one, and neither offered much hope of a peaceful solution to France's problems. The extent of these problems might well have defeated any parliament, since the Assembly had committed itself to the transformation of virtually all of France's institutions. This was not possible without pain and protest, but the intensity of the hatreds that developed cannot be explained solely in terms of the reluctance of the losers to accept the sacrifices that were demanded of them. What set the deputies at each others' throats was not so much their divergent policies as their perception of the other side's intentions. The apocalyptic dimensions of the ensuing conflict were a product of both politics and ideology. To discover how the two interacted, one has to look in some detail at one or two of the more important areas of disagreement.

8

Foreign Policy

THE fundamental conflict between the views of Montesquieu and Rousseau was perhaps most obvious and irreconcilable when they considered the relationships that ought to prevail between nations. Montesquieu, true to his universal perspective, gave the cosmopolitanism of the Enlightenment a particularly personal emphasis: 'If I knew of anything useful to my own nation that would be ruinous to another, I should not propose it to my prince, since I am a man before I am a Frenchman, or rather, I am a man by necessity and a Frenchman by accident.' His own country must by judged by the same universal standards that applied to any other. He was not one of those who transfer to a different country the allegiance that they cannot give to their own, but his admiration for the British constitution gave that country privileged status. He was an advocate of commerce which 'cures destructive prejudices and is conducive to peace. Two nations which trade with each other become dependent on each other.' All this set Rousseau's teeth on edge. He detested any idea of dependence, personal, political or economic. He had no particular regard for England and his conception of a general will implied the total sovereignty of each nation-state. Sparta was his ideal, a state not exactly renowned for its eagerness to subordinate its own interests to the general good.

Every partial society, when it is confined and closely knit, alienates itself from the mass. Every *patriote* is hard on foreigners: they are merely men, they are nothing in his eyes. This is an inevitable inconvenience, but of no great consequence. What matters is to behave well towards the people with whom one lives. Abroad, the Spartan was ambitious, miserly, unjust, but disinterestedness, equity and peace reigned within his walls. Beware of those cosmopolitans who go hunting far afield in their books for the duties that they will not condescend to fulfil around them.

Where foreign policy was concerned, the immediate inclination of the men of the Constituent Assembly was towards Montesquieu. Their attitude looked backwards towards Voltaire's *Candide* and forwards towards twentieth-century radicalism. Wars were due to the dynastic ambitions of autocratic rulers. Except in the case of wars of national independence – William Tell was a great revolutionary favourite – an elected government, genuinely representative of the people, would fight only in self-defence. One of the most important ways in which the regeneration of France would lead to the emergence of a better world was therefore the withdrawal of one of Europe's most powerful states from the rat-race of the despots. Even the long-standing animosity towards the British had perhaps been France's fault. Such, at least, seems to have been the view of Mirabeau, speaking in the name of the diplomatic committee, in 1790: 'We regard no people as our enemy. That country is no longer one, which insidious policy presented as our rival, the country whose footsteps we follow.' England and France might not be able to impose peace on the squabbling 'tyrants' of central Europe, but at least they would never fight each other again and sooner or later their example would prevail everywhere. The prospect of universal peace was one of the reasons why 1789 seemed to so many people the Year I of a new and better world.

If this was one of the more estimable ways in which the French revolution marked the beginning of the modern world, old attitudes were easier to repudiate than to eradicate. Conflicts of what was assumed to be national economic interest, as the example of England already showed, could be as bloodily aggressive as those of dynastic ambition. A new sense of pride in belonging to a regenerated nation, in a world that was still full of tyrants, transferred to the French people as a whole some of the arrogant self-assertion that had characterized, at the personal level, the old aristocratic sense of honour.[1] The conviction that the millennium had already begun, the sense of belonging to a community that had proclaimed its regeneration by the conclusion of a new social contract, created problems of its own. What was distinctive about the new France, what made it superior to the other states of Europe, even including England, was its proclamation of the rights of man – the rights of all men. These were imprescriptible rights that could not be renounced by individuals or alienated by treaty. By definition, they applied equally to all peoples, but it was only in France that they had been made the basis for the legitimacy of all political action. When their assertion came into conflict with treaty obligations or the claims of foreign governments, there could be no question of France departing from universal principle in order to appease those whose pretensions were founded on the discredited practices and false maxims of the past. The result of all this was a somewhat ambivalent attitude on the part of the Constituent Assembly. Arrogant lectures on political theory, which could easily take on a nationalist accent, coexisted with what were generally conciliatory actions, since the majority of the deputies were not yet ready to do anything practical about smiting the unrighteous, whom they tended to regard with more pity than anger.

Some of the seigneurial rights abolished on 4 August 1789 were exercised

[1] See N. Hampson, 'The French Revolution and the nationalization of honour', in *War and Society*, ed. M. D. R. Foot (London, 1973) and G. Best, *Honour among Men and Nations*, (Toronto, 1982).

by German lords over manors held in France. In theory at least, these rights had been renounced by their beneficiaries and the Assembly had endorsed their renunciation. When the German seigneurs objected that Frenchmen had no right to deprive them of their property, it was Rewbell, a deputy from Alsace, who replied that it was not for foreigners to criticize French legislation. After two years of inconclusive argument - the two viewpoints were irreconcilable but no one was going to go to war over them - Rewbell again made aggressive noises but the deputies preferred to follow the advice of their diplomatic committee and offer compensation to the German feudatories. A similar issue arose in connection with a Genoese claim to have preserved some residual rights over Corsica when the island was transferred to France in 1768. The Assembly had declared Corsica to be an integral part of France and Barnave defended its action on the ground that this was the wish of the Corsicans themselves. Since they were not actually asked to express an opinion, this was a case of the thought being father to the wish. Even the Genoese cannot have expected their protest to have any practical effect. There was nothing they could do about it and the European Powers had more important fish to fry. Nevertheless, the French assertion of the right to popular self-determination that was implicit to Barnave's argument, was of wider application. If it was true of the Corsicans, it was presumably relevant to the Belgians, the Poles and the Irish, and the revolution had opened up a distant prospect of dubious plebiscites and wars of national liberation.

Robespierre, as usual, thought that his colleagues were guilty of credulity and irresponsible over-confidence. What was significant about the Genoese incident, unimportant in itself, was its exposure of yet another plot, devised by an unholy alliance of French and Genoese aristocrats. This exposed him to the charge that he did not know much about the social structure of the Genoese republic and his speech had little influence on his colleagues, who were used to his eternal cries of 'wolf' as he detected a counter-revolutionary intrigue behind every political issue. The more level-headed deputies were inclined to laugh at Robespierre's alarmism, but he was merely giving dramatic expression to a point of view that the deputies of the Left were inclined to take seriously. France had, by the mere fact of its regeneration, made itself the natural enemy of foreign tyrants, to whose oppressive rule it was a standing reproach. They might shrink from attacking a nation that would defend itself with enthusiasm and induce their own enslaved subjects to revolt, but they would go as far as prudence permitted to weaken and discredit a revolution from which they had so much to fear. In this they could naturally count on the support of all those in France who refused to recognize the legitimacy of the new revolutionary order. French aristocrats were the natural allies of foreign tyrants and French ministers had more in common with foreign courts than with the national Assembly. This was an inevitable consequence of the Manichean attitude that divided all Frenchmen into those who identified themselves with 'the revolution' and those who would stop at nothing to subvert it.

From enthusiasm for regeneration it was an easy transition to assertions of national superiority. This therefore tended to be particularly pronounced on the Left. As early as August 1789 Rabaut Saint-Etienne, who might have been expected to have more reservations about a country where his fellow-Protestants had been persecuted until very recently, was urging his colleagues to disregard whatever foreigners did, on the ground that it was for France to set an example rather than to follow others. Robespierre held that it was in the interest of all nations – by which he presumably meant peoples rather than governments – to protect France 'since it is from France that the liberty and happiness of the world must originate'. Charles Lameth was even more emphatic: France was a scarecrow to all tyrants, with whom French ministers were in league; 'it is time for the peoples to take concerted action against the tyrants.' Logically, this implied the kind of revolutionary crusade that was to become official policy in 1793. During the session of the Constituent Assembly, the deputies contented themselves with declamation and they do not seem to have alarmed any foreign statesmen except Burke. They had no intention of giving any practical help to the Poles or the Irish and there was little protest when the French government allowed Austrian troops to march through French territory on their way to subdue the Belgian revolt. There was a sense, though, in which Burke was right and the weapons for an ideological war were being forged, even if the Constituent Assembly had no intention of taking them out of the armoury.

All this made it very difficult to know what to think about England. For the royalists, things were comparatively straightforward and 'proud Albion' remained the national enemy. Mounier and the Monarchiens saw the country as an example for France to emulate. The men of the Centre, who had more reservations about the beauties of the British constitution, nevertheless regarded England as a free country that would be the natural partner of the new France. Even the Left, which adopted a rather patronizing attitude towards the British, was still inclined to think that a constitutional monarchy would not indulge in the counter-revolutionary mischief-making that was to be expected of despots. As the months went by and the centre of gravity in the Assembly shifted towards the Left, uncritical admiration tended to give way to an understandable irritation at the constant citing of alleged British practices in defence of French conservatism. This encouraged the re-emergence of suspicions and animosities that had never been altogether overcome, and the memories of the Bretons reinforced the condescension of the Rousseauists.

During the crisis of July 1789 the British Ambassador became worried about 'insinuations which might prove essentially injurious to the English, now resident in Paris, having been industriously propagated for some days past and instilled into the minds of the populace, tending to make it believe that Emissaries from England have been actively instrumental in fomenting the disorders that have lately been committed in this Town.'[2] Since the Parisian

[2] *Despatches from Paris, 1784-1790*, ed. O. Browning (London, 1910).

insurrection had, of course, been a glorious affair, to blame the British for having had a hand in it certainly seemed rather curious. The ambassador asked Montmorin, the French foreign minister, to publicize through the Assembly the fact that, a few weeks before, when a group of men had asked for British help in their attempt to burn the Brest fleet, he had promptly reported the fact to the French foreign office. Montmorin complied with Lord Dorset's request and the ambassador professed himself satisfied with the consequent change in public opinion. He seems to have been easily pleased: on the day after his letter was read out to the Assembly, one of the deputies referred to Brest having been almost handed over to the British. Dorset's revelation of what sounds like a singularly unconvincing plot immediately became the evidence for British intrigue.

In September 1789 there was applause for a noble who announced that Eden, who had negotiated an unpopular commercial treaty with France in 1786, was at present in Spain, trying to cheat the French a second time. The ambivalence of the deputies was particularly obvious on 15 May 1790 when one deputy was applauded for proclaiming that, in the event of war, 'we will go and attack England on British soil' and another was booed for calling England 'our eternal rival and enemy'. Even the apparently innocuous remark that England and France were unfortunately national rivals, when advanced by a noble of the Right, brought cries of 'no'. This did not deter a noble of the Left, the duc d'Aiguillon, a fortnight later, from accusing England of supporting French counter-revolutionaries. The deputies could never make up their minds whether their neighbour was perfidious Albion or the home of constitutional liberty. If one remembers the secular antagonism between the two countries and the single-minded determination with which the British government pursued what it took to be its economic advantage, the strength of French goodwill is more remarkable than the persistence of suspicion and dislike. It was, however, already apparent that, if the national interests of the two countries brought them into conflict, it would be easy for a revolutionary government to rekindle the old emotions and to give to a war against England a particularly virulent character. The fact that the British could not be represented as the victims of their despotic government would quickly transfer this animosity to the people as a whole.

Foreign policy, like every other aspect of the Assembly's business, was seen as part of a struggle for power between the deputies and the executive. The simple equation that absolutism meant war and constitutional government, peace, made the radicals all the more determined to deprive the king of the means of involving the country in a conflict that might enable him to recover his lost authority. This led the royalists to accuse them of being so obsessed with party politics that they were prepared to compromise French national security in pursuit of party advantage. National safety implied an effective executive in charge of both military and foreign policy and that meant reinforcing the power of the king. As usual, there was enough justification for each point of view to give its advocates plausible grounds for suspecting the motives of their opponents. This made it difficult to treat any case on its merits and the French were lucky in not being confronted with the need to make any decisive choices. The one international crisis that blew up and blew over illustrated the complexity of the factors that came into play whenever the Assembly confronted a major problem.

In 1788 Captain John Meares set up a trading post at Nootka Sound, on Vancouver Island, and built a schooner there. A year later the Spaniards, who claimed sovereignty over the entire Pacific coast of America, seized the ship and began to fortify Nootka Sound. Meares protested to the British government, which threatened war in support of his right to trade. France and Spain, both ruled by Bourbons, were united in a 'family compact', an alliance that committed each to the unconditional support of the other. The Spanish government therefore requested French backing in its quarrel with England. On 14 May 1790 Montmorin transmitted this request to the Assembly and the deputies found themselves in an awkward predicament. The origin of the conflict did not lend itself to easy dramatization in terms of ideology or revolutionary principle. Spain was the *bête noire* of the Enlightenment, the home of the Inquisition and all things backward, obscurantist and oppressive, whereas England, even for those who did not share Montesquieu's idolatry of its constitution, looked like the natural ally of regenerated France. On the other hand, England and France were commercial rivals, Spain was entitled to French military support and to default on the alliance might leave France dangerously isolated in an unregenerate world.

Montmorin merely informed the deputies that instructions had been given for the commissioning of fourteen ships of the line, for which he professed himself confident that the Assembly would find the money. This set off a debate in which the Right was content to propose a vote of thanks to the king, while the Left insisted on discussing who should be responsible for the conduct of foreign policy. This was the kind of issue that generated both daydreams and a certain amount of paranoia. Robespierre proclaimed the interest of all nations in protecting France as the hope of the world; Rewbell denounced family compacts and ministerial wars and thought that France should ally herself only with just peoples, without suggesting how that fitted the particular situation; the duc d'Aiguillon thought the whole crisis was a ministerial plot, which provoked the retort that the British government was unlikely to go to the expense of commissioning thirty-two ships of the line merely to serve France's ministers. Mirabeau persuaded the Assembly to endorse the king's decision and leave the general issue of the control of foreign policy to the following day.

When the debate was resumed it took some time to disentangle the issue of principle from the particular circumstances of the Spanish request. Charles Lameth, in a speech whose inconsistency revealed the multiple preoccupations of the Left, argued that the right to declare war was too important to be entrusted to the king, at least for the time being. As a general principle, any such enunciation of the general will must be done by the nation. The Assembly's control of the purse would not be an effective way of keeping the executive in line. Since, in large assemblies, generous passions would prevail over perverse ones, there was no danger in leaving decisions of this kind to the deputies. Even Montesquieu, whose audacity was not up to the profundity of his genius, had not explicitly said that the right to declare war belonged to the king. The present crisis was largely the product of the private interests of the Bourbons and of Spain's fear of revolution. War would play into the hands of the enemies of the revolution in France, by which he meant the rich. This was followed by the somewhat contradictory argument that it would prejudice the sale of Church property, on which the Assembly was pinning its hopes of solvency. To entrust the right to declare war to a king as virtuous as Louis XVI would be safe enough, but so virtuous a man would not want to be responsible for ordering the shedding of blood. He did not explain how this last argument applied to the Assembly.

The Left as a whole saw the decision to declare war as one of the most important manifestations of the general will. The right to do so therefore belonged exclusively to the nation and, as usual, they identified the nation with themselves. Montlosier, with his customary bluntness, reminded them that the king was the nation's agent and not theirs. Some of the Right accepted the Rousseauist argument about the general will but maintained that the need for secrecy in diplomacy and promptness in military action obliged the nation to delegate this particular manifestation of its will to the king. As usual, what divided the deputies was the question of how much power to give to the king. D'Aiguillon, pursuing his old vendetta against a monarch who he thought had slighted him, was for entrusting everything to the Assembly. This was the theme of the Left as a whole, to which the Extreme Left provided more or less picturesque variations. Pétion was in favour of open diplomacy and a statement that France renounced ruse and guile in favour of justice and probity. He was one of those who favoured a declaration to the effect that France renounced aggressive war. He even wanted to deprive 'the executive' of its control over the armed forces. Robespierre got into trouble for describing the king as a *commis*, or mere agent, whose role was to enforce the general will rather than to participate in deciding what it was. He supported Pétion and thought that the moment had come to 'begin this great revolution that will spread throughout every part of the world', though he did not specify how this was to be done peacefully. Rewbell believed that a great nation which relied on Providence, justice and its own strength, had no need of allies. Menou countered the argument that national defence might mean taking precautions well in advance of a declaration of war, with the absurd claim that the army could be mobilized in 24 hours and the fleet in a fortnight.

The Right took its stand on what it claimed to be practical common sense. Whatever one thought about the general will, the effective conduct of foreign policy demanded allies and alliances implied secret diplomacy. Offensive wars were sometimes necessary. The comte de la Galissonnière, a naval officer, disliked the idea of any declaration of non-aggression, although Montlosier thought that France should cure itself of the 'mania of conquest'. The most surprising speech came from Cazalès:

> Legislators should not base their opinions on vague humanitarian principles . . . having nothing to do with such sentiments, which are mere ostentation; the exclusive object of our love must be the *patrie*. Love of the *patrie* creates more than men, it creates citizens. It creates Spartans . . . As for me, I declare that it is not Russians, Germans or Englishmen that I love; it is Frenchmen; the blood of one of my fellow-citizens is dearer to me than that of all the peoples of the world.

This met with general disapproval; three years later it was to be orthodox Jacobinism. Cazalès went on to denounce the Enlightenment for withering men's hearts and demeaning their spirit. Offensive war might be necessary. England would attack and France was now the weakest state in Europe. If the Assembly took control of foreign policy it would have to assume the responsibility for appointing diplomats and generals. The legislature should stick to formulating general laws, which was all that it could do well. All of this would have delighted Rousseau, as Cazalès must have been well aware, when he paraphrased *Emile* so carefully. His speech is a useful reminder of the fact that the influence of Rousseau was almost universal and that it helped to determine the ways in which most of the deputies responded to political issues. How his principles were to be interpreted and, if need be, modified, and when they were to be invoked, were matters of political tactics, as is always the case when ideology has to be translated into politics. This did not mean that they were mere window-dressing.

The debate on the right to declare war and make peace was unusual in the sense that the deputies of the Centre had the better of the argument and won the eventual vote. Malouet, who usually devoted his considerable talent to finding reasons for strengthening royal authority, this time opted for a compromise and tried to steer the debate away from ideological platitudes. He rejected as meaningless the idea of a declaration of non-aggression, on the ground that the policy of assemblies and nations was determined by the calculation of advantages rather than by principle. Free peoples were just as likely as despots to engage in aggressive wars. France needed her colonies, Spain her alliances and British ambitions were liable to endanger both. The king should have the power to defend the country against attack, but needed the assent of the Assembly to commit France to any other kind of war. He should have the power to make peace treaties, but not to transfer territory or conclude alliances without the approval of the Assembly. Dupont de Nemours said that even nations were not entitled to wage offensive wars, but to pretend that France did not need allies was 'noble folly'. Duquesnoy warned his colleagues of talking in terms of a monarchy whilst actually creating a republic; an assembly in permanent session could scarcely help becoming an aristocracy. 'I want neither a despotic monarchy nor an aristocracy; I want liberty.'

The whole debate was dominated by two speeches from Mirabeau, who had recently succeeded in being taken on as the secret adviser of the king and was perhaps eager to show that he could provide value for money. In his first intervention he lent his reputation, his eloquence and his lungs to the support of Malouet's case. He did accept a declaration of non-aggression, presumably on the ground that it would win friends on the Left without actually committing anybody to anything. He quoted the applause for the deputy who had talked of invading England as evidence that assemblies were no more pacific than individuals, and he confronted his colleagues with the permanent dilemma of the Left: 'Do you count as nothing the danger of importing republican attitudes into a government that is both representative and monarchical?' When Barnave accused him of wanting to reserve too much power to the king and advanced the familiar argument that 'the expression of the general will can only emanate from assemblies elected by the people', Mirabeau returned to the battle, denouncing his opponents for trying to silence him by incitement to mob violence. The suspensive veto was the proof that executive and legislature were both involved in the formulation of the general will. Barnave was confusing legislative *power*, which rested in the nation, with the specific rights of a legislative *body*. Both the king and the Assembly were delegates of the nation and the most immediate danger was that the constitution would become purely aristocratic. 'We did not delegate power to the king; we recognized that delegated power as existing before our constitution.' 'I want the participation of the executive power in the expression of the general will . . . my adversaries do not.' He was so confident of victory that he demanded that Barnave be given the right to reply, but the Assembly had heard enough. The Left, as a tactical move, tried to have the vote taken on a royalist motion of Maury and Cazalès, that they thought they could defeat. When that move was rejected, an amended version of Mirabeau's proposal was passed by a large majority.

The final resolution recognized that the right to declare war and to make peace rested with the nation. A declaration of war required a proposal from the king and its endorsement by the Assembly. The actual conduct of foreign policy and defence was left in the king's hands. If war should break out, the deputies could impeach ministers accused of provoking aggression and the Constituent Assembly declared that 'The French nation renounces any war of conquest and will never employ its forces against the liberty of any people.' During a war the legislature was free to demand peace at any time and as soon as hostilities were over the military budget would be automatically reduced to its peacetime level. The king retained the sole responsibility for the negotiation of peace treaties and alliances, but they only became effective when ratified by the Assembly. It was a reasonable compromise that could have fitted into a constitutional monarchy. As Malouet predicted, its future would be determined by politics rather than by ideology. Two years later it was a bellicose Assembly that forced an unwilling king to declare war on Austria and within six months of becoming a republic, France began hostilities against Holland, England and Spain.

In the meantime, the Nootka Sound affair resolved itself. In August 1790 Mirabeau, whilst still conciliatory towards England, persuaded the Assembly to raise the operational fleet from fourteen to thirty ships of the line, on the ground that it was better to be safe than sorry. On 25 November Montmorin announced to the deputies that Spain had given way and the crisis was over. In rather more than six months France had managed to commission seventeen ships of the line, which was rather a contrast to Menou's claim that the entire fleet could be mobilized in a fortnight.

If compromise carried the day in the debate on the control of foreign policy, this may have owed something to the fact that it was only the more dedicated deputies who could present the whole issue as essentially ideological. Where politics alone was involved, it was possible to work out a compromise that was acceptable to the majority. The case of Avignon proved more difficult to handle.

Both the town of Avignon and the neighbouring Comtat Venaissin had been under Papal rule since 1273 and 1348 respectively.[3] They were situated well inside France and French monarchs had been in the habit of occupying them whenever they wanted to put pressure on Rome, most recently, from 1768 to 1774. The Papacy imposed no taxes but the local population paid dearly for the services of rapacious Italian officials. This was more of a nuisance to the better-off business and professional people of Avignon than to the more rural inhabitants of the Comtat. The former looked back nostalgically to the French occupation and the economic opportunities it had brought them, whereas the Comtadins tended to think that they had more to gain from continued tax exemption than from access to French markets. Although both territories were ruled by the same vice-legate in Avignon, they had retained their separate identities and their suspicions of each other. In the heady summer of 1789 both aspired to imitate what was happening in France, but in different ways. Food rioting and fear of brigands led to the creation of an armed municipal guard in Avignon. In the Comtat, an irregular assembly of the three Orders, rather like that of Dauphiné in 1788, demanded the restoration of the old Estates General. When the Provençal deputy, Bouche, urged the Constituent Assembly to declare both areas part of France, on 12 November 1789, the deputies dismissed the idea without debate. Both Avignon and the Comtat then affirmed their loyalty to the Pope, which did not prevent them from pressing on with their separate constitutional demands. In Avignon a more or less irregularly appointed municipal government declared that it adopted the French constitution. When the Pope sent out a special envoy to assert his

---

[3] For an account of what happened in Avignon and the Comtat, see A. Mathiez, *Rome et le clergé français sous la Constituante* (Paris, 1911).

authority, in the spring of 1790, the Avignonese refused to receive him and appealed for support to Paris. The Papal envoy therefore made his way to Carpentras, in the Comtat, where he was welcomed – but bullied into accepting the convocation of a representative assembly, which was the Estates General in all but name. This in turn adopted the French constitution. Although the two areas had so far proceeded along roughly parallel courses, they remained as suspicious of each other as ever. The assembly at Carpentras refused to accept representatives from Avignon and one or two of the towns in the Comtat broke with Carpentras and declared their support for Avignon. Possibly encouraged by the growing ill will of the Comtat, opponents of the Avignon municipality began to assert themselves and on 10 June 1790 fighting broke out. The 'aristocrats' had the worst of it and some of them were massacred. National Guards from neighbouring parts of France intervened to prevent further slaughter and the defeated 'aristocrats', together with the Papal vice-legate, fled to the Comtat, where there were attacks on the supporters of the Avignon *patriotes*. As the Papal territories drifted towards civil war, the surrounding parts of France became involved, the département of the Drôme supporting the Comtat while the Bouches-du-Rhône backed Avignon. It was at this stage that Avignon applied to the Constituent Assembly for incorporation into France and the deputies had to decide whether or not to intervene.

As always, it was impossible to conside the case purely on its own merits. The Assembly had begun a major reconstruction of the French Church, for which it was hoping to obtain Papal approval.[4] The Right, as usual, disapproved of the way that everything was going. With the exception of a few conservative anti-clericals, it disliked the new religious policy, had no sympathy for the Avignon radicals and supported the Pope's claim to sovereignty over his French territories. The Centre was more concerned about the religious settlement than about the future of Avignon and the Comtat. It hoped to use the territorial question to put pressure on the Pope to accept the Assembly's religious policy – which meant not pressing him too far. The Left had no use for half-measures and was inclined by principle and temperament to see everything in black and white. As usual, it rejected compromise and was prepared to use whatever force was necessary for total victory, regardless of the consequences. It was the old problem of how to treat the monarchy, reappearing in a new form.

When the Assembly debated the issue in November 1790, Pétion and Robespierre challenged the validity of the Pope's claims to sovereignty. Robespierre denied his legal title and Pétion argued that the Avignonese request for union with France was an expression of the general will of a population that had always had a separate identity, and could not therefore be considered as wanting to secede from the country to which it belonged. He dismissed the danger of foreign intervention with the dangerous argument that the European Powers were already hostile to revolutionary France but would

4 See below, Chapter 9.

not dare to provoke a war that might expose them to revolutions at home. Robespierre, always inclined to see questions of foreign policy in terms of revolution and counter-revolution, argued that the preservation of Papal sovereignty would turn Avignon and the Comtat into an asylum for those who were plotting against the revolution in France. The Right replied that the Pope's title was valid in international law and there was no proof that the majority of the Avignonese population wanted to be united with France. To take over the territories, in these circumstances, would be an aggressive act in violation of the recent declaration against expansionism. Malouet accused the Left of appealing to principles only when they worked to their own advantage, which was true enough, but equally applicable to his own side. Mirabeau, looking for a middle way, proposed sending in French troops to stop the local population massacring each other. Maury could not resist adding an amendment that French forces were to act in the name of the Pope. This was too much for the Assembly, which adopted a counter amendment by Bouche, insisting that they were to act in concert with the revolutionary authorities in Avignon.

The Assembly would have been happy to leave it at that, but its hand was forced by events in the south. An Avignonese force, which included some of the French troops, invaded the Comtat. This provoked the département of the Drôme to send some of its National Guards to defend Carpentras. When civil war broke out in April 1791, the Assembly had to decide whether or not to intervene. By this time attitudes had evolved. It was becoming clear that the Pope had no intention of accepting the religious settlement and there was nothing to be gained from appeasing him. The Assembly's diplomatic committee, which had previously opposed incorporation, and the moderate Left in general, now favoured taking over the territories. Even the Right, in the persons of Maury and Cazalès, seemed to concede that self-determination took precedence over treaty rights. They therefore based their argument on the claim that there was no proof that the majority of the local population wanted union with France. It was Clermont-Tonnerre, a deputy of the Centre, who pointed out that to enforce all of France's territorial demands would mean re-creating the empire of Charlemagne. His reward for this was to be attacked in the streets and to have his house looted. Robespierre and Pétion, faced with the awkward fact that most of the communes in the Comtat seemed to have voted against union – perhaps because they were afraid it would imply union with, and under, Avignon – took up what had formerly been the tactic of the Right and claimed the support of the silent majority. The majority 'must have' wanted what the speaker thought was good for them, even if they had been bullied into voting for its opposite. As Robespierre put it to the Jacobins, 'One must not evaluate those who detest tyranny by the number of those who denounce it, but by each man's inner feelings. That part of the population of the Comtat which has not pronounced itself in favour of union must be regarded as oppressed.' He said much the same thing in the Assembly. Avignon and the Comtat had always been French. 'The majority for union with France must have existed by the very nature of things . . . The people of Avignon and the Comtat must want liberty.' He may have been right, in the sense that there was so much intimidation by both sides that it was impossible to know for certain what anyone actually wanted, but the logic of his argument was to allow the French, in the future, to annex as much territory as they wanted, under the pretext that they were liberating it, whatever the inhabitants protested to the contrary. This was one of the consequences of assuming France to be the only free country in an unregenerate world. It was still a minority opinion: when the Assembly was invited to vote on whether or not Avignon and the Comtat were part of France, it decided in the negative by 481 votes to 316.

The question had perhaps been tendentiously put, so as to neutralize the votes of all those who thought that the two territories were not French but should be allowed to become so. As a general rule, since any vote in the Assembly was held to express the general will, no question could be reopened. This did not prevent Pétion from demanding a new debate at once, on the ground that the previous vote had not dealt with the central issue. Maury predictably protested that the Left refused to abide by the rules of its own devising and had raised the issue of Avignon on four different occasions. That was the trouble about the general will: if one knew what it was, and it could only be what one sincerely thought one's self, the fact that one was in a minority merely meant that most people were ignorant, selfish or intimidated and, like the Comtadins, would have to be forced to be free, in their own interest. At the end of the new debate the Assembly voted on a motion from its diplomatic committee, to incorporate Avignon alone and pay compensation to the Pope. This was defeated by 376 votes to 368. Yet again Maury demanded that the Left accept the verdict of the majority and they replied that the vote could not prejudice the future. The Assembly, in fact, virtually reversed its decision when it decided to send more troops to the disputed territories, accompanied by commissioners who would see to the restoration of order.

On 14 September 1791, when the king had accepted the constitution and the Pope had rejected the religious settlement, the question of Avignon and the Comtat came before the deputies for the last time. By now the Right had stopped trying to moderate the course of a revolution from which it felt totally alienated and the political struggle was between the old and the new Left, both of whom favoured the incorporation of the territories. This was also the view of the commissioners and it seems to have enjoyed a fair amount of local support, whether the Comtadins had been enabled at last to express their true feelings or prevented from doing so. This time the decision to absorb them went through with a minimum of debate and little serious opposition.

On the whole, the Constituent Assembly handled problems of foreign policy with reasonable success. It was lucky, in the sense that Spain climbed down over Nootka Sound and there was no war for it to approve or veto. The division of authority that it worked out between the executive and the legislature was not unreasonable and could have been made to work. In the case of Avignon and the Comtat, it certainly overcame its usual inclination towards impulsive action and held its hand as long as there was any prospect of agreement with the Pope over the religious question. The eventual decision to incorporate the territories can be seen, with hindsight, to have raised the spectres of indefinite conflicts over the right to national self-determination, the right of provinces to secede and the meaning of plebiscites, but Avignon and the Comtat constituted a special case. Nowhere else did a European ruler claim sovereignty over European territories so remote from his own country, set within the heart of another state. The Papal title to the territories was not beyond dispute and the other European Powers did not react – although not for Pétion's reasons. The French could claim with some justification that they had not wanted to intervene but had been forced to do something to stop the local people massacring each other.

When the Constituent Assembly dispersed, nothing irrevocable had been done and nothing suggested that France was on the threshold of twenty years of virtually uninterrupted aggressive war. This raises the insoluble question of whether the straws in the wind should be dismissed as unimportant or treated as portents of the future: the old (and well-justified) suspicion of England; the occasional readiness of the deputies to forget their pacific principles and respond to an outburst of chauvinism; above all, the conviction of the Left that France, as the hope of humanity, *must* have right on its side. Popular sovereignty, the belief in the general will, the right of peoples – or at least of those with the right ideas – to self-determination, could not be reconciled with the sanctity of treaty rights. The basic attitude of the Assembly was pacific, indeed, it believed peace to be one of the foundations of the new order. At the same time, the majority of the deputies were opposed to the idea of compromise in domestic policy and convinced that they were waging a moral crusade against the forces of darkness. To be a revolutionary was to believe that one's opponents would stop at neither deceit nor violence in their attempt to safeguard their own selfish interests by sabotaging the work of those who aspired to create a better society. The minority saw themselves as victims, refused even the right to personal security and absolved from any obligation towards those who denied them the right to their opinions. There was a belief, common to both sides, that since one's own conviction represented the general will, one's opponents knew it to be in the general interest and opposed it for their own sectional advantage. This meant that there was never any room for compromise. The same moral absolutism applied in foreign policy. The assertion of French superiority and suspicion of foreign powers as the agents of counter-revolution, fuelled a new kind of nationalism and conferred ideological respectability on old xenophobia. It had not come to this by 1791. Perhaps it need never have done so, but the seeds were in the wind and if they germinated they would bear poisonous fruit.

9

Religion

As an Estate of the Realm, the clergy in 1789 had few friends. The clerical hierarchy reproduced in its own way the anomalies of lay society. If the whole Order was privileged, in the sense of being self-taxing and self-administered, most of the rewards were reserved for a minority of its members, distinguished by birth rather than by piety or devotion to its pastoral duties. All of the bishops were noble and the more able of them were often more concerned with secular administration than with spiritual matters. As a powerful corporate body, the Church had played a vigorous part in the interminable trench warfare that had almost paralysed eighteenth-century France, fending off attempts by the government to subject it to direct taxation and fighting a war of attrition against the Parlements for influence and authority. As a result, it was disliked by both conservatives and radicals. To the former it was a rival, to the latter a particularly provocative example of the arrogant and ostentatious domination of the country by the 'privileged Orders'. Such consideration as it had derived from its claim to the special status conferred by ordination and its unique position as the mediator between heaven and earth had been eroded, so far as many of the educated were concerned, by the deist tendency of the Enlightenment. Few Frenchmen were atheists, but the acceptance of the claim of the Roman Catholic Church to incarnate the only true religion and to hold the keys of salvation was on the wane, especially in the higher reaches of society. Almost everyone believed in the existence of some kind of a Supreme Being, but not one whose service implied that the cardinal de Rohan should try to buy the queen's favour by the present of a diamond necklace. Most people thought that some kind of cult was necessary to keep other people in order and to preach morality to those too ignorant to work out a moral code for themselves, or too fallible to adhere to it without the fear of some kind of divine retribution. Intellectuals tended to subscribe to a 'natural' religion, centred on the service of Man, rather than on devotion to God, which held no place for clerical celibacy or a life of prayer and contemplation. The way in which the Church was administered meant that those most directly concerned with the provision of help to the poor, the parish clergy, were often amongst its bitterest critics. For the population of France as

a whole, religious attitudes varied enormously in different parts of the
country. There were areas of relative indifference and others where religious
practices were the most important things that bound communities together.
Where the country people were most 'fanatical' or 'superstitious' - in the
west for example - educated townsmen could be the most provocatively anti-
clerical. Two Frances confronted each other even before 1789 and the collapse
of royal authority was to set them at each other's throats. Elsewhere - in
Alsace and parts of the South - the presence of a substantial Protestant
minority gave rise to different hatreds. Opinion here was already polarized
along religious lines and the revolution provided new liveries for factions that
were already in being.

Whatever eventual support the Church was to get from sections of the
peasantry, it derived little initial sympathy from the political Right, which
shared to the full the secular attitudes of the radicals. The conservative deputy
and diarist Duquesnoy referred to episcopacy as 'an office conferred by
society'. He commended a fellow-deputy for having the courage to 'manifest
religious principles in an Assembly where they were more or less ridiculed.'[1]
Ferrières, who usually voted with the majority of the nobility, was a
pronounced anti-clerical. Malouet refused to sign a protest when the Assembly
declined to declare Roman Catholicism the state religion, and said that a
hundred other deputies of the Right did the same. He favoured suppressing
some bishoprics, selling some of the property of the Church and closing
religious houses where there were fewer than a dozen monks or nuns. He
agreed that the nation was entitled, if it wished, to change the religion of the
state and differed in this from the radicals only in his insistence that the will of
the nation could not be equated with a vote of the Assembly. Montlosier,
original as ever, thought that man was a superstitious but not a religious
animal. He seems to have been apprehensive about the political consequences
of provoking religious unrest, but his cast of mind was secular and when he
produced the draft of a personal declaration of the rights of man, it included the
elevation of the king to the headship of the Church: in other words, a French
Reformation.[2]

Faced with this formidable army of adversaries, the clergy were hopelessly
divided amongst themselves. Many of the parish clergy subscribed to
Richerism, a kind of parish priests' trade union movement for the democra-
tization of the Church. This had made enough headway for the king to think it
necessary, in 1782, to forbid the *curés* to form leagues or to deliberate without
royal permission. In some constituencies the clerical elections to the Estates
General had paralleled the offensive of the Third Estate against the 'privileged
Orders'. Religious divisions within the clergy were not confined to this version
of the class struggle. The conflict between the monastic orders and the secular
clergy was age-old and, to make matters worse for the regulars, some of their

---

1 *Journal d'Adrien, Duquesnoy*, ed. R. de Crèvecoeur (Paris, 1894), 2 vols, I/307, I/426.
2 *Essai sur l'art de constituer les peuples* (Paris, 1790), appendix.

opponents had come to share the views of the laity about the uselessness of a life of meditation. One of the deputies, the *curé* Thomas Lindet, declared himself to be 'both a priest and a citizen'. His correspondence suggests that he was rather more of the latter. He thought that it was 'of the essence of the clergy to be useful'; the priesthood was 'a kind of magistracy'; the state should supervise its exercise, reduce its cost and circumscribe its jurisdiction. He was in favour of election to clerical posts, disapproved of those who wanted to declare Roman Catholicism the state religion and complained that his fellow-clergymen preferred to lose all by fanaticism rather than identify themselves with the nation.[3] Before the session ended he had been made a bishop.

An even more serious threat to the ecclesiastical status quo came from those who wanted to reform the Church for its own good. They were to lead the attack, and their blows were all the more damaging since their motives could not be impugned. The entire French Church was influenced by a Gallican insistence on its corporate autonomy and relative independence of Rome. According to Duquesnoy, the abbé de Montesquiou, the *Agent-Général* of the clergy, joined in the vote for the suppression of the payment of annates to Rome. Gallicanism was a vague term that could encompass anything from the desire for a little more elbow-room to the fringes of a Protestant Reformation. It overlapped with Jansenism, which was equally imprecise. Both contemporaries and historians tended to use the two terms somewhat indiscriminately.[4] Jansenism could mean anything from a theological attitude to a political programme. It had begun as the former but by the latter half of the eighteenth century the term was being applied to anyone who wanted to reform the Church by restoring it to what was believed to have been its apostolic purity. Such motives, together with theological attitudes towards grace, gave some Jansenists a vaguely Protestant air. The attack on ecclesiastical affluence that was reserved for men of noble birth, meant that Jansenists had something in common with Richerists, while Papal hostility ensured that they would get some sympathy from Gallicans. Whatever it implied, Jansenism involved dislike of the ecclesiastical status quo. The motives of the purifiers were very different from those of the secular-minded, who saw the clergy merely as *officiers de morale*, but in their shared hostility to the existing state of affairs they could go a long way together.

The deputies most commonly described - rightly or wrongly - as 'Jansenists' were the lawyers Camus, Fréteau, Treilhard and Martineau, all attached to the Paris Parlement, Lanjuinais from Brittany, Durand de Maillane from Provence and the *curés* Grégoire and Expilly. Several of them were members of the ecclesiastical committee. Lanjuinais, who had been made a professor of ecclesiastical law at the univeristy of Rennes at the age of twenty-one, had distinguished himself before the revolution as one of the leading

[3] *Correspondance*, ed. A. Montier (Paris, 1899), pp. 52, 127, 145, 147.

[4] See J. McManners, 'Jansenism and politics in the eighteenth century', *Studies in Church History*, no. 12, 1975.

opponents of the Breton nobility. After 1789 he continued to combine radical politics with the vigorous defence of what he conceived to be the real interests of the Church. Grégoire's career too showed him to be a man of courage and piety, but this was of little immediate comfort to the Church. He believed that religion was the necessary foundation of civil society and that lack of religious principle was the most immediate threat to political liberty. However, since the clergy had proved to be incapable of reforming themselves, it was up to the state to recall them to a life of disinterestedness and austerity.[5] Faced with arguments of this kind, coming from some of its more able and altruistic members, it was difficult for members of the Church hierarchy to carry conviction when they claimed that they could be trusted to implement reforms that were beyond the competence of the temporal power. To a sceptical and secular-minded Assembly, this sounded like a defence of fat livings. Events were to prove that this was far from being the case, but not until it was too late to repair the damage. Of all the sections of French society in 1789, the clergy were the most vulnerable and had the most to lose.

When the Estates General met, the anti-clericalism of the Third Estate was at first muted by its hopes of persuading the clergy to join it. The latent hostility towards the clergy surfaced on the night of 4 August, despite offers by some *curés* to surrender their *casuel* (occasional payments for particular services) and the holding of benefices in plurality. This did not deter the radical deputy Buzot from contrasting the generosity of the nobility and the Third Estate with the selfishness of the clergy, all of whose wealth, he claimed, belonged to the nation. The leading role in the attack on the clergy was taken, not by the Left, but by the nobility. When the issue of tithes was fought out on 10 August, the clergy showed their apprehension at the prospect of being reduced to salaried officials: Mirabeau described them as *officiers d'instruction*. Lanjuinais declared tithes to be sacred and Grégoire and the abbé Gouttes – no friends of the ecclesiastical establishment – proposed that, if they were abolished, they should be replaced by a grant of land that would ensure the continuing independence of the clergy. Sieyès, who usually preferred to see himself as a citizen rather than as a priest, argued that to abolish tithes would be to make a present of 70 million livres to landowners and complained that anti-clericalism was being mobilized to give an air of respectability to avarice. The southern deputy Ricard replied that the clergy were in favour of sacrifices – so long as they were made by someone else. Since privileges were held to be a kind of property, they could only be abolished if their beneficiaries agreed to renounce them, which meant that nothing could be done unless the clergy themselves agreed to give way. Eventually they did, and the archbishop of Paris and cardinal de La Rochefoucauld surrendered tithe without any promise of an alternative source of revenue that would guarantee the independence of the clergy.

[5] *Légitimité du serment civique* (Paris, 1791), pp. 4, 5, 31.

Attention then shifted to the drafting of the declaration of the rights of man and the first major debates on the constitution. This raised the question of the place of religion in French society. Already, on 4 August, Grégoire and Camus had failed to persuade the Assembly to include man's duties in the declaration of his rights. Grégoire wanted the declaration to contain a reference to God, 'the source of all rights and duties', but had to be content with an invocation of the Supreme Being, which was not quite the same thing. The debates on the constitution itself began on 27 August with the rejection of a proposal that Roman Catholicism be declared the state religion. What is most striking about these early debates is the tendency of some of the future leaders of the reform movement, particularly Grégoire and Camus, to speak up in defence of the Church. This may have been partly due to the hostility that the clergy in general were meeting outside the Assembly. Grégoire was reluctant to follow the king to Paris in October because of the 'most frightful threats' to which the clergy were exposed in the streets of the capital. He was not a man who was easily scared.

The independence of the clergy was bound up with its ability to finance itself from its own resources. It was already clear that, if it were to depend on the goodwill of the Assembly, it could expect short rations and much interference. This independence had already been severely compromised by the loss of the tithe. It was further threatened by the tendency of the population at large to treat the revolution as a pretext for not paying their taxes, which brought Necker before the Assembly with desperate appeals for subsidies. On 29 September, when the finance committee supported his demand for more money, someone obligingly pointed out that the Church owned plate to the value of 140 million livres, and the archbishop of Paris agreed to surrender as much as was compatible with the decency of church services. Two days later, in an evening session when many of the Third Estate were absent and the clergy were out in force, this offer was withdrawn. It was not always the upper clergy who were the most reluctant to make sacrifices. So far the clergy had been invited to surrender what was recognized to be its own. The next move was more threatening.

It was Talleyrand, nominally a bishop, who on 10 October argued that most of the Church's assets had been given to it for the relief of the poor, who were henceforth to be cared for by the state. The wealth of the clergy was not property in the usual sense and it should therefore be restored to the nation, which would use two-thirds of it to pay clerical salaries. Connoisseurs of irony will appreciate a debate in which Talleyrand cast himself as the voice of disinterested spirituality and Grégoire tried unsuccessfully to get his motion adjourned. In the ensuing argument, the abbé Maury deployed eminently secular tactics, warning the deputies that the wealthier of them might come to regret having encouraged speculation about the origin of property rights. Malouet complained that it was dishonourable for the Third Estate to despoil the clergy after having begged for its support earlier in the year. He denied that the general will favoured the sale of Church property and warned the Assembly against dismantling the present system of poor relief before it had provided the funds for an alternative one. Even he proposed selling off about a quarter of the estates of the Church and suppressing some religious orders. Pétion was censured by the Assembly – but defended by Camus – for saying that the wealth of the clergy had corrupted its morals. It was left to Mirabeau to sum up: everyone was agreed that the state was composed only of individuals and had no room for 'great political corporations'. No one would be in favour of such corporations if he were founding a new society. The Assembly was, in effect, doing just that, since 'there is no legislative act that a nation may not revoke and alter whenever it wishes'. Since the Assembly had constituent status, it possessed 'all the rights that the first men who created the French nation could exercise'. His conclusion was a good deal less radical than his premises and the Assembly voted his motion, not to sell Church property, but to put 400 million livres of it 'at the disposal of the nation'.

If the clergy thought that they had got off lightly, they were badly mistaken. Five weeks later, when the Assembly had yielded to the irresistible temptation to print its way out of its difficulties by the issue of paper money, the deputies voted to sell the 400 million livres of property, as backing for the new *assignats*. In April 1790 the 'Jansenists' took the field: Martineau proposed doubling the amount of Church property to be offered for sale, while Treilhard suggested selling it all. On 25 June he got his way. The clergy were henceforth to be entirely dependent on the salaries voted them by the Assembly and on the conditions which it chose to impose on them.

In confiscating the property of the Church, the Assembly could, at a pinch, claim to be merely exercising rights that had always been claimed, if not enforced, by the monarchy. By making itself responsible for the payment of the clergy, it now had to decide how much should be given to whom. Since its immediate motive had been to meet the demands of a desperate fiscal situation, it was bound to save as much money as it could, by reducing payments and suppressing ecclesiastical offices. Sooner or later this was going to lead it to encroach on what the clergy believed to be spiritual matters. What made things particularly serious was the fact that the attack was led, not by disreputable rakes like Mirabeau or by rabid anti-clericals, but by 'Jansenists', some of whom were themselves members of the clergy, and often some if its more impressive priests.

The first bastion to fall was that occupied by the monks and nuns. In November Martineau, a member of the ecclesiastical committee, spoke in favour of the suppression of all benefices without cure of souls, the virtual abolition of pluralism and the closure of all religious houses containing less than twenty members. A month later Treilhard, in the name of the committee, proposed that the state should cease to recognize monastic vows and that monks and nuns who wanted to leave their convents should be given pensions. The bishop of Clermont denounced this as going beyond the limits of the temporal power, and described the monastic state as 'the most fitting for the support of the nation, because of the influence of prayer on the success of human affairs'. Outside the clergy, there were probably few deputies who believed the latter part of the sentence, and, even including the clergy, even fewer who were convinced by the first part. On 13 February 1790, in a decision that went farther than some of the 'Jansenists' would have liked, the Assembly decreed that religious orders were abolished and the law would take no cognizance of perpetual vows. Those in monasteries or convents not involved in charitable or educational work were entitled to leave or, where the men were concerned, to be regrouped in a small number of religious houses where they could continue to lead a communal life. Alarmed by the 'philosophical ideas' that had been aired during the debate, the bishop of Nancy asked for a declaration that Roman Catholicism was the state religion. He did not get it.

The deputies believed themselves responsible for providing 'constitutions' for every aspect of the French state: local government, the magistracy, the armed forces. Taking it for granted that the Church was an integral part of the state, they assumed themselves to have the same authority in this sphere as they had in all the others. The ecclesiastical committee therefore set to work to prepare a 'civil constitution' for those aspects of the Church which it regarded as coming within the authority of the secular power.[6] In November 1789 Durand de Maillane produced a relatively moderate document for consideration by the Assembly and eventual submission to the Pope. Very unwisely, the two bishops on the committee vetoed it. Faced with disagreement on the committee, the Assembly enlarged its membership in February 1790, when the sitting 'Jansenists' - Martineau, Treilhard, Camus, Durand de Maillane and the abbé Gouttes - were joined by the abbé Expilly. Soon afterwards the two bishops and seven other members resigned. The 'Jansenists' were still in a minority but they seem from then onwards to have made most of the running.

Alarmed at the apparent intentions of the committee, one of its members, the Carthusian Dom Gerle, again tried to have Roman Catholicism declared the religion of state. This seems to have embarrassed the Left, who did not wish to appear openly hostile, but disliked the implications of the motion. By this time, the polarization of Right and Left was beginning to offer the clergy more lay support than they had had in the past, but at the price of offering a new ground for disliking them, without giving them a majority. When the Right demanded an immediate vote, the president adjourned the session. On the following day, Gerle was induced to withdraw his motion and the Assembly passed a vague resolution to the effect that it had no power over consciences and that religion was too majestic a matter to form the subject of political debate. This was not going to afford anyone much protection.

On 29 May 1790 the committee produced its report. In essence, this proposed to 'rationalize' the Church by reducing the episcopate from 135 to

[6] See A. Mathiez, *Rome et le clergé français sous la Constituante* (Paris, 1911).

85 (one bishop to each département) and allocating one *curé* to every 6,000 inhabitants in the towns. All dignities other than those of bishop, rector and curate were abolished. All of the clergy were to be elected by the same colleges that chose local government officials, and the Pope was merely to be informed of the election of bishops, without being invited to give them canonical institution. This was when the irresistible force of popular sovereignty, embodied in the Assembly, encountered the immovable object of canon law. The bishops were eager for compromise and were prepared to accept the civil constitution, provided that what they considered spiritual matters were referred to ecclesiastical authorities, either a council of the French clergy or the Pope. What they could not do was accept the claim of the Assembly to total sovereignty in everything. They did not challenge popular sovereignty in temporal matters and they hoped that the Pope would make it possible for them to accept the civil constitution, but if he did not, they could not. Although they would scarcely have approved of the parallel, they were echoing Luther's 'Here I stand. So help me God, I can do no other.' The deputies, for their part, insisted that the civil constitution did not trespass on matters of faith. They saw it as relating merely to the organization of the Church, and therefore within their competence. Some of them went further, insisting that the general will of the nation was sovereign in all things, including matters of belief. What happened was, in fact, a head-on collision between two different kinds of faith. The anti-clericalism of many deputies and the enthusiasm of the 'Jansenists' for a return to the conditions of the primitive Church, complicated and obscured the issues, adding acrimony and suspicion to the basic deadlock.

When the committee had produced its proposals, the archbishop of Aix replied with a speech on the 'sacred principles of the ecclesiastical power'. 'What is at issue is an order of things where magistrates and kings must obey.' No human power was entitled to interfere with the organization of the Church. When their request for a council was rejected, since it would have involved reviving one of those corporate bodies that Rousseau had taught the deputies to detest, the bishops took no further part in the debate. The Assembly was not much concerned about kings, or even magistrates, but it could not accept any restriction on the omnicompetence of the sovereign people, whom it claimed to represent. Camus, seconded by Treilhard, read the archbishop of Aix a lesson in political theory. 'The Church is part of the state. The state is not part of the Church.' He went on to say that the Assembly, as a convention, was entitled to change the religion of the nation if it so wished. This was going well beyond 'Jansenism', whatever that might be taken to mean, in its assertion that the national religion rested, not on revealed truth, but on a political decision.

With the clerical party abstaining, the result of the debate was a foregone conclusion and all that happened was a certain amount of minor skirmishing that revealed some of the nuances of attitude within the majority. Roederer thought that one bishop to every two départements would be enough since 'public functionaries must not lead idle lives.' A group of civic-minded *curés* promised their support in advance for whatever the Assembly could decide. Martineau, in his zeal for a return to the ways of the primitive Church, sounded like an anti-clerical. He persuaded the Assembly to reduce the proposed number of seminaries, defeated a motion by Grégoire and Camus to retain archpriests and, despite the opposition of Lanjuinais, imposed on each bishop a council that he was obliged to consult on all matters of policy. The Assembly went its own way, confident that, in the end, the clerical deputies would bow to the general will and the population at large would welcome whatever was decided in its name and in its supposed interest. Reality did break through once or twice: the deputies heeded the warning of Camus not to suppress rural parishes, on the ground that the country people were attached to their familiar churches, but for the most part the urban intellectuals had very little idea of what religion meant to their constituents.

The debate on how the clergy were to be elected exposed one or two mental attitudes. Martineau, in the name of the ecclesiastical committee, recommended election by the laity, on the ground that this had been the practice of the primitive Church. This was too much for the abbé Jacquemard, who thought that, in contrast to those far-off days, the eighteenth century was an age of vice and the laity would choose badly, perhaps on purpose, if they were Protestants. Robespierre could not miss such an open goal. After pointing out that Jacquemard's objection would apply to all elections, he went on, 'The right to elect cannot belong to the local administration [that had been a suggested compromise]; only the body in which sovereignty resides is entitled to choose . . . that branch of public officials known as bishops.' When the question arose of whether or not a bishop could veto the election of a *curé* whom he considered unsuitable, it was a priest who objected that this would over-rule popular suffrage, and a layman – Lanjuinais – who accused the Assembly of confusing the temporal and the spiritual: 'Either the Assembly intends to legislate for the Catholic religion, which is the state religion, or for whatever religion it chooses to create.' Eventually Camus secured a compromise that gave bishops a veto on grounds of doctrine and morals, subject to a right of appeal by the *curé*.

When the deputies considered how much the new 'public officials known as bishops' were to be paid, there was not much disagreement, although Robespierre tried to have their salaries reduced. When it was a matter of the salaries of the *curés*, the tone was lowered by the fact that one or two of them had fewer inhibitions than the bishops in defending their own interests. Jacquemard in particular more or less accused the Assembly of spoiling a good career: 'In the villages, the house of the *curé* is the only one where a gentleman can alight.' His lamentations were indignantly repudiated by Grégore and Gouttes, although both of them thought the proposed salaries too low. This provoked the reply from a farmer that, since most *curés* were sons of 'petits-bourgeois', what was proposed would look like a fortune to them.

Even before the debates on the civil constitution had dragged to a close, news reached the Assembly of the *bagarre de Nîmes*, an outbreak of street-fighting between Protestants and Roman Catholics in which about 300 of the latter were slaughtered.[7] This was the product of complicated local hatreds, embracing politics and religion, that had no direct connection with the reorganization of the Church. It was nevertheless a warning that the Assembly was making a big gamble when it assumed that its religious dispensations would be accepted without demur by an obedient clergy and a grateful people. At the same time no one was looking for a fight. Ferrières thought that the civil constitution did not trespass on matters spiritual and that it was being exploited by enemies of the revolution. Even he, however, regarded its leading advocates, Camus, Fréteau, Martineau and Treilhard, as 'extreme Jansenists'. He thought that the new clerical salaries were far too low and he signed the protest against the refusal to declare Roman Catholicism the state religion. His way of dealing with his own chapel was typical of Ferrières: he did not want it raised to the status of a parish church, with an elected *curé* since 'it is more than likely that the most hare-brained, intriguing and factious people will be elected'. When it came up for sale he did not intend to bid for it and thereby 'give an example of such an open violation of property rights'. He would, however, agree in advance to pay more than the highest offer, and hand over the chapel to a priest whom he liked, whose parish he expected to be suppressed. It did not seem to have occurred to him that the priest in question might refuse to accept the civil constitution.[8] Perhaps the most surprising thing about the new proposals, in view of the sacrifices they imposed on bishops not hitherto conspicuous for their indifference to worldly possessions, was that the great majority of them were looking for ways in which the civil constitution could be reconciled with their consciences. Even the abbé Barruel, who was later to acquire notoriety for his theory that the entire revolution was part of an international Masonic plot, wrote at the time that the civil constitution would be legitimate if it was endorsed by the Church. The controversy that was eventually to tear the country apart began as a conflict about means rather than ends. If the French clergy had been allowed to summon a council, it would probably have advised acceptance and the Pope would then have been offered the choice between bowing to the *fait accompli* or facing a revolt of the French clergy. When he opened the debate, the archbishop of Aix had proposed this solution, but it was anathema to an Assembly obsessed with its own sovereignty and indoctrinated on the evils of corporate bodies. Rejecting a council threw the deputies back on the Pope.

Pius VI had no sympathy with the aspirations of the revolutionaries but he could not ignore the fact that they held as hostages both the French Church and Avignon. In March 1790, before the debate on the civil constitution began, he condemned the declaration of the rights of man for its commitment

[7] See G. Lewis, *The Second Vendée* (Oxford, 1978).
[8] *Correspondance inédite*, ed. H. Carré (Paris, 1932), pp. 307-8.

to popular sovereignty and to religious toleration, but he did so in a private consistory that left him with a free diplomatic hand. During the summer of 1790 no one was in a hurry. The Assembly realized that Papal approval would dispose of its problems; Pius hoped that the deputies would be accommodating over Avignon while they waited for his reply, and possibly believed that the difficulties in the way of implementing the civil constitution would incline the deputies towards a compromise. In the meantime the religious life of the country went on as before. The great festivals held in Paris and the provinces to commemorate the first anniversary of the July revolt had their presiding priests and their *Te Deums*. They were the last occasion during the revolution when throne, altar and people combined in a common commitment to regeneration. The prevailing atmosphere was one of rejoicing, so much so that some of the more jaundiced radicals were uneasy at all the premature fraternization. They need not have worried: the religious time-bomb had a long fuse but nothing was going to extinguish it.

In July the Pope wrote to the king and to the ministers, threatening them with schism. Later in the month Louis, who took no action on religious matters without clerical guidance, accepted the civil constitution but declined to promulgate it until 'necessary measures' had been taken, which implied winning the Pope's consent. Even the Papal nuncio urged Pius to accept it, lest he be repudiated by the French episcopate. The Assembly was patient but to wait indefinitely would have been to concede a Papal veto. In August some deputies began to complain and on the 24th Louis agreed to promulgate. From now onwards confict was inevitable and attitudes were bound to harden when the declaration of the bishops that they would be unable to accept the civil constitution was translated from the conditional to the present tense. When Expilly, one of the leading reformers in the Assembly, was elected to the vacant see of Quimper, the bishop of Rouen refused to give him canonical institution. The Assembly had little alternative but to decree that, in such cases, the local authorities were empowered to approach any bishop, instead of the metropolitan. The random incidence of vacancies due to death or retirement forced the issue out into the open in some places and the anti-clericalism of the local authorities precipitated it in others. The officials of the département of Puy-de-Dôme lamented that 'The sovereignty of the nation is ignored; one section of its officials has the pretension to hold the general will in bondage.' Within the Assembly, pressure built up to force the clergy to bind themselves by oath to the civil constitution. According to Durand de Maillane, who had himself been one of the reformers, this came, not from his own ecclesiastical committee, but from the police committee. Even Grégoire denounced 'the tyrants, or rather the municipal executioners [*bourreaux en écharpe*] for whom the needs, the sufferings and the grief of the priests were a source of enjoyment'. On 30 October the bishops in the Assembly drafted an *exposition de principes* which was signed by thirty of them and by ninety-eight other clerical deputies. This was in conformity with their previous attitude, repeating the necessity for Papal approval and urging the clergy to oppose the implementation of the civil constitution by the mildest forms of passive resistance. The exposition was sent to the Pope who was urged to give at least provisional assent in principle to the civil constitution. The bishops could scarcely have done less or done it in a more conciliatory way. It was a sign both of the fanaticism of the more radical deputies and of the hardening of attitudes that their exposition should have been treated as a declaration of war.

On 26 November Voidel, of the police committee, presented a motion on behalf of the combined ecclesiastical, reports, alienation and police committees. According to Durand de Maillane, he and the majority of the members of his ecclesiastical committee were opposed to it. Religion was henceforth to be treated as a question of public order. The report proposed the imposition of an oath of acceptance of the new constitution on all priests exercising public functions. Those who refused the oath were to be dismissed, forfeit their entitlement to a pension and be deprived of their civic rights. Anyone who incited opposition to the law or continued to officiate after his dismissal, would be prosecuted. Voidel's proposal was greeted with loud applause. Cazalès was heard with less sympathy when he warned of the danger of creating a threat to public order, and yet another request for permission to convene a Church council, by the bishop of Clermont, met with *grandes murmures*. Maury, in an uncharacteristically temperate speech, warned the deputies against creating martyrs. All that the opponents of the civil constitution could suggest was that the Pope should be given more time, which, in view of the time that he had already had, was not very persuasive. The most striking feature of the debate was an extraordinarily violent diatribe against the clergy, by Mirabeau, who accused them of being ready to endanger religion if only they could mobilize opposition to the revolution. He denounced the secret of the confessional, complained that there were too many clergy and threatened to have them all sacked. He recommended the Assembly to dismiss all those who refused the oath, prosecute those who protested, and suspend all ordinations.

Mirabeau, whose past life had perhaps exposed him to more sermonizing than he cared to remember, had been consistently anti-clerical, but this speech was so abusive as to suggest that the real motive of that devious and impenetrable man was to do the very thing of which he accused the clergy: to stir up popular opposition to the revolution and to discredit the Assembly.[9] Some of his colleagues seem to have suspected as much. Even Pétion thought that Mirabeau had gone too far with his proposed ban on ordinations, which suggested that the long-term aim of the Assembly was to do away with religion altogether. Camus was no friend of the clergy: he took advantage of the opportunity to repeat his old argument that the 'nation' was free to choose its own religion; legislation on matters of religion had needed Papal approval in the past, but this was no longer necessary, now that the 'nation' was assembled. Even Camus, however, attacked Mirabeau for saying things that

9 See below, p. 158.

were 'inexcusable and unjust'. Disregarding Mirabeau, the Assembly voted the motion proposed by its committees, which was penal without being abusive.

Once again the king dragged his feet and the deputies paused in their reluctant progress along the road to which they had committed themselves. For almost a month nothing happened, apart from an indignant protest against the *exposition de principes* by a deputy who denounced it as a crime against the nation; clemency had merely encouraged ingratitude and the *patrie* was now demanding vengeance. It had to wait a little longer, but whatever apprehensions they may have felt, the deputies had eventually to reap where they had sown. On 23 December Camus asked why the king had not promulgated the decree requiring the taking of the oath. Louis replied on the same day that he was taking the most conciliatory means to get the civil constitution implemented – which Camus interpreted as a kind of royal strike. He warned the king that it would be bad for royal authority if the Assembly was constrained to disregard the king's silence. When he went on to claim that Christ was the only sovereign pontiff and that Papal sovereignty was contrary to the spirit of the Gospels, a deputy of the Right understandably expressed some scepticism about Camus's own religion. The Assembly demanded immediate promulgation and, as usual, the king gave way.

On 27 December the clerical deputies began to take the oath. It had been generally taken for granted that the great majority of the clergy, in the Assembly and in the country, would resign themselves to the inevitable. Thomas Lindet even thought that this would restore peace to the Church and force the Pope to capitulate. He circulated a petition in support of the civil constitution, but abandoned it when he got no more than thirty to forty signatures. When it was becoming apparent that there would be a great deal of resistance to the oath, there was a curious debate on 3 January 1791. Cazalès repeated Montesquieu's old argument that religion and honour were the strongest obstacles to despotism, and demanded that the Assembly should only order what was *faisable*.[10] Unless it was claiming infallibility [which, of course, it was, since it regarded itself as embodying the general will], it must respect the right of individuals, even if they were mistaken, to reject what they believed to be contrary to their honour and conscience. Charles Lameth gave him the Rousseauist reply that matters of conscience were not for the individual to decide, but the deputies were always sensitive to an appeal to honour, and they refused to call Cazalès to order. For a moment he seems to have had their sympathy, if not their support, but he, like everyone else, was a prisoner of the situation and all he could suggest was that the clergy be given more time to make up their minds. The Assembly gave them until 1 pm on the following day.

The original intention of the deputies was to give maximum publicity to the taking of the oath, by making it an *appel nominal*, in which each member of

10 An apparent reference to a striking passage in *The Spirit of the Laws*, IV/2.

the clergy would come forward in turn. This misfired rather badly. When the first three rejected the oath, the *appel nominal* was hastily abandoned. Less than one-third of the deputies signed, with Talleyrand as the only bishop sitting in the Assembly. In the country as a whole, the clergy divided more or less evenly, although with very wide regional variations. Only four bishops, excluding those *in partibus*, took the oath and Talleyrand, who was on the point of resigning his see, was the only one who was prepared to consecrate new bishops. When the clerical deputies had announced their decisions, Barnave carried the inevitable motion to replace all the clergy who refused to take the oath. According to the *Moniteur*, the deputies were well aware that things were not working out as they had intended; there were long silences and predictions of troubles to come.

Mirabeau, at least, seems to have been in his element. On 7 January he persuaded the Assembly to waive the requirement that the new bishops and parish clergy must be men with considerable local experience. In view of the large numbers that had to be recruited, this was inevitable, but the fact that so many of the new men were outsiders was a major reason for their unpopularity, especially in some of the more remote rural areas. A week later he produced another diatribe, in terms so offensive that his mischievous intentions were rather too obvious. He suggested that the real motive of the bishops was to 'restore to their palaces the gold that was their scandal and shame'. He then tried to make them the target for revolutionary hatred by accusing them of organizing resistance to the law of the land in the hope of restoring the double despotism of throne and altar. The result of their hypocrisy would be to drive the laity towards deism. 'It will want to offer up its sacrifices only on the altar of the *patrie* and come to believe that it has been the puppet of imposters and the victim of lies.' The Catholics were saying that freedom and religion were incompatible but no one was entitled to base his conscience on false and arbitrary principles. 'The duty to construct one's conscience comes before the duty to follow it.' Mirabeau's intention was presumably to convince public opinion that the Assembly was hostile to any form of Catholicism, in the hope of arousing fanaticism on the one side and intolerance on the other. Somehow or other, he had persuaded the religious committee to endorse his speech, but it created an uproar in the Assembly. Many of the clergy walked out, Camus denounced its 'abominations' and the deputies referred it back.

When the committee produced a draft of its own, the tone was very different. Roman Catholicism was declared to have been established by God, which must have made the Protestants uneasy; the Assembly was not interfering in spiritual matters and its only concern was the public good. Those unable to accept the oath were not to be punished, although the organization of resistance to the civil constitution was to be a criminal offence. The deputies presumably felt that they could not have been more conciliatory, which, from their point of view, was true. Educated men of the Enlightenment, whose own beliefs leaned towards 'Jansenism' or a latitudinarianism that shaded imperceptibly into deism, few of them had any idea of what religion meant to the majority of the population. The Right - whether or not it welcomed the fact - was perhaps more aware than the Left that the country was splitting in two.

On 26 January the ecclesiastical committee moved to replace the non-juring clergy and Cazalès made a last attempt to avert the inevitable. He argued that Catholicism, unlike Protestantism, with its 'monstrous' opinions, implied obedience to the universal Church. If the Pope were to condemn the civil constitution, Catholics would have to obey and the principles of the non-jurors were 'superior to your laws'. Their eviction would be the first step on the road to some illusory millennium. Those excluded would excommunicate their successors, part of their congregation would follow them, leading to religious war, with the cause of the faith offering a convenient banner for anyone who wanted to stir up trouble. 'If you are wise and humane legislators . . . you will not sacrifice all these victims to your insane pride.' Even if the Church was wrong, the Assembly was still acting foolishly: 'If your laws can only be executed by force, beware of the convulsions that will drench France in blood.' It was too late for this kind of talk. A deputy of the Left accused Cazalès of preaching civil war and Maury blamed him for trying to deprive the Right of the grievance it wanted: 'Let the decree pass; we need it. Two or three more like that and it will all be over.'

When the Assembly discussed what pensions to give the non-jurors - despite its recent vote to give them none - the new polarization of opinion was revealed. The old reformers, whose concern throughout had been primarily religious - Camus, Treilhard, Martineau and Lanjuinais - had to defend the non-jurors against a new Left, which the *Moniteur* was beginning to describe as the 'Left of the Left'. Some of the Right had openly adopted the *politique du pire*: one of them introduced an ironical motion for the toleration of the private practice of Catholicism.

The Assembly's chickens were not long in coming home to roost. On 25 January there was news of religious troubles in Amiens. In mid-February commissioners sent into Alsace reported general religious disaffection that was already reinforcing the political opponents of the revolution. The National Guard at Colmar, one of whose companies was sporting the colours of the comte d'Artois and the white cockade of the Bourbons, refused to receive the commissioners, who were defied by the local authorities. Things got worse in March, when there was a riot in Strasburg after a non-juring priest refused to vacate the cathedral and struck the new bishop. Rohan, the previous incumbent, who wisely lived on the far bank of the Rhine, excommunicated his successor and condemned as schismatical anyone inducted by him. He put the cathedral out of bounds to the faithful and was said to be recruiting for the army of liberation that the French princes were raising in Germany.

At the opposite end of France there was trouble in Brittany, where the overwhelming majority of the clergy had refused the oath. The country people said that religion had been abandoned and they marched on the towns in the hope of sacking the offices of local government. In their petitions they claimed that the civil constitution was contrary to the faith and that 'the property given to the clergy by the people has been taken from it without the people's consent'. 'We want peace, we want to live in peace and not to be driven to resistance.' The town of Vannes was attacked by a peasant army of between 1,200 and 1,500 and was saved only by the National Guards from the naval base at Lorient.

In March there was rioting in Douai, where the municipality refused to declare martial law even when two men had been lynched. This was ostensibly a food riot but local grain prices were exceptionally low and the deputies from the Nord believed that the real cause of the unrest was the election of a new bishop. Whatever its regrets and apprehensions, when faced with violent outbreaks of this kind, the Assembly had no alternative but to despatch troops, suspend local authorities and put its trust in force.

The religious history of the Constituent Assembly occupies a place of its own. The opponents of the status quo came from opposite directions: secular-minded anti-clericals and those who aspired to create a more spiritual Church. Entangled with this was the campaign of the Richerists against the ecclesiastical hierarchy, and the hostility towards Rome of the Gallicans, both clerical and secular. The result was that the Church was open to attack from a variety of directions and was unable to rely on the support of many of its priests. When battle was eventually joined, over the civil constitution, the issue shifted to a conflict between canon law and popular sovereignty. This further confused matters, since many of those who had gone over to the Third Estate in 1789 refused to take the oath. Some of the clergy claimed to be able to reconcile the roles of priest and citizen, which enrolled them, will-nilly, in the army of those who saw the clergy as public officials, paid by the state, which was entitled to determine their rights and duties. Similar conflicts of loyalty have arisen in other countries at other times. What gave this one its particular character, and excluded any possibility of compromise, was the obsession of many of the deputies with a Rousseauist conception of popular sovereignty, which made the general will the infallible source of moral, as well as political authority. This emerged starkly when Charles Lameth told Cazalès that it was not for the individual to determine the bounds of his own conscience. Rousseau's influence also helped to rule out the possibility of calling a Church council. The French bishops were eager for a compromise. If the Assembly made the worst of all worlds and played into the hands of its enemies, much of the responsibility lay in its own arrogance and insensitivity.

The development of the religious conflict also owed something to class incomprehension, if not to class conflict in the economic sense. In the closed world of the Assembly, religion was a matter of theology for a minority and morality for the rest. Fear of damnation, if it had ever been invoked as an argument, would have been greeted with general ridicule. The reformers were intent on turning the Church upside down and the secular-minded were looking for moral tutors who would glorify the revolution at the same time that they preached the Ten Commandments. For the mass of the population, religion was something entirely different, even if it is hard for a twentieth-century observer to know exactly what it was. It was darker, more parochial, more bound up with traditional practices and confidence in the saving authority of the priest, an authority derived ultimately from God and not from man. The two Frances spoke different languages – they were often literally incomprehensible to each other – and in some areas they lived in a state of mutual fear and suspicion. Townsmen may have despised peasants but they had no illusions about the formidable power of the rural ocean that surrounded them. One or two deputies had an inkling of this, but their warnings were disregarded and the rural revolt was all the more violent since the peasants saw themselves as fighting to defend their way of life.

The civil constitution, however, was a political act and to ignore its political dimension is to make it incomprehensible. During the autumn of 1789 the Assembly, which had been summoned because the government was going bankrupt, was desperate for new sources of revenue. It was the need to raise money quickly, and on a massive scale, that drove them to seize the assets of the Church, which implied reorganizing it from top to bottom in order to make the necessary economies. Initially, the Right had been, if anything, more anti-clerical than the Left. It was the evolution of the political situation in general that threw monarchists and clergy together. For a long time the Right fought a tenacious rearguard action but by the end of 1790 it was increasingly tempted by the *politique du pire*, as practised by both Maury and, in disguise, by Mirabeau. Whatever other factors were involved, there was always a political dimension to the revolution. Calculation and miscalculation played an important part in deciding whether or not conflicts of ideology or interest could be accommodated within a working compromise.

10

The Watershed

A s the year 1790 drew to a close, the thoughts of the deputies turned more and more towards the future. The Assembly was approaching the end of its formidable agenda and would complete its work during the following year, leaving France with a written constitution and no sovereign constituent body. The powers of the next assembly would be circumscribed by a text that it was not allowed to modify and the political future was supposed to conform to rules that only the Constituent Assembly had the authority to draft. This concentrated everyone's minds. The business of tidying up all the loose ends of the Assembly's work would offer plenty of opportunities for its more or less discreet revision, in either a radical or a conservative direction. The time was approaching, in other words, when those who had thought it necessary to bully the king into submission before proclaiming the end of the revolution and restoring to him the power he needed for the constitution to function, were going to have to strike a compromise with the 'executive power'. When the constitution was finished, Louis would have to make up his mind or, if that was expecting too much of him, at least decide whether or not to take an oath to implement it. What was at issue was how to bring the revolution to a satisfactory end or, where the Extreme Right was concerned, how to prevent the rest of the deputies from doing so. The strategic objective might seem straightforward enough, and likely to command the support of the great majority, but the actual conduct of politics had become so involuted and so bedevilled by suspicion on all sides that its achievement would be no easy matter.

The most obvious political leader, who combined a clear awareness of the problem with the parliamentary influence that might enable him to solve it, was Mirabeau. An examination of Mirabeau's position indicates some of the difficulties. He had been recruited as a secret adviser to the king and queen by his 'friend', La Marck, who sat in the Assembly as a member of what had originally been the Second Estate. La Marck, despite his professions of esteem and admiration to Mirabeau, had told *his* 'friend, the Austrian Ambassador Mercy Argenteau, that he only kept up his contact with Mirabeau in the hope of serving the queen. Marie Antoinette herself told Mercy that she did not trust La Marck with anything. She had no confidence in any of the ministers either and even less in the 'factious intriguers with whom we have the appearance of being in league'. The money to pay Mirabeau had presumably come from the king, but the forty-fifth of the notes with which he bombarded his royal paymasters, suggests that they were intended for the queen alone.[1] He was denied any contact with the ministers who – officially at least – were unaware of his contact with the Court. Whoever it was that was reading, or failing to read, the notes, presumably thought that Mirabeau's pension was the price of his services and whenever he made what looked like a radical speech he was accused of breaking his contract. Mirabeau, whatever he may actually have thought, protested that he was serving the king and queen on grounds of constitutional principle, as their political consultant. When discouraged by their habitual neglect of his advice, he threatened from time to time to abandon their service. He also objected to their taking advice from anyone else, and when he heard of their doing so, he complained to La Marck about the behaviour of the royal 'cattle'.

During the autumn of 1790 the ministers, who had been in office since the summer of 1789, were violently attacked in the Assembly. A vote of no confidence was narrowly defeated – it was one of the few victories of the Right – but one by one each of the ministers resigned, with the exception of Montmorin, the relatively popular foreign minister. Mirabeau saw this as his opportunity. He hoped to persuade the Assembly to reverse its vote of 7 November 1789, debarring deputies from ministerial office, and to become chief minister himself. It was presumably with this in mind that he urged the king to choose his new ministers from the majority in the Assembly and even from members of the Jacobin Club. As always, he saw Lafayette as his main rival and urged Louis not to appoint any of Lafayette's protégés. He wanted Montmorin sacked, since he suspected him of being one of them. Louis, if he was actually responsible for the choice, agreed with Mirabeau, although for reasons of his own, about the undesirability of Lafayette. La Marck, on the other hand, whom Mirabeau regarded as his spokesman at the Tuileries, was pressing for the appointment of Lafayette's men.

Towards the end of November, Mirabeau suddenly reversed his policy, for two reasons. The completion of the ministerial reshuffle put an end to his hopes of office and Montmorin approached him, saying that he had broken off contact with Lafayette and asking Mirabeau to help him to win the confidence of the queen, whom he suspected of turning the king against him. This suited everyone. La Marck told Mercy – it was not necessarily true – that Louis paid more attention to his ministers than to the queen and it was therefore necessary to find a minister who could be persuaded to act as the queen's agent. Montmorin would fill this role very well, especially since he was quite

---

[1] *Correspondance entre le comte de Mirabeau et le comte de La Marck*, ed. A. de Bacourt (Paris, 1851), 3 vols, II/382-5.

well regarded in the Assembly. Mirabeau, if he could not become a minister himself, could hope to have one at his disposal, who would act as his mouthpiece and keep him informed of what went on in the royal council. He also took advantage of the opportunity to ingratiate himself with the queen by betraying Montmorin's confidence and promising Marie Antoinette to keep her informed of all Montmorin's activities. He asked her not to tell the king of the relationship between Louis's foreign minister and the man who was supposed to be his confidential adviser! This was a game that more than one could play: La Marck reported to Mercy that he had promised the queen to keep an eye on the coalition between Mirabeau and Montmorin. If the implications of all this are a little difficult for us to follow, things were presumably not much clearer to any of the participants.

It was perhaps because his prospects of ministerial influence seemed to be rising, when his chances of becoming a minister himself had been destroyed and he would not have to defend in the Assembly the policies that he advocated in the king's name, that Mirabeau now switched abruptly to the *politique du pire*. This was the subject of his forty-seventh note, undated, but apparently written in mid-December.[2] He still argued that there could be no question of restoring the *Ancien Régime*. Even civil war and a successful invasion would not do that. The constitution could, however, be revised. Since the Constituent Assembly would never agree to destroy its own handiwork, this would have to be done by its successor, which must somehow or other be given the same constituent powers. In the meantime the existing Assembly must be encouraged to destroy its popularity in the country as a whole by encouraging it to discredit itself by extremism, voting privileges to Paris, usurping more and more powers and imposing unpopular policies on the provinces. The deputies of the Right must stop trying to moderate radical and unrealistic policies and give the extremists their head. In the meantime, everything must be done to prepare public opinion for the next election. Montmorin could coordinate the activities of sympathetic deputies, who were to be kept in ignorance of the grand strategy. A Parisian agency would win the support of the press and popular agitators by persuasion and bribery. Two more agencies were to organize public opinion in the provinces, without understanding the real purpose of what they were doing. Only Mirabeau and his royal clients would know the whole plan. Even he admitted that his tactics were based on 'dark intrigue and cunning dissimulation'. They also implied that he alone had the complete confidence of the king and queen and that he would be allowed to supervise everything on his own.

It was presumably as a first step towards implementing his new policy that he made his wild attacks on the clergy, on 27 November and 14 January. These immediately revealed one of his difficulties. His language was so extreme, and his probity so suspect, that some of the deputies correctly divined

2 Ibid., II/414-504.

his real intentions. Mirabeau promptly drew in his horns and stopped trying to provoke the Assembly into unpopular legislation by his own speeches. His concern for his popularity in the Assembly immediately aroused Mercy's suspicion that he was hedging his bets and might eventually opt for a career as a revolutionary. Malouet, whom he approached, rejected the *politique du pire* and condemned his plans as counter-revolutionary. Optimistic claims by Mirabeau and Montmorin to 'dispose' of influential deputies seem to have had little foundation: everyone was confident that he could manipulate everyone else. The Parisian agency does seem to have come into being, even if it did not do very much, but Mirabeau was not the man to get down to the laborious administrative work involved in setting up the provincial agencies – or to entrust it to anyone else. His whole grandiose scheme did not amount to much more than an elaborate daydream.

The situation at Court was equally complicated and confused, although the king and queen were at least resolute about one thing: they would have nothing to do with Artois who, from his safe retreat abroad, was boasting of his plans to start a civil war and to invade France at the head of an army of *émigrés*. Artois had not much prospect of inheriting the throne himself and he liked to pose as the head of the aristocratic party that had started all the trouble in 1787. His irresponsible posturing could only jeopardize the king's policy of at least seeming to want to work with the Assembly, and might even endanger his safety. In April 1791 Artois virtually threatened to set off an insurrection unless his brother renounced all contact with revolutionaries and produced a plan of action that Artois recognized as satisfactory. Fortunately for Louis, Marie Antoinette's brother, the Habsburg emperor, had enough problems on his hands in Belgium and Hungary and he was extremely reluctant to intervene in France. His influence restrained the minor German princes and Artois's father-in-law, the king of Savoy, from giving active support to the *émigrés*. In view of this, the counter-revolutionary plot was more of an irritant than a serious threat, although this was less obvious at the time than it is now.

When Marie Antoinette had married the heir to the French throne she had espoused the French king but not his country. Her mother, the formidable Maria Theresa, saw her daughter as the instrument by which Austrian policy could be made to prevail at Versailles, especially since, as Mercy had reported to her as early as 1772, the character of the future king made it seem virtually inevitable that Marie Antoinette would eventually become the effective ruler of France. That this had not happened by 1789 was partly due to the frivolity of the queen, who saw politics essentially in terms of advancing the careers of her friends and their dependents. Louis, who does not seem to have been enthusiastic about the Austrian alliance, was also quite capable of opposing a bland resistance to her attempts to influence him. Whatever the extent of that influence, she had been a political force in her own right, under Mercy's guidance. This was even more the case during the revolution. Mercy was still her *éminence grise* and La Marck considered himself to be her man. How far she was able to make Louis do what she wanted, it is impossible to say. She herself wrote to her brother in October 1791 that people greatly exaggerated the extent of her influence and that she did nothing to undeceive them since, if they knew how little it actually was, she would have even less. Mercy, on the other hand, wrote that, in his official capacity as ambassador, he was never received by the king without the queen being present. He told Montmorin that the king was quite useless. The foreign minister also insisted on Marie Antoinette being present at his audiences with the king, but that may have been due to his own concern to convince her that he was her man. Marie Antoinette certainly had her own advisers and confidants and she was more determined than her husband to have nothing to do with 'this monstrous constitution. Any agreement with these people is impossible, but until the last minute we must keep up the appearance.' At the same time, her refusal to contemplate 'liberation' by Artois and his cavaliers set her against the idea of armed insurrection and her instinct was to play for time and hope that something would happen to allow her to escape from a situation that she had no intention of accepting.

Doing nothing was a policy that always appealed to Louis. On the other hand it was he, and not the queen, who had to sign things and commit himself. His acceptance of the civil constitution of the clergy was a heavy burden on his conscience and from the end of 1790 he had taken up more seriously the idea of escaping from Paris that had been at the back of his mind since October 1789. As usual, there were many conflicting plans, each involving a separate group of advisers. Mirabeau wanted the king to leave his capital publicly and to head for Normandy, away from the frontier garrisons and their suggestion of an appeal to armed force. Montmorin agreed with the idea of a public departure, but favoured the garrison towns in eastern France. Louis was inclined to prefer a secret flight to the army of Bouillé, which was thought to be reliably royalist. Marie Antoinette told her brother in April that only four people knew of his plan: Bouillé, Breteuil (who had been authorized by the king to act in his name), the queen's admirer, the Swedish count Fersen, and Bombelles, the royal family's agent in Vienna. Louis's idea was that the Austrian emperor should concentrate troops on France's eastern frontier, which would provide a pretext for the king to join his army and offer to mediate between the Assembly and the threatening invaders. The emperor, while professing his readiness to play his part, was unwilling to move his troops before the king was safely out of Paris. Perhaps both monarchs were rather relieved to have reasons for not making the first move.

All his advisers seem to have told Louis that there was no prospect of restoring the old order. Mirabeau, La Marck and Bouillé himself were all agreed on that. How far Louis shared their opinion, what he would actually have liked and what he was prepared, if necessary, to accept, he perhaps did not know himself. The king's counsellors were as suspicious of each other as were those of the queen. Lafayette wrote repeatedly to Bouillé, who was his cousin, in the hope of establishing some sort of an understanding between the commanding officer of the Parisian National Guard and the general in charge of the last reputedly royalist troops on the frontier. Bouillé rebuffed him, which he later came to think was a mistake. The king's spiritual adviser, the archbishop of Toulouse, disapproved of the employment of Mirabeau and tried to put an end to it. The king had no confidence in his new ministers and kept his plans from them. With the exception of his ministers, his inclination was to consult as many people as possible and to trust none of them. Where the deputies were concerned, he seems to have assessed them on the basis of what he believed to be their personal loyalty to himself. Sooner or later he might have to take a stand, and perhaps leave Paris in order to do so, but there was never any need for immediate action and one day was as good as the next.

So far as Louis was concerned, there was nothing particularly new in all this. Ever since he came to the throne he had been surrounded by problems that he could not solve and ministers whom he did not entirely trust. It was what he knew as politics and he had spent his reign wondering what to do next and parting company with opinionated ministers whose brilliant schemes seemed only to have made things worse. He was used to rival clans intriguing against each other and presenting their schemes in the name of the public good. Things had changed a good deal since 1789; he missed his hunting and even Louis must have realized that he was living in a more violent and dangerous world. He was not likely to forget the night of 5-6 October and he remembered what had happened to England's Charles I. He was less of a fool than his nervousness in public made him appear to be, but he had no experience of life outside the Court. He was a conventional man with old-fashioned ideas of his rights and obligations, adrift in a new world that he did not understand. Like a good many other people, he did not know how to stop the drift towards extremist views in the Assembly and organized violence outside it. He was being asked to surrender more than anyone else and the fact that he was continually being assured that this was for his own good did not make the prospect any more palatable. He must have found it all intolerable, even if he could not face the alternative to tolerating it.

All the political actions of the king had to be counter-signed by ministers who were theoretically responsible for governing the country, while the Assembly reformed its institutions. In fact, the deputies encroached so comprehensively on the sphere of what they loved to denounce as the 'executive power' that it executed virtually nothing. Most matters of importance were decided by the Assembly, and local authorities, if they had any contentious problems on their hands, looked to the Assembly for guidance. The impotence of the ministers and their timorous attempts to escape criticism by inactivity, did not preserve them from the suspicion and denunciation of the more radical deputies, to whom their very title acted as a kind of provocation. 'Ministerial despotism' had had such a good run for its money that deputies like Robespierre, and the more vituperative press, found it impossible to conceive of a minister who was not a despot or aspiring to become one. The men who had been appointed in the autumn of 1790 were a colourless lot whose main concern was to keep out of trouble. Some of them were believed to be clients of Lafayette, but this did not do him much good. In his memoirs he claimed to have been responsible for the nomination of Duportail to the War Office, but the new minister was so frightened of the Jacobin Club that he immediately transferred his allegiance to the Lameths. Whatever the outcome of the political imbroglio, it would not be the result of any ministerial initiative.

Within the Assembly itself, some of the deputies had moved so far to the Right that they were literally out of sight. In February, La Marck told Mercy that 200 of the clergy and nobility were habitual absentees. Since the majority of votes for the Left was small and fluctuating, the votes of the missing men could often have tipped the scale. One can sympathize with their reasons for preferring to be somewhere else: if they spoke, they were denounced in the Assembly, insulted in the press and liable to be mobbed in the street. By their absence they were, however, abandoning the attempt to get the future settled by debate and, by implication, opting for latent or actual civil war. Some of them were aware of it. Maury had advised Cazalès to let the Assembly pass the kind of extremist measures that would destroy its reputation, but he himself was too much of a gladiator to resist the call of the arena. He still intervened in debate, from time to time, to flagellate the Left with his bitter and incisive wit. This put him, and many of the Right, in a false position since they made it clear that they felt under no moral obligation to accept the policies that they had been unable to defeat.

The problem for the moderates had always been to realize that their similarities were greater than their differences. As the majority had become more radical, there was a steady trickle of deputies towards the Right, but the oldest inhabitants of those unpopular benches were somewhat cool towards the new recruits who had recently been denouncing them. Outside the Jacobin Club, it was also difficult for men of similar convictions to coordinate their policies. There was a good deal of talk about who could dispose of whom. Montmorin boasted to Mirabeau that he was sure of Le Chapelier, Talleyrand and, perhaps, Barnave. Mirabeau added half a dozen names of his own. Malouet, in an optimistic assessment of the strength of the conservatives, thought that he could command fifty followers, Mirabeau twice as many, and the king ought to be able to persuade a considerable number of the clergy and nobility to turn up, shut up and vote. He had hopes of winning over Barère, although he recognized that the king would have nothing to do with either Barère or Lafayette. A good deal of this was idle speculation or whistling in the dark. What *was* happening was that some of the former radicals - men like Le Chapelier and Sieyès - had become worried by the continuing instability and the tendency of the Assembly to opt for extremism. They believed the time had come to bring the revolution to an end and to restore order. Lafayette had reached this conclusion by the summer of 1790, which had isolated him from his former allies on the Left. By the spring of 1790, Barnave's name was being mentioned as a possible convert to conservatism, although his associates, the Lameths and Duport (who were particularly obnoxious to the Tuileries as former members of the Court nobility and of the Paris Parlement) were still committed to revolutionizing.

Increasingly visible – and vocal – on the Extreme Left was a group of deputies centred round Robespierre, Pétion and Buzot, whom Mirabeau had denounced as the 'thirty voices' when he ordered them to keep quiet. Whatever their actual numbers, their influence was mainly due to their rigid adherence to the principles affirmed in the summer of 1789, when the Assembly had been fighting to protect itself from a government that still had at least the appearance of power. These principles were essentially concerned with the protection of the legislature. They had proved very useful in their time but their literal implementation was liable to paralyse the executive and endanger public order. The problem now was to create institutions that would work. That meant compromise, on matters of principle as well as constitutional machinery. Both moderates and radicals were agreed that revolutions were exceptional periods in the history of states, when the normal rules were suspended. From one point of view, the question was whether or not it was now safe to return to constitutional government. That was a matter of political judgement, which might have admitted of agreement to differ, if each side had not suspected the motives of the other and accused it of selling itself to the Court, or of secretly hankering after a republic. Those who favoured compromise recognized that the royal government would have to be handed back some of the authority that had been taken from it in the dangerous days of 1789 – which exposed them to plausible accusations of backsliding. This was a permanent dilemma when men moved from opposition to government: Pétion, Buzot and Robespierre were going to jettison a few principles of their own when their hour came. If one followed the logic of the Extreme Left, the revolution would go on for ever. They replied that those who were moving from Left to Centre were prepared to endanger the gains that had been achieved for the illusion of power, in the hope of becoming partners of a king who would never accept even their attenuated view of the revolution and who intended to use them merely to subvert the cause in which they still pretended to believe.

As usual, there was something to be said for each point of view, but the Extreme Left occupied the more defensible ground. Their opponents *were* trying to go back on decisions made in more radical days; they *were* trying to restore the ability of the government to maintain order and to escape from some of the more awkward consequences of an unqualified belief in the virtues of popular sovereignty. The course of the revolution and the hysteria of some of the newspapers had generated a quite extraordinary amount of suspicion of the king, the clergy, the nobility, the ministers, in fact, of anyone with whom one disagreed. This made back-bench deputies, whose political virginity was not compromised by any offers of power, only too likely to believe that anyone whose policies were evolving in a more conservative direction must have sold himself to someone or other. Faced by a divided Centre and an alienated and often absent Right, the influence of the Extreme Left was therefore much greater than one would have expected from its limited numbers.

In the presence of so much confusion, indecision and suspicion, it is tempting to sweep the whole unintelligible imbroglio under the carpet and opt for some comfortable theory that makes the outcome inevitable. This certainly encourages the production of less complicated books and makes everything more convenient for those who like to have their minds made up for them. If one actually looks at the rise and eclipse of such global explanations, however, it is hard to resist the temptation to see them either as creeds of the age in which they were written, or as intellectual games. There is not much point in arguing about creeds – which tend to imply a generous element of determinism – and history ought to be more than a skating rink for the performers of elegant pirouettes. If one aproaches the history of the revolution from the angle of a particular teleology, the meaning of the whole experience depends on each aspect of it being a necessary development from what had gone before. No one applies this kind of determinism to the evaluation of present-day politics and it seems a little hard to foist it on our predecessors. The political entanglements of 1791 were to have a particular outcome. If one investigates this, one can see how the various factors involved contributed to that outcome. This does not mean that other combinations would not have been possible. If Artois had succeeded in setting off his insurrection and led his ramshackle army into France, everything might have developed differently. What actually happened can – after a fashion – be explained, but it could not have been predicted and it need not have happened that way. This is perhaps a pity. The reader and I might have got more enjoyment out of a proper ballet, in which all the dancers stuck to the parts allotted to them by some transcendental choreographer. All that I have to offer is the confused spectacle of a crowd of intelligent but bewildered men bumping into each other in a fog as they try to persuade everyone else to go in their particular direction. This is a poor substitute for a ballet but it has at least the merit of respecting their individuality and not reducing them to performers in someone else's puppet theatre.

During the first six months of 1791, the Assembly was in a fluctuating mood, with extremists of both Left and Right inclined to challenge its legitimacy and the majority wavering between its automatic suspicion of ministerial authority and its realization that, before the Assembly dispersed, it would have to set up a government that would work. Where religion was concerned, there were still anti-clericals around, ready to denounce priests who refused to take the oath as factious and seditious rebels, but the reports of rioting and disaffection in the provinces were a sobering warning that a settlement that had seemed so reasonable and progressive to most of the deputies, was providing the enemies of the revolution with their first mass support. All that the deputies could do now was to limit the damage as best they could. When they decided to replace non-jurors, they gave them pensions. Where extremists saw refusal to take the oath as a political commitment against the revolution, the majority treated it as a religious decision that any priest was free to take, which merely debarred him from continuing to act as a public official. In April, the département of Paris decided to restrict the city's churches to the constitutional clergy, to ban public worship in private chapels and to regulate religious services in private buildings. This was, in effect, to begin the proscription of the non-juring clergy and their adherents. It was badly received by the Assembly. Treilhard was applauded when he demanded freedom of worship and the advocates of religious toleration received unexpected support from the Left, which took exception to a local authority trespassing on matters that should have been decided by the Assembly. Talleyrand had little difficulty in persuading his colleagues to authorize any religious group to hire its own buildings (which could include disaffected churches) for its own services. This produced an outraged protest from a non-juring deputy that Catholic churches might be converted into temples of Baal, which provided the Assembly with a little light relief. When the eighty-year-old cardinal de La Rochefoucauld prohibited two members of the constitutional clergy from preaching and hearing confessions, the Assembly voted not to take any action against him. Its intentions were conciliatory enough but it was the prisoner of its past decisions. As Cazalès had warned it, opposition to the civil constitution was going to turn ordinary people against the revolution; the Assembly would have no alternative but to defend its own and whatever counsels of moderation it offered to local authorities would be disregarded in areas where the religious division was fuelling the forces of counter-revolution.

It was religion that induced the king's pious aunts to leave France for Rome, in February 1791. The aunts were political ciphers but the obsession of the Assembly with seeing an issue of principle behind every specific event set off a debate on the right of public servants – and more specifically members of the royal family – to leave the country. This was given a new twist when a crowd at Arnay-le-Duc refused to allow the aunts to proceed, and the local municipality concurred. The Left demanded a law against emigration and the Right replied that any such law would violate the declaration of the rights of man. Answering the argument that it was fear for their security which made people want to emigrate, Pétion said that the unrest was due to 'the revolt of the minority against the majority'. This earned him a lecture from Malouet on the meaning of the general will. In terms that might well have appealed to Rousseau, Malouet said that the general will, in the sense of a popular consensus, was quite capable of deciding upon the basic principles of a regime, but that their implementation demanded 'the application of the intelligence of the most upright and enlightened men'. Rousseau was never far from their minds. One deputy reminded his colleagues that Rousseau had approved of the denial of the right to emigrate in times of crisis, as though that ought to clinch the matter.

The Assembly solved the problem of the aunts in the usual way, by ordering their release without blaming those who had arrested them. That left it to deal with the general question of the right of the royal family, and of the king himself, to leave the country. The Left wanted a declaration that if he left France without the consent of the Assembly, the king would be judged to have abdicated. Cazalès, equally predictably, replied that any talk of deposition was unconstitutional. Disgruntled members of the Court nobility, like the Lameths and d'Aiguillon, were the most concerned to impose restrictions on the king, whose interests were defended by minor nobles such as Cazalès, d'Eprémesnil and Montlosier. In terms of abstract principle the question was insoluble. The royalists argued that the Assembly had not created the monarchy but inherited it and the inviolability of the king antedated the constitution. When Le Chapelier replied that monarchy was an office rather than a possession, the Right answered that if the definition of the king's powers depended on the will of the Assembly, France was effectively a republic. Cazalès took the sensible point of view that it was impossible to legislate in advance for cases where insurrection would be legitimate. 'If the king can be tried, he is not independent and if he is not independent, the executive power is enslaved.' He rather spoiled the effect by adding that this would still be the case, even if the king were to lead an army against his people. The Left made equally heavy weather of the debate. Pétion got lost trying to prove that French citizens were subject only to the law and that the nation as a body owed no obedience to the king. Since he also said that sovereignty was located in the nation, which meant the Assembly, this made the king the servant of the Assembly. In terms that would have scandalized Rousseau, he made out that the general will was the sum of all the particular wills of a community. Everyone was therefore entitled to criticize the law and invitations to disobey it might well be justified. In case this gave anyone the wrong ideas, Rewbell pointed out that circumstances altered cases: a ban on emigration would have been tyrannous under the *Ancien Régime*, but it would be legitimate if it was necessary to defend the revolution. Le Chapelier, for the constitutional committee, reported that it was impossible to draft an acceptable law controlling emigration. When nevertheless ordered to do so, the committee produced a project so extreme and arbitrary that it was immediately rejected, which was presumably what they wanted. Where the king was concerned, a law ordering his residence in France was passed by a large majority after the Right had declared itself unable to take part in the debate.

As the Assembly began to make preparations for winding up its session it faced the question of whether or not its own members should debar themselves from election to the next assembly. Those whose main concern was to make the constitution work wanted the new legislature to include men with some political experience. This exposed them to the suspicion that they were mainly concerned about their own careers. Mirabeau advised the king against re-election since it was likely to perpetuate the policies that both of them were trying to defeat. The Right as a whole shared his point of view. So did Robespierre, either because Rousseau, 'a philosopher whose principles you honour', had seen the role of legislator as advisory rather than executive, or more prosaically, to stop the triumvirate of Lameth, Duport and Barnave dominating the next assembly. A self-denying ordinance was the kind of disinterested gesture that appealed to the theatrical sense of the deputies. Anyone who opposed it looked as though he was out to feather his own nest and the bill went through with comparatively little debate.

When the deputies began to discuss the organization of the future legislature they came up against the rather different question of the eligibility of their successors for repeated re-election. It was one thing for the present deputies to agree to stand down; prescribing to the sovereign people whom it might or might not choose to represent it, was rather a different matter. Pétion favoured giving the electorate a free choice, but Robespierre dissented – even though someone pointed out that inexperienced deputies might prove particularly vulnerable to the wiles of the dreaded 'executive power'. Robespierre justified what might look like a high-handed restriction on the rights of the sovereign people, on the disingenuous ground that the 'nation' (which he identified with the Assembly) was free to prescribe rules to protect itself from its own mistakes. That could take one a very long way, as the future was to show. It was too much for Le Chapelier, who objected that any law that violated reason, justice and popular sovereignty was a scandalous example of tyranny that local authorities would be entitled to defy. Tactical considerations got everyone on the wrong foot. Extremists of both kinds, for different reasons, opposed re-eligibility, while those whose main concern was to make the constitution work, were in favour of it. The one thing on which they were all agreed was that there would be permanent hostility between legislature and executive. In the end they opted for a rather unsatisfactory compromise: future deputies could be elected to two successive legislatures, but had to miss the next one.

Amongst all the abuse and bad temper it was possible to make out signs of a growing conservatism that might have isolated both the cavaliers and those whose attachment to what they saw as principle would make the country ungovernable. Cazalès was trying hard to make the best of a bad job and, except where the sacred person of the king was concerned, was looking for compromise solutions. Not a great deal separated him now from former radicals like Le Chapelier. On 28 February the latter argued that liberty depended on the rule of law. This had necessarily been 'hidden in the clouds of a great revolution' but it must now reveal itself to an exhausted nation as 'the centre of regular and peaceful movement'. It might have been Malouet speaking. Le Chapelier therefore proposed that the Assembly should recognize that sovereignty belonged only to the nation as a whole and not to any of its constituent parts and that any invitation to disobey the law was a crime against the constitution. This scandalized Pétion and Robespierre – who complained that it might imply a restriction on the freedom of the press – but it seems to have gone down well with the Assembly and it was even applauded in the public galleries. In April Le Chapelier again took on Pétion, who wanted the tenure of office of ministers to be restricted, with the legislature deciding on their re-eligibility. What Pétion really wanted, said Le Chapelier, was a republic. It was perhaps a sign of the times that, a month later, the conservative d'André defeated Charles Lameth in the fortnightly election for president, or Speaker, of the Assembly.

Le Chapelier pressed on with his campaign. On 9 May he proposed, in the name of the constitutional committee, the banning of collective petitions by clubs and other local bodies. The Sections, into which towns were divided for electoral purposes, were not to assume any administrative function and were only to discuss the specific issues for which meetings had been called, since they were not organs of administration, this function belonging exclusively to the town councils. Le Chapelier then delivered an extraordinary tirade against passive citizens (those who did not pay a minimum of three days' wages a year in direct taxation), as vagabonds. 'Someone who is nobody is not a part of society; one can only participate in its advantages when one shares in its burdens.' Passive citizens were even to be denied the right to petition. By implication at least, this was contrary to the declaration of the rights of man. This naturally provoked an outcry from Robespierre and Pétion, with Grégoire protesting against passive citizens being called vagabonds, but Le Chapelier got his motion voted, with relatively minor amendments.

On 17 May he received the unexpected support of Duport, in the debate on re-eligibility. In a sombre speech, Duport complained that 'step by step you have been led to the complete disorganization of society'. The revolution had prevailed and the danger now was of a new despotism, based on popular violence and civil war. 'We had to destroy; now we must re-build.' This was the opposite of what Duport's ally, Alexandre Lameth, had said in February, when he had denounced talk of the revolution being over as intended to give people a false sense of security and encourage them to relax their vigilance. The deputies seem to have listened to Duport with respect and they voted to have his speech printed, which was always a sign of approval. Contemporary rumours that the triumvirate was making overtures to the Court are strengthened by the recent publication of a letter from Marie Antoinette to Mercy, warning him against her banker, Laborde, who had told her that his son (a deputy), Duport and especially Barnave were less ill-intentioned than was generally believed. She told Mercy that, as usual, she had pretended to agree with everything that was said.[3] This suggests that any revolutionaries who were hoping to arrive at a working agreement with the queen were going to have a difficult time.

---

[3] Quoted in P. and P. Girault de Coursac, *Enquête sur le procès du Roi Louis XVI* (Paris, 1982), p. 258.

A month later Le Chapelier introduced the Bill that was henceforth to be associated with his name, prohibiting collective action by journeymen. This was subsequently to be used to outlaw trade unions and there is a natural temptation to regard it as a piece of class legislation - all the more so in view of Le Chapelier's unkind remarks about passive citizens. There had recently been labour troubles in Paris, but Le Chapelier's objective was primarily political What worried him was the threat to public order. There was therefore clear signs, in the spring of 1791, that the tide was setting in the direction of moderation. Granted a minimum of cooperation from the Right, there was the prospect of a conservative majority emerging in the Assembly, committed to the stabilization of the revolution.

This process was probably facilitated by the death of Mirabeau on 2 April. He had been an impossible colleague, always trying to discredit possible rivals and recently committed to the *politique du pire*. No one trusted him and so long as he and Montmorin thought they had the ear of the queen it was going to be very difficult for anyone else to strike a bargain with the king. This was the logical conclusion to the political evolution of Le Chapelier and Duport. If the revolution was over and the peaceable rule of law was to take its place, there must be some sort of compromise with Louis XVI. The difficulties were formidable, since the merest suspicion of collusion with the 'executive power' would prompt accusations that a man had sold himself to the Court. Unless one actually committed one's self - perhaps even if one did - there was no means of knowing whether the king was prepared to cooperate or whether he was merely buying time by a pretence of interest. In the end everything turned on that irresolute and vacillating man.

Since the beginning of the year Louis had been working on the manifesto that he would leave behind when he escaped from Paris - if he could bring himself to go.[4] It was a strange document that said virtually nothing about religion and combined substantial constitutional grievances with complaints about such trivialities as the lack of comfort in the Tuileries when he was taken there in October 1789. From the king's point of view, all the sacrifices that he had accepted had merely encouraged the factious to slander him. His tone was that of a benevolent and paternal ruler, always ready to sacrifice himself for the welfare of his subjects - but on his own terms. This was no doubt how he himself viewed his situation, but it did not suggest that there was much basis for compromise. One of his grievances was the Assembly's divorce of the idea of the state from the person of the king. If he was not prepared to accept that, which, in a sense, was what the revolution was all about, there was perhaps no ground for any agreement at all.

On 18 April the royal family prepared to leave for St Cloud, where they had spent part of the previous summer. A crowd at the gates of the Tuileries prevented them from leaving. Lafayette appeared but his National Guards

4 J. Dreyfus, 'La manifeste royale du 20 juin 1791', *Revue Historique*, 77 (1908).

refused to clear the way. Lafayette was threatened, the king and queen insulted and the royal family was obliged to return to what Louis described as their prison. This time he had had enough. On 21 June the Assembly learned that the royal family had escaped from Paris during the previous night.

11

'The Revolution is Over'

WHEN they heard that the king had left, the deputies could only guess which way he had gone, and hope that they would be in time to catch him.[1] Faced by this new challenge, they behaved with a quiet self-confidence that reminded Ferrières of the Roman Senate in its prime. Although he himself had no inhibitions about referring to the king's 'escape', the official version, from the start, was that he had been 'abducted', a sensible, if implausible, way of putting it, that kept all the options open for the future. Barnave moved quickly to exonerate Lafayette who, as the man responsible for the custody of the royal family, was immediately accused by the street politicians of conniving at his flight. This produced a rapprochement between Lafayette and the triumvirate, who had gone their separate ways since the autumn of 1789. The leaders of the majority in the Assembly could now rely on the support of the Parisian National Guard.

The deputies declared themselves in permanent session, voted that the royal sanction was no longer necessary for legislation and ordered the ministers to report to them. They complied, and the king's attempt to paralyse the administration by forbidding his ministers to sign decrees in his absence merely showed how easily the regime could be transformed into a de facto republic. A republic, however, was not what the great majority wanted, and a proposal to elect an executive committee of five deputies was rejected. A new oath of allegiance was imposed on army officers and the elections to the next legislative assembly were suspended. Fifteen deputies were sent into the provinces with the power to dismiss civil and military authorities whose loyalty was suspect. The Left stressed the need for everyone to respect law and order, posting up a proclamation to this effect in Paris, and the Right - or most of them - were prepared to cooperate in measures of national defence to protect France from possible foreign invasion. For the moment, the king's flight seemed to have brought the deputies together in defence of national independence, if not of the revolution. Montlosier, in his memoirs, wrote that if the king had got away,

[1] Despite all the re-telling, the story of the king's flight is still contested. The account by the Girault de Coursacs, *Sur la route de Varennes* (Paris, 1984), stretches credulity too far, but it contains enough documentary evidence to suggest that all is not yet known.

he, Malouet and Cazalès would have been prepared to come to terms with the triumvirate. Louis almost did get away, but late in the evening of 22 June the Assembly heard that he had been intercepted at Varennes, within a few miles of Bouillé's army. Three deputies were sent to escort him back.

Louis, as usual, had made the worst of a bad job. If he had escaped, he and his family would at least have been safe and he might have been able to talk the Habsburg emperor into the kind of military support that would have allowed him to dictate some sort of compromise to the Assembly. If he had stayed at home, the former radicals were looking for an understanding with him and if he had exerted his authority over deputies on the Right who claimed to be royalists, a majority in the Assembly was there for the asking. What he had actually done was to destroy what was left of his credibility. Thomas Lindet reported that, all over Paris, royal inn signs and street names disappeared. A popular print showed the royal family transformed into a litter of pigs. In Paris at least, all that had gone to make monarchy much more than one constitutional option amongst others had been lost on the road to Varennes. The king's manifesto was not going to convert anyone and it offered an unflattering commentary on the sincerity of his past professions of support for the constitution. No one was going to believe him any more, including the political leaders who, for their own tactical purposes, had to pretend that they did.

The immediate consequences of the flight were less catastrophic than its long-term effects. Montesquieu and Rousseau had persuaded almost everyone that a country the size of France had to be governed as a monarchy. If Louis were deposed, there would have to be a regent for his six-year-old son. The order of succession to the regency prescribed by the constitution consisted of Provence (who had succeeded in getting out of France at the same time as Louis's unsuccessful flight), Artois (abroad since July 1789) and Orléans. The first two were obviously impossible and Orléans was unpopular and suspected of every kind of intrigue. There was therefore no alternative - apart from a republic - to the restoration of Louis XVI. This was accepted by all but a handful of deputies of the Extreme Left, who wanted the king to be tried, without having any clear idea of what they would do if he were found guilty. Keeping Louis on the throne was going to call for exceptionally heavy doses of equivocation and pretence, of which the fiction that he had been abducted was merely the first instalment. Such finesse was lost on the Parisian radicals, who had little difficulty in whipping up vociferous support for the trial of the king.

The result of all this was an evolution in political attitudes within the Assembly. Hitherto, when the Right had appealed to the sovereignty of the silent majority, they were thinking of the wishes of the countryside, as expressed in the *cahiers* of 1789. The Left, while recognizing the right of the sovereign people to engage in the appropriate kind of insurrection - as in July 1789 - insisted that sovereignty had been transferred to the Assembly. They repeated this all the more insistently, now that they were losing touch with the

Parisian radicals. Duport told his colleagues on 29 June, 'Your charge is to express the people's will for it; its will lies here.' The Extreme Left, which on the whole had concurred in stressing the sovereignty of the Assembly, rather belatedly remembered what Rousseau had written against representative government and were inclined to locate sovereignty on the streets of Paris. This led to their taking up the old cry of the Right that the majority in the Assembly was tyrannizing over public opinion. This would not have cut much weight if the royalist Right had joined forces with the Centre and the old Left, in order to save the monarchy. With their usual preference for what they presumably regarded as chivalric values over political common sense, they did the opposite. Offended by the proposed treatment of the king, Montlosier, who ought to have known better, helped to organize a kind of sit-down strike. A group of more than 290 deputies were persuaded to sign a declaration that they would abstain from voting, except on matters directly related to the interests of the king. Ferrières quite rightly called this proclamation a 'capital fault' – and then signed it! Noblesse might have been abolished, but it still obliged. Cazalès, who was perhaps finding himself pulled in too many different directions, resigned from the Assembly, depriving the Right of its most intelligent and constructive leader.

This act of collective hara-kiri by the Right still left the moderates with an overwhelming majority for the first stage of their strategy, when the immediate need was to balance the king once more on what was left of his tottering throne, and to face up to the resulting fury in Paris. The trouble would come later, when they tried to revise the constitution so as to make the monarchy viable, and to persuade Louis to accept it with more sincerity than he had shown in the past. The logic of the situation drove the leaders, especially Barnave and Duport, further and further along the road of compromise. The 'thirty voices' naturally accused them of having sold themselves to the Court. Without necessarily believing that, a good many deputies were understandably reluctant to make concessions to the king in return for nothing more than the kind of assurances that did not seem to have meant much to him in the past. Thomas Lindet's reaction was perhaps typical: he did not believe that either the king or the Right wanted to make the constitution work, but he was worried by the signs of republicanism in Paris and saw no alternative to a conditional restoration, even if this meant defying public opinion.

On 23 June the Assembly issued a proclamation describing the king's repudiation of the revolution as 'extorted before his departure from this misled king'. This allowed the deputies to justify their past record and to go on denouncing the executive power without specifically accusing Louis. Monarchy was necessary, but only for the welfare of the people. The Assembly had admittedly encroached on the sphere of the executive, but the king's flight had proved that it had been right to do so. The proclamation closed with an expression of thanks to the political clubs, whose love of liberty had done so much for the revolution. That was how the majority saw things on the day after they heard of the king's capture. If they were going to get him to stick on his throne they would have to go a good deal further. Whatever they did, unless they merely pretended that nothing had happened, was bound to expose the fiction that both the king and the Assembly shared in sovereignty, as agents of the general will. The Assembly was no longer negotiating with the king; it was telling him the conditions on which it would allow him to reign.

To ensure that Louis himself did not spoil the delicate manoeuvring that was being done on his behalf, it was decided – in the teeth of violent protests from the Extreme Left – that he should not be subjected to a public interrogation about his flight, but that he could make a private declaration to three deputies (one of whom was Duport), which they were therefore free to write for him. This was read to the Assembly on 26 June and it said all the right things: the king's flight had been prompted by his fears for the safety of the royal family and by his desire to prove to the Powers of Europe that he was a free agent. The protest he left behind had not attacked the fundamental principles of the constitution and his voyage, which had really been a kind of peripatetic public opinion poll, had allowed him to see for himself that the French people were in favour of the revolution. It was not very convincing but it was the best that they could do.

During the first half of July, pressure mounted in Paris for bringing the king to trial or making his restoration dependent on the result of a referendum. The Jacobin Club was torn apart by the conflict between Left and Extreme Left. Although they included almost all the deputies, the moderates made the tactical mistake of walking out, to create a new club at the Feuillants, leaving Robespierre and Pétion to preside over what looked like the wreck of the Jacobins. Control of the premises and custody of the magic name were eventually to enable them to triumph over the Feuillants, but during the summer of 1791 it looked as though the Jacobins had destroyed themselves.[2] It was not until 13 July that the Assembly debated the king's fate. A report in the name of no less than seven of its committees reminded the deputies that they had committed themselves to a monarchy. The king had broken no law – he insisted that he had never intended to leave the country – and he could not be held to have violated a constitution that had still not been put together. He had therefore committed no crime – and even if he had, he was protected by his inviolability. Not surprisingly, the Extreme Left did not find this very convincing. Pétion, Buzot and Grégoire wanted him to be tried; Vadier thought he should be considered to have abdicated, and Robespierre wanted a referendum on his fate. The triumvirate, who might once have used the same arguments themselves, were now staking everything on making a consti-tutional monarchy work, even if they could not feel confident that they could dispose of a constitutional monarch. They confronted the Assembly with the hard facts of the situation. Duport told the deputies bluntly that if they did not

[2] See G. Michon, *Essai sur l'histoire du Parti feuillant: Adrien Duport* (Paris, 1924).

want a republic they must settle for an inviolable monarch and have the courage to brave public opinion. Barnave said that the only alternatives were to bring the revolution to an end or to start it all over again - and any further move in a radical direction would involve a threat to property. The Centre and the Left carried the day and the Assembly voted that the king should be suspended until the constitution was finished and restored to his throne only after he swore to observe it.

This was the decisive vote. It was the suspension of the king that led the 290 deputies of the Right to abstain from future voting. For those who equated the general will with the majority in the Assembly, the issue had been settled. Vadier explained that he had always detested republicanism and Robespierre dissuaded those who still attended the Jacobin Club from supporting petitions for the trial of the king that were now illegal. This was not going to stop the movement in the streets, where radical agitators were rather less convinced of the sovereignty of the Assembly, but it more or less united the deputies. The Paris Commune and the ministers were reminded that they were responsible for preserving order and when, on 17 July, it was reported that a crowd had lynched a couple of men (wrongly said to have been appealing for calm), a deputy demanded the imposition of martial law in Paris.[3] What followed was, if not inevitable, at least fairly predictable. Under repeated pressure from the Assembly, when the Commune heard of the lynchings, it proclaimed martial law. Lafayette led his National Guards to the Champ de Mars, where a peaceful crowd was signing an illegal petition on the king's fate. Greeted, as they approached, by a shower of turf and stones, the Guard opened fire, a fair number of people were killed or wounded and the crowd fled. On the following day the president of the Assembly (Charles Lameth) and Barnave applauded the action of the National Guards and demanded the prosecution of the leaders of the crowd. A Bill was hastily passed, making incitement to break the law, provocative cries during riots and attempts to tamper with the loyalty of the National Guard, criminal offences. Martial law remained in force in Paris for the best part of a month. Some of the popular leaders were arrested; others fled or went underground. During the next few days, messages of support for the Assembly poured in from the provinces. The moderates, at the cost of cutting themselves off from their popular base, had won the first round. To an extent that had not obtained since they had come to Paris, in October 1789, the deputies were free to work out the terms of a compromise with the king and the Right, without having to face mob violence on the streets.

A week before the shooting on the Champ de Mars, the Lameths, Duport, Barnave and Lafayette had given Mercy Argenteau a letter for the queen. This stated fairly bluntly that if the monarch and the monarchy were to be preserved, Louis would have to win back the confidence of the nation. This

---

[3] For the best account of the extremely complicated situation in Paris, see A. Mathiez, *Le Club des Cordeliers pendant la crise de Varennes et le massacre du Champ de Mars* (Paris, 1910) and M. Reinhard, *La Chute de la Royauté* (Paris, 1969), Pt 1.

time, a mere oath would not do and the French people would require proof of
the king's good intentions. He must obtain the return to France of his brothers
and the other *émigrés* and persuade France's allies, Austria and Spain, to
recognize her constitution. If the king complied, he would gradually win back
all the authority that he needed. If he did not, the revolution would continue
and might develop into a crusade against monarchies, which was something
that the king, the foreign Powers and the moderates had a common interest in
preventing.[4]

Mercy passed this on to the queen with the helpful comment that its authors
were obviously frightened of foreign intervention and that there was no ground
whatever for believing in their good intentions. Marie Antoinette scarcely
needed such advice. She warned Mercy, in her turn, that he should beware of
Duport and especially of Barnave. It was not a promising start. There was
probably something in what Mercy wrote: Barnave and his friends *were*
concerned about foreign support for Louis and, if they approached the queen, it
was perhaps mainly in the hope that she could exert some influence over her
brother, Leopold. She duly sent him a letter that was more or less dictated by
Barnave, a fact that she made abundantly clear to him. 'I have been asked, my
dear brother, to write to you . . .' She passed on to him the gist of the
communication she had received from Mercy, adding that Varennes had
actually improved the situation. Those in control of the Assembly had
committed themselves to the preservation of the monarchy and the restoration
of order. The more moderate deputies had abandoned their opposition and
staked everything on cooperation with the monarchy. This would give the
government a breathing-space and the hope of recovering some of its former
power.

In her vulnerable situation after Varennes, the queen was certainly sincere
in not wanting any impulsive action, so much so that Mercy began to have
doubts about her intentions. He told his Chancellor, Kaunitz, that he feared
that she was serious about negotiating with the 'villains' and informed Kaunitz
that, when he wrote to the queen, he pretended to share what he imagined to
be her views of them. Since her actual opinion was the same as his, this cannot
have made for clarity on either side. What Marie Antoinette actually feared
was the kind of irresponsible sabre-rattling that appealed to Artois, who was
now seconded by Provence. They wrote to Catherine II of Russia, inviting her
to put up the money for an *émigré* landing in Normandy, denouncing the
entire work of the revolution and 'the mad hope of an ignominious
accommodation'. Catherine gave them her blessing – and told them that it was
up to France's neighbours to do something about the situation.

---

[4] For this correspondence see *Louis XVI, Marie Antoinette et Madame Elisabeth. Lettres et
documents inédits*, Feuillet de Conches (ed.) (Paris, 1864), 4 vols, II *passim*, and *Marie
Antoinette et Barnave. Correspondance secrète*, A. Söderjhem (ed.) (Paris, 1934). Some of the
documents quoted by Feuillet de Conches were apparently of his own manufacture.

That was what Marie Antoinette thought too. Her hopes were centred on persuading her brother at least to threaten armed intervention - which might eventually commit him to undertaking it. It was not until September that she had an opportunity to tell him what she actually thought. He should not pay any attention to what she had written in July: 'what it cost me to write a letter of that kind!' Unfortunately for the queen, Leopold was no crusader for absolutism - at least in France - and he had enough problems of his own. He therefore pretended to take his sister's first letter at its face value and, to her fury, chose to regard it as indicating her willingness to negotiate with the triumvirate, when what she wanted was an ultimatum.

The political situation, in other words, was in a state of extraordinary confusion, with no one trusting any of the people with whom he or she would have to come to terms. The queen was pretending to listen to the Feuillants, as the moderates were coming to be called, while actually trying to pursue the opposite policy to the one they recommended. She and they agreed only in their hostility to Provence and Artois, who were pursuing their own interests with complete disregard to the safety of the royal family. Since their determination to bring the revolution to an end had led to a bloody confrontation with the Parisian radicals, the Feuillants were more than ever committed to striking a bargain with rulers whom they did not trust. For the time being, they could hope to control both the Assembly and Paris, but their long-term prospects depended on the cooperation of Louis and Marie Antoinette, who dared not defy them but were determined to frustrate them. Whatever Barnave and Duport may have suspected about the real intentions of the king and queen, they had to pretend to accept their assurances and try to persuade their colleagues to revise the constitution to an extent that Louis would find acceptable. Every move in this direction would be denounced as a betrayal of the revolution by the thirty voices, whose appeals to the deputies to stand by their principles were still persuasive, even if the radicals themselves had no solution to offer to the constitutional deadlock. The less embattled deputies were impressed by their arguments and still motivated by the suspicion of the 'executive power' that the triumvirate itself had worked so hard to create. The overwhelming majority that had shown itself ready to stand up to the challenge from the Parisian radicals melted away in the face of these new doubts. This need not have been decisive if the Right had come to the support of the moderates - who had insulted it for so long. Its deputies still attended the Assembly, but only to observe the conflicts amongst the Left with ironical detachment. The loss of almost 300 potential votes, and this demonstration that the Right was repudiating the revolution as a whole, prevented the moderates from making any substantial changes to the constitution.

Malouet at least had learned something from the rigorous political apprenticeship of the past two years and he was much less fastidious than he had been in 1789. In his memoirs he wrote that it would have been wiser to give Barnave and his allies credit for the fact that they were abandoning their 'bad company and evil principles', rather than to reproach them for the 'dangerous errors and heresies' to which they still clung. He himself made approaches to Barnave in the colonial committee, where both of them supported the white settlers, and he also made contact with Le Chapelier. They told him that they now shared his detestation of political clubs and his contempt for *la canaille révolutionnaire*, but that they could not risk abandoning their former allies so long as the Right was still intent on their destruction.[5] Malouet admitted to his readers that his reply that the Right was prepared to cooperate with its former enemies, rested more on hope than conviction. It was agreed that, when the debate opened on the revision of the constitution, Malouet should attack it and Le Chapelier would then denounce him, while at the same time saying that he did not need Malouet's help to realize that it needed revision, and to present as his own the amendments on which both sides were agreed.

On 8 August Malouet therefore opened the debate by protesting that if the constitution could deliver all that it promised, he would be its most fervent advocate. He then went on to repudiate the intellectual basis on which it rested. 'By a retrogression of 2,000 years you have identified the people with sovereignty and offered it that continual temptation, whilst at the same time denying it the actual exercise of sovereignty.' Rousseau's doctrines were erroneous and they were also irrelevant since he had insisted that the general will could not be expressed through representatives. It was better to define law as justice, since there could be no guarantee that the general will would not be unjust. He was going on to propose the restoration of an Upper House, the strengthening of the executive, an absolute veto for the king and his right of dissolution, when the Left lost its nerve, perhaps because Malouet seemed to be winning rather too much sympathy from his audience. It was Le Chapelier himself who carried a motion that Malouet should not be allowed to continue. The scene was typical of a situation that had reproduced itself over and over again during the revolution. People whose objectives were close enough to have provided the basis for an agreement were kept apart by mutual suspicion, misunderstanding of each other's motives and the need to preserve allies - however compromising - in case they should be attacked by those with whom they would have preferred to cooperate.

The hostility of the Right and the success of the Extreme Left in playing on old fears of corruption and the machinations of an 'executive power' that scarcely existed in fact, meant that the majority was saddled with a constitution that its leaders did not have the power to change to any significant extent. Thomas Lindet's reactions were probably typical of many deputies. He approved of the restoration of the king but he was morbidly suspicious of Barnave, whose only motive, he suspected, was to make himself a minister. Even if the Feuillants had been able to offer the king substantial concessions,

[5] Malouet. *Mémoires* (Paris. 1874). 2 vols. II ch. XVII.

his view of things was so different from theirs that any understanding would have needed more time and patience than were likely to be available. Each side had plausible grounds for clinging to its inflated fears of the other and the only beneficiaries, in the long run, were those who preached indefinite mistrust and the continuation of the revolution.

The Feuillants could win minor tactical victories but they were condemned to a strategic retreat. They defeated a motion by Roederer, to the effect that executive power was delegated by the nation, and got the king's status as one of the organs of the general will written into the constitution, but that did not change very much. Robespierre and Pétion won little support when they objected to the prohibition of direct action by the sovereign people; as Pétion put it, 'People want to reduce us to the system that has destroyed liberty in England.' One of the more peculiar debates concerned the right of a free citizenry to libel civil servants. This was rejected, despite violent protests from Pétion, that the virtuous would have nothing to fear, from Roederer, who said the rejection was a ministerial plot and the final blow against liberty, and from Robespierre who, perhaps remembering some of his own performances, said that the Assembly itself had been in the habit of denouncing people without proof. If the arguments of the moderates strained logic and credulity, those of their opponents were sometimes no better. The radicals could afford to lose debates on points of detail, since fear of being denounced by them deterred the Feuillants from trying to make substantial changes to the constitution.

One or two amendments did go through, notably the removal of the civil constitution of the clergy from the constitution itself, which meant that it could be modified or repealed by a simple vote of any subsequent legislature. The qualification of payment of taxes to the annual value of a *marc d'argent*, previously required of deputies, was transferred to the electors who chose them. As the radicals realized, the conservatives stood to gain more by restricting the number of electors than by preventing them from picking impoverished candidates. This debate produced a fair amount of special pleading on both sides, with Robespierre developing the curious argument that the man who paid only ten days' wages in taxation was more independent than a wealthier man, since his needs would be even more modest than his fortune. There was a good deal of talk about whether or not Rousseau would have been eligible and the kind of electorate that would have been most likely to have chosen him. The Extreme Left seems to have won a good deal of support for its attack on the restriction of the suffrage but Barnave had a point when he replied that a relatively wide franchise would lead to the election, not of working men, but of carpet-bagging journalists. It was decided that deputies must live in the départements in which they stood as candidates, which was intended as another spoke in the wheel of Parisian extremists.

The Feuillants had more difficulty when they tried to do something to improve future relations between the legislature and the executive. The spokesman for the constitutional committee wanted to abolish the provision that no former deputy could become a minister until four years after the expiration of his mandate, on the ground that this was to treat the executive as a source of corruption, when it would be preferable for a kind of shadow cabinet to emerge within the Assembly, as happened in England. 'Anglomania' seemed to be coming back into fashion. The proposal immediately created the suspicion that its advocates were thinking of their own future and there was laughter on the Extreme Left when Duport said that the Assembly did not want the executive to be unpopular. What this implied was that the radicals had nothing better to offer than a future of endless instability. This particular battle was drawn: Buzot persuaded his colleagues to decide on a gap of two years before an ex-deputy could become a minister, which would keep the triumvirs out of office for the time being. Strengthening the executive had been the *leitmotiv* of all those trying to effect a transition from opposition to government. It had been the policy of Mounier and the Monarchiens in 1789; it was now taken up by the Feuillants and it was to become the slogan of Buzot and Pétion, and eventually of Robespierre himself. Everyone was agreed that the revolution could not go on for ever – and everyone denounced as treason any attempt to bring it to what he considered a premature conclusion.

The question of how the new constitution was to be amended in the future provided the occasion for a last Rousseauist field day, and a demonstration of the absurdities that arose from every attempt to construct a workable political system on the basis of popular sovereignty. One deputy struggled to make sense of it all: if the nation was indeed sovereign, the Constituent Assembly could not dictate to the future, by means of an unchangeable constitution. The sovereign people was entitled to do whatever it wanted – but only to resort to violent insurrection if it was unanimous [in which case it would presumably have had no one to fight]. On the other hand, reliance on insurrection would give every crackpot an incentive to try his luck, and it raised the interesting question of the status of an unsuccessful insurrection. When a free people was blessed with a good constitution, an insurrection could never be legitimate, in any case. The mandate of the Constituent Assembly had been conferred on it by the deliberations of the *bailliages* in 1789 and the electorate must therefore be allowed to convene similar sovereign assemblies in the future, in order to revise or replace the constitution. It would be rather inconvenient, however, if it were to do so straight away, so this right could not be exercised until after a decent interval. This was to expose the contradictions of the theory rather baldly. Most of the deputies wrapped things up more plausibly, but they were all confronted by the same impossible choices. Since the people ruled, it was an abuse of power for the Assembly to prescribe their future conduct – for example, by instructing them to go to the polls on a particular day, when they might prefer another. On the other hand, one could argue that the Assembly was free to draw up as many rules as it liked, since the people were equally free to defy them by insurrection. As always, behind the theoretical speculation were hard-headed calculations about which way the political cat was likely to jump, and what was proposed owed as much to tactics as to ideology.

Malouet produced an argument that was all the harder to refute since many of the deputies accepted his premises and only objected to their likely consequences. Revolutionary and constitutional government were incompatible and the immediate need was to substitute the latter for the former. This involved the offer of a general amnesty to political offenders, an end to persecution and the repeal of all the various loyalty oaths (which included that to the civil constitution of the clergy). There must be no conventions, with sovereign powers, and future legislatures must be prevented from following the example of the Constituent Assembly and claiming sovereign powers. The constitution should therefore be submitted to a referendum, but not until January 1793, to give the country time to settle down. When it had been approved, a majority of the 83 départements would be able to propose amendments, which the king would be empowered to veto. Any future assembly that claimed constituent powers would be automatically dissolved.

There was not much support for a referendum amongst the self-styled partisans of popular sovereignty. Le Chapelier said that public opinion was almost unanimously in favour of the constitution and that Malouet's motives, in proposing a referendum, were counter-revolutionary, which sounded rather like a non sequitur. Pétion's proposal for regular conventions was rejected almost unanimously, as a recipe for perpetual revolt. After conceding that the nation was free to do whatever it liked, the Assembly advised it to wait for thirty years until it revised its constitution. That satisfied the *amour propre* of the deputies without solving their long-term problem. A noble pointed out that those who had elected the Constituent Assembly had intended the king to have a veto on all its activities, including the drafting of the constitution. This was true, but not very helpful, since it would have implied starting all over again. Robespierre was for leaving the total revision of the constitution, as distinct from its amendment, to be decided by insurrection. That was perhaps logical but it was not very helpful either.

Gradually the admirers of Rousseau succeeded in adapting his arguments to their political needs. As one of them put it, what was needed was to guarantee the people their constitution, even despite the people themselves. Their general will took shape in the legislature, whereas the individual citizens had each no more than a particular will. The revision of the constitution, which must embody the general will if it was to be legitimate, could therefore only be undertaken by the Assembly. This was the old game of the Left, to transfer sovereignty from the electorate to the elected. By this time, Barnave was ready to jettison Rousseau altogether. He said that representative government was the best system, while direct democracy was 'the most odious, the most subversive and the most harmful to the people itself'. It had been a scourge in city-states and it was an absurdity in large nations. He got into rather a tangle over the history of the Constituent Assembly, which had 'called for' an insurrection. The people had then endorsed its legislation [presumably by not revolting against it too comprehensively], even when its policies were very different from those the people had wanted when they elected it. This proved that the nation did not really know what it wanted until its legislators made up its mind for it. 'The people are sovereign but only their representatives can act for them, because their own interests are almost always attached to political truths that they are incapable of understanding clearly and in depth.' That was getting dangerously close to a repudiation of every kind of representative government.

In the end the Assembly decided that there would be no referendum and no conventions. Leaving the sovereign people with its uncontested, but somewhat nebulous, right of insurrection, the deputies decided that the constitution would be revised by votes in three successive legislatures, and that the whole business could not start before 1797. They were not to know that the entire constitution was to disappear within less than twelve months.

The revision of the constitution did not therefore amount to very much and the document that was presented to the king on 3 September was essentially what he had denounced when he left for Varennes. Louis, as usual, consulted widely before opting for what looked like the easiest solution. Maury and Cazalès advised rejection, in which they were supported by the *émigré* chorus. Mercy passed on Burke's advice in the same sense: the revolutionaries were traitors, the *émigrés* would do whatever the king told them and the Powers would come to the rescue of the royal family. This was not Burke at his most prescient. Malouet favoured trying to bargain, but the king opted for unconditional acceptance. On the 13th he told the deputies, in a speech that sounds as though it had been written for him by Barnave, that when he had fled, he had not been able to regard a situation in which the laws were unenforced, as in conformity with the general will. Since then, however, the Assembly had voted to maintain law and order and to enforce military discipline, and had withdrawn the civil constitution of the clergy from the text of the constitution itself, which he was therefore able to accept. This, no doubt, was what the Feuillants hoped; what Louis actually believed was perhaps another matter.

In a final flurry of activity, the Assembly annexed Avignon and the Comtat, denied political rights to free coloureds in the colonies, voted them to all Jews, left the passing of an education act to its successors and voted an innocuous bill against political clubs. It was Le Chapelier – once a founder-member of the Breton Club from which the Jacobins had sprung – who had waged the attack on the clubs, saying that everyone wanted to bring the revolution to an end and that its only enemies were those who preached mistrust and attacked authority. He got his Bill through, but had to abandon the clause that prohibited clubs from corresponding and affiliating with each other, which left it not much more than a pious exhortation. On 30 September the Assembly declared its session closed.

Marie Antoinette at least had no doubts about where that left her. In mid-August she had had a chance to tell Mercy what she really felt. Open opposition to the constitution would merely encourage more people to support it. There was no immediate prospect of military intervention by either the Powers or the *émigrés* - and rescue by the latter would mean even worse enslavement. The only course was therefore for the king to accept the constitution when it was offered to him, keep within the law and wait for public opinion to change. This would be misunderstood, both by the Court and by the 'aristocrats', who were still cherishing idle dreams of recovering everything that they had lost. It was impossible to know what the king would actually do: 'one thinks one has persuaded him one minute and then a word or an argument turns him round without his realizing it.' 'You know the kind of person with whom I have to deal.' She was pinning her hopes on her son and hoping that he would grow up to be worthy . . . not of the Bourbons, but of Maria Theresa. Not for nothing did her enemies describe her as 'l'Autrichienne'. Not opposing the constitution did not imply any intention of eventually coming to terms with it. It was 'so monstrous that it cannot possibly survive for long' and her intention was to overturn it at the first opportunity. As for the Feuillants, 'It is a matter of lulling their suspicions and winning their confidence so that we can thwart them all the more effectively later on.' Three weeks later she wrote to Mercy again, complaining that the king's acceptance speech was too weak. 'Can it be that, born with my spirit and so conscious of the blood that runs in my veins, I should be destined to pass my days in a country like this and with men like these?' Lafayette had summed her up when he had written that she was more concerned to put on a brave front in the face of danger than to avert it.

Where the king stood, and indeed, if he could be described as standing anywhere in particular, is as problematical as usual. When Moleville was made a minister in October, he asked Louis how he regarded the constitution and received the reply that the king had sworn to maintain it, with all its faults, and that he intended to keep his oath. Moleville, who was writing royalist history, long after the king's execution, rather spoiled his effect by claiming that this was also the view of Marie Antoinette. For the moment, neither the king nor the queen saw any way of challenging the constitution, but neither regarded it as acceptable in the long run.

The princes made the king's position more difficult by writing him an open letter in which they said he was not a free agent and could only be considered to have accepted the constitution under duress. They rejected all the work of the Assembly, on the ground that it was contrary to the general will, as expressed in the *cahiers*. The king, in any case, did not have the right to sign away the fundamental rights of a monarchy in which he had only a life interest. If he were to order them to abandon their opposition to the revolution, they would respect his real intentions by disregarding what he had been forced to say. One can understand why Marie Antoinette found them so insufferable.

184 'The Revolution is Over'

Assessments of the situation naturally varied with the perspective of the observer. Barnave, writing a little later, encouraged himself to think that, if the constitution had been given a chance, order could have been restored within three months. The electoral system would have entrusted the actual business of government to men of leisure and enlightenment, who would have had to respect the interests of the majority of the population, in order to get themselves elected. Things had already begun to move in a promising direction, towards the end of the Assembly's session, and each step forward would facilitate the next.[6] He was bound to take an optimistic view of the prospects of a policy on which he had gambled everything, including his life, but the fact that it was not to be, does not mean that it could not have been.

Montlosier was less sanguine. The constitution was 'tyranny reduced to an art and subjected to rules'. Nevertheless, the nobility could have been induced to accept it if they had not been insulted as well as expected to foot the bill for all the changes. Some of the revolutionaries were intent on making a career out of revolution but others were ready to settle for what they had got and some of the original leaders were genuine in their conversion to monarchical principles - but he published this in a pamphlet with the uncompromising title, *On the need for a counter-revolution in France*.

Robespierre put his faith in the readiness of the newly elected deputies to 'defend the rights of the nation against the guile of false men who only praise liberty in order to attack it with impunity'. The country was still full of hypocrites, intriguers and ambitious men, whose only objective was personal power. The future was as dark as ever and if liberty was to be preserved, it could only be by eternal mistrust.

La Marck's view was the mirror-image of Robespierre's. The king was unfit to rule and the queen allowed every opportunity of taking charge to escape her. Their only hope rested on foreign intervention and luck. 'If one considers their conduct in conjunction with the mad agitation of 24 million lunatics, how can one look forward to anything but the most deplorable future?'[7]

Perhaps the last word should go to the duc de Lévis: 'A revolution is a very interesting thing to read about in history, and even to watch, provided that one can keep one's distance; close up, one is revolted by all the injustice, unhappiness and crime that defile it.' There had been plenty of those, but also plenty of altruism and disinterested enthusiasm. The bright hopes of 1789 had not been enough, but the path to Hell was nevertheless paved with good as well as bad intentions.

[6] *Introduction à la Révolution française*, in *Oeuvres*, ed. Béranger de la Drôme (Paris, 1843), 4 vols, I/201-7.
[7] *Correspondance entre le comte de Mirabeau et le Comte de La Marck*, ed. A. de Bacourt (Paris, 1851), 3 vols, III/247-9.

12

Conclusion

THIS book was not conceived as a history of the Constituent Assembly. Its pursuit of a different objective has inevitably directed the reader's attention away from the almost incredible achievements of that assembly which transformed virtually all of France's institutions and created, not merely a new society, but new ways of looking at man as a social animal and new ideas about the scope of political action. When Burke attacked the French revolution he argued that it was impossible to pull a country up by the roots and make a fresh start. The Constituent Assembly showed that the process was liable to get out of control and the final cost might prove more than anyone would have cared to pay if they had foreseen it, but that it could be done. The aim of the revolutionaries was to substitute for a chaotic inheritance of provinces, privileges and prejudices, a new order that would be national, rational and founded on the principle that power should be entrusted only to men who had been chosen by their fellow-citizens, whether this meant officers in the National Guard, judges or bishops. The new conception of liberty went deeper than that. Based on the belief in fundamental rights, common to all men, that transcended positive law, it involved religious toleration, civil and political rights for Jews, the freedom of the press and the security of any individual who had not been convicted by an independent jury of having broken a pre-existing law. From one point of view, the declaration of the rights of man was a collection of aspirations, but it was also the blue-print for a programme of positive action that was largely implemented within the space of two years. The British Ambassador knew what he was talking about when, in July 1789, he wrote that the French had become a free people. Despite the appalling difficulties in translating these aspirations into action in a country whose communications, administrative techniques, level of literacy and standard of living could not escape from their eighteenth-century limitations, France *was* transformed, in a way that many, probably most, of its educated citizens passionately believed to be for the better. The new institutions were made to work, as a result of the dedicated enthusiasm of thousands of anonymous Frenchmen who believed themselves to be creating a better society than any that their ancestors had ever known. These institutions took root and were to survive all the political changes of the nineteenth century and provide the basis for both the structure and attitudes of present-day France. All this was achieved within two years. No other parliament has ever done anything remotely comparable.

This must be the starting-point for any inquiry into why this transformation should have torn the country apart and prepared the way for civil and foreign war and a reign of terror as extraordinary as the bright hopes of that dawn when Wordsworth had felt it bliss to be alive. It would be contrary to the tenor of everything that I have written in the rest of the book if I were to argue that, in the autumn of 1791, this grim sequel was inevitable. The whole course of the revolution was transformed by the war that broke out in 1791 and lasted with scarcely a break until 1815. The war was not the inevitable response of the European Powers to a threat that their rulers dared not tolerate; it was begun by France, as a matter of internal politics. Some of the revolutionaries opposed it and the decision might have gone the other way. Thomas Paine, who had been as eager as anyone to welcome and defend the revolution, understood very well that the reasons why it degenerated into a nightmare were to be found within itself. He wrote to Danton in the spring of 1793, 'my despair arises not from the combined foreign Powers, not from the intrigues of the aristocracy and priestcraft, but from the tumultuous misconduct with which the internal affairs of the present revolution are conducted'. Whether or not this bloody sequel was already inevitable when the Constituent Assembly closed its session is an insoluble problem, and perhaps a meaningless one. All that the historian can do is to recognize that the seeds of the Terror had been sown and to show how they germinated. If the climate after 1791 had been different, the harvest would not have been the same. Nevertheless, French society was already beginning to fall apart by the time that the exhausted deputies of the Constituent Assembly made their way home. Many Frenchmen already regarded the revolution as an intolerable threat. In the latter days of the Assembly its two sides had not been on speaking terms, with each denying the right of existence of the other. The worst had not yet happened and perhaps it need never have happened, but the almost unanimous belief in national regeneration had given way to equally universal hatred and suspicion. Even the enthusiasm now had an inquisitorial edge to it. We therefore return to the question that I set myself at the outset: why?

It has, I think, become clear that the answer is not to be found in the kind of explanation that can be offered for the civil war that followed the Russian revolution. What happened in France was not due to the determination of the leaders of one social class to expropriate and destroy another. Initially, the French revolutionaries saw themselves as leading a national movement whose only enemies were the handful of agents of illegitimate and discredited 'ministerial despotism'. Even when the Second and Third Estates were at loggerheads in the spring of 1789, this was a quarrel about political power and concepts of social organization - hierarchical or egalitarian - that did not call into question the right of those with property to continue to enjoy it, even if they might have to forfeit some of the traditional sources of income that they were inclined to regard as property. Noble status was eventually abolished but nobles were never proscribed, nor was their property confiscated unless they fled the country or were executed as traitors. If a good many nobles lost some of their wealth and standing, this was perhaps on a smaller scale than the losses of the British middle classes in the generation after the Second World War – which did not provoke them to armed insurrection, even if a few of them 'emigrated' to tax havens with agreeable climates. Some peasants may have lost more than their seigneurs, as a result of increased taxation. It was not proscription or intolerable material burdens that drove nobles to emigrate or peasants to revolt.

Religion was another matter. Although the intention of the Assembly had been to improve the Church rather than to destroy it, the deputies blundered into a conflict that convinced many Frenchmen that they had no alternative but to take up arms against a government intent on destroying something that was of vital concern to them. This was the product of a tragic misunderstanding rather than a clash of incompatible interests.

There was therefore no obvious necessary reason why the members of the Constituent Assembly should have come to feel that their aims were irreconcilable. The initial objectives of the great majority had much in common. What at first divided them was disagreement about means, above all, about what powers should be given to the king in a constitutional monarchy that was accepted as both necessary and desirable. This conflict of means led men with no experience of parliamentary politics to take parades of principle and grandiloquent gesturing at their face value and to create myths about each other. A certain amount of myth-making is an ingredient in all parliamentary politics but it does not usually prevent those who have been denouncing each other from enjoying a drink together afterwards. Things were different in 1789. The magnitude of the issues involved, the July crisis that had almost led to civil war and the absence of any rules or precedents, made it harder for men to separate fact from fantasy, but there was more to it than that.

The eagerness, not merely to denounce one's opponents as essentially evil, but to believe that that was what they actually were, was one of the consequences of making a particular ideological choice. In the summer of 1789, the Assembly rejected the conception of politics as being about the balanced representation of necessarily divergent interests, for a belief in popular sovereignty and the construction of the ideal society. The former view implied that differences were legitimate and respectable and that the objective of political action was to represent them in such a way that no one interest or coalition of interests would be able to dispose of the power of the state for the attainment of its own sectarian purposes. The alternative view implied that any healthy society was a unanimous one. Politics was a matter of putting *vertu* on the statute book. The French people formed an organic unit with a single general will. What was in accordance with that will was not merely in the interest of the people as a whole but morally incumbent upon each one of them. Once this general will was known, opposition to it was therefore illogical, unjustifiable and immoral.

This immediately raises the question of why the Constituent Assembly preferred one creed to the other. Part of the answer lies in the extraordinary vogue for Rousseau's ideas that permeated the entire educated population.[1] To some extent, the answer was also a question of politics. A policy of constitutional equilibrium implied a bicameral parliament, like those of England and America. The exaggeration of the alleged virtues of the British constitution irritated deputies who were not lacking in a sense of their own importance and an awareness of the magnitude of the work of national regeneration to which they were committed. A bicameral assembly also looked to the Third Estate like a return to the concept of separate Orders whose liquidation had been necessary in order to set the whole revolutionary process in motion. The rural nobility saw it as the creation of a House of Peers for the benefit of the Court aristocracy. The policy of balance also implied giving the king a veto over legislation and the power of dissolution. It was not unreasonable to shrink from entrusting this kind of authority to the man who had just sacked Necker. Whatever the abstract merits of the British constitution, England and France were different countries, with different political traditions, and what worked tolerably well in one of them could not simply be exported to the other. This was something that Burke, like the Monarchiens, failed to understand. For all kinds of reasons, the British plant could not be expected to strike root in French soil, as Burke, with his penchant for organic imagery, ought to have understood. The French deputies could not be expected to envisage progress as the gradual improvement on past precedent. They *had* no precedents, or at least, none that they were not determined to repudiate. Their mission was to draft a constitution for a country that had never had one.

If their choice of ideology was influenced by the needs of politics, once it had been made it became a political force in its own right. Popular sovereignty had a superficially modern ring to it and it was going to inspire the political theorists and revolutionary activists of the nineteenth century. In fact, it meant opting for the past, for a way of looking at things that reached back, through Rousseau and Machiavelli, to the classical republics of Greece and Rome. As Montesquieu had realized, it was the alternative view, despite its appearance of seedy expediency and the sanctification of the status quo, that corresponded to the complex needs of an integrated but diverse and economically interdependent society. Popular sovereignty also had another drawback: it led to an inescapable logical impasse. If, as Rousseau had argued, sovereignty was inalienable and could not be transferred by a people to its representatives, it

---

[1] For an examination of this, see R. Barny, *Rousseau dans la Révolution: le personnage de Jean-Jacques et les débuts du culte révolutionnaire (1787-1791)* (Oxford, 1986).

could only be effectively exercised within a city-state. Any government other than direct democracy would always be liable to misinterpret the general will. One could devise means of palliating this, by frequent elections, the right of electors to recall their deputies and referenda on laws, but only to a limited extent. Popular sovereignty logically implied imperative mandates, which would have made any kind of representative government unworkable. Its advocates, if confronted by an insurrection, could only wait to see if it succeeded before deciding whether or not it reflected the general will. In their efforts to escape this horn of the dilemma, the deputies impaled themselves on the other one. If one ignored Rousseau, as they did, and asserted that the general will could only emerge within a body that represented the entire nation, sovereignty was transferred from the electors to the elected. Whenever the assembly found itself out of step with public opinion, it would be the latter that was mistaken, and the duty of the deputies to bring it into line, by education or coercion. This was not to become official dogma until 1793 but it was already rather more than implicit in the debates in the Constituent Assembly.

It is not very meaningful to blame that assembly for choosing the option it did, unless one can point to a better, and none existed. The problems of the location of sovereignty and the limits to the legitimacy of a modern state *are* insoluble. Things work because those who work them steer clear of the 'deep questioning that probes to endless dole'. Parties usually agree to work within a framework of precedent. When they quarrel about principles, the issues involved are usually minor frontier disputes. If they involve something more basic, an electorate that is reasonably satisfied with its constitution – whatever it may think about a particular government – will desert a party that tries to rock the boat. If the electorate behaves in the opposite way, neither politics nor ideology can prevent the country from falling apart. Here Rousseau and Burke find common ground.[2] If the general will implies an unspoken agreement that politics shall continue to be conducted within a traditionally accepted framework, acceptable changes will be the ones that respect that framework. If public opinion comes to reject it, it will pull the system down.

In the France of the summer of 1789 there was no past that anyone was prepared to invoke as a proof of legitimacy. Behind them, the deputies had the exhilarating and almost incredible triumphs of July. Ahead lay a future whose possibilities seemed unlimited. If anything is surprising, it is that some of the heroes of the earliest days, such as Mounier, who had proposed the Tennis Court Oath, should have been saying that France would not be doing badly if it emerged from its dizzying adventure with a constitution no worse than that of England. It was asking too much to expect the majority of the Assembly to settle for so little. It is not surprising if they preferred Sieyès's exhortation to aim for 'ideal models of the beautiful and the good'. It was this that gave the revolution its unique resonance, both in France and throughout the world.

[2] See D. Cameron, *The Social Thought of Rousseau and Burke* (London, 1973).

There was a price to pay. The option of regeneration, the pursuit of *vertu* and the unanimity of the ideal society was perhaps what gave the deputies the courage to attempt - and achieve - so much. Inevitably, the loftiness of their aspirations, their belief in a general will and their often justified sense of their own disinterestedness, left no room for opposition. The minority, and those who were being regenerated against their will, protested that the Assembly had usurped a power that it had stolen from the people in whose name it claimed to exercise it. It was the height of their aspirations that led men to perceive their opponents as the incarnation of evil and thereby gave the revolution its tragic dimension. If the Assembly failed in its impossible task of effecting national regeneration by consent, this was due to what was best, much more than to what was worst in it. Counter-revolutionaries were eventually to denounce the revolution as Satanic and they were right in a way that they did not intend, for Satan was an angel before he became a rebel and his sin was to reject the limits that even he could not transcend.

Bibliography

F OR the debates in the Constituent Assembly I have relied mainly on the reports in the *Moniteur*, supplemented by editions of the speeches of some of the deputies and by the 8° Lc²⁹ series in the Bibliothèque Nationale. This contains the text of speeches that were ordered to be printed by the Assembly, together with others, privately printed by the deputies themselves, usually when they had been unable to deliver them on the floor of the House.

PRIMARY SOURCES

Adhémar, comtesse d', *Souvenirs sur Marie Antoinette*. Paris, 1836, 4 vols.
Bailly J-S., *Mémoires d'un témoin de la Révolution*. Paris, 1804, 3 vols.
Barère B., *Le Point du Jour* (newspaper).
Barère B., *Montesquieu peint d'après ses ouvrages*. Switzerland, an V.
Barnave A., *Oeuvres*, ed. Béranger de la Drôme. Paris, 1843, 4 vols.
Besenval P-J-V., *Mémoires*. Paris, 1821, 2 vols.
Bouillé F-C-A., *Memoirs Relating to the French Revolution*. London, 1797.
Brissot J-P., *Plan de conduite pour les députés du peuple aux Etats-Généraux de 1789*. n.p., 1789.
Browning O., *Despatches from Paris, 1784-1790*. London, 1910, vol. 2.
Camus A-G., *Mes pensées et ma Déclaration sur la religion*. Paris, n.d.
Chastenay Mme de, *Mémoires*, 3rd edn. Paris, 1896, 2 vols.
Chevallier P. (ed.), *Journal de l'Assemblée des Notables de 1787*. Paris, 1960.
Creuzé-Latouche J-A., *Journal des Etats Généraux*. Paris, 1946.
Desmeuniers J-N-D., *Avis aux députés qui doivent représenter la nation dans l'Assemblée des Etats-Généraux*. n.p., 1789.
Dubois-Crancé E-L-A., *Le Véritable Portrait de nos législateurs*. Paris, 1792.
Dumont E., *Souvenirs sur Mirabeau*, ed. J. Bénétruy. Paris, 1951.
Duquesnoy A., *Journal*, ed. R. de Crèvecoeur. Paris, 1984, 2 vols.
Ferrières C-E., *Correspondance inédite*, ed. H. Carré. Paris, 1932.
Ferrières C-E., *Mémoires*. Paris, 1821, 3 vols.
Gower Earl, *Despatches*, ed. O. Browning. Cambridge, 1885.
Grégoire H-B., *Avis aux citoyens des campagnes du département de Mont Blanc*. n.p., n.d.
Grégoire H-B., *Légitimité du serment civique*. Paris, 1791.

Lafayette M-J-P-Y-R-G-M., *Mémoires, correspondance et manuscrits*. Paris, 1837-1838, 6 vols.

Lally-Tollendal T-G., *Notice historique sur la vie de M. Mounier*. n.p., n.d.

Lameth A. de, *Histoire de l'Assemblée Constituante*. Paris, 1818-1819, 2 vols.

Lanjuinais J-D., *Examen du 8è chapitre du Contrat Social de J-J. Rousseau*. Paris, 1825.

Lanjuinais J-D., *Oeuvres*, ed. V. Lanjuinais. Paris, 1832, 4 vols.

Lindet T., *Correspondance*, ed. A. Montier. Paris, 1899.

Louis XVI, Marie Antoinette et Mme Elisabeth. Lettres et documents inédits, ed. Feuillet de Conches. Paris, 1864, 4 vols.

Malouet P-V., *Collection des opinions de M. Malouet*. Paris, 1791, 2 vols.

Malouet P-V., *Mémoires*. Paris, 1874, 2 vols.

Marat J-P., *Les Pamphlets de Marat*, ed. C. Vellay. Paris, 1911.

Marie Antoinette et Barnave. Correspondance secrète, ed. A. Söderhjelm. Paris, 1934.

Maury J-S., *Opinion sur la souveraineté du peuple*. Avignon, 1852.

Mirabeau H-G-R., *Collection complète des travaux de M. Mirabeau l'ainé à l'Assemblée Nationale*. Paris, 1791-2, 5 vols.

Mirabeau H-G-R., *Correspondance entre le comte de Mirabeau et le comte de La Marck*, ed. A. de Bacourt. Paris, 1851, 3 vols.

Moleville B. de., *Histoire de la Révolution de France pendant les dernières années du Règne de Louis XVI*. Paris, 1801, 10 vols.

Montlosier F-D-R., *De la nécessité d'une contre-révolution en France*.

Montlosier F-D-R., *Essai sur l'art de constituer les peuples*. Paris, 1790.

Montlosier F-D-R., *Mémoires*. Paris, 1830, 2 vols.

Mounier J-J., *De l'influence attribuée aux Philosophes, aux Franc-Maçons et aux Illuminés sur la Révolution de France*. Tübingen, 1801.

Mounier J-J., *Exposé de la conduite de M. Mounier dans l'Assemblée Nationale et des motifs de son retour en Dauphiné*. Paris, 1789.

Mounier J-J., *Recherches sur les causes qui ont empêché les Français de devenir libres*. Geneva, 1792, 2 vols.

Necker J., *De la Révolution française*. Paris, 1797.

Pétion J., *Appercu sur la situation politique actuelle de la France*. n.p., 1790.

Pétion J., *Avis aux Français sur le salut de la patrie*. n.p., 1788.

Pétion J., *Oeuvres*. Paris, an I, 3 vols.

Rabaut Saint-Etienne *Considérations sur les intérêts du Tiers-Etat, adressées au peuple des provinces par un propriétaire foncier*. n.p., 1788.

Rabaut Saint-Etienne *Précis historique de la Révolution française*, 6th edn. Paris, 1813.

Recueil de pièces intéressantes. Sens, 1788.

Recueil de pièces intéressantes pour servir de l'histoire de la Révolution de France. John Rylands Library, Manchester. R65600, vols 1-9.

Robespierre M., *Oeuvres*, vol. 2, ed. E. Lesueur, Paris, 1914; vol. 6, ed. M. Bouloiseau, G. Lefebvre and A. Soboul, Paris, 1950.

Roederer P-L., *L'Esprit de la Révolution de 1789*. Paris, 1831.

Sieyès E-J., *Collection des ecrits*. Paris, n.d.

Vaudreuil J-H. de R., *Correspondance entre le comte de Vaudreuil et le comte d'Artois pendant l'Emigration*, ed. L. Pingaud. Paris, 1889, 2 vols.

SECONDARY SOURCES

Alexeev-Popov, 'Le Cercle Social 1790-91', *Recherches Sovietiques*, 1956.
Aulard A., *La Société des Jacobins*. Paris, 1889, vols 1-2.
Barny R., *J. J. Rousseau dans la Révolution française*, 1789-1801. Paris, 1977.
Barny R., *Rousseau dans la Révolution: le personnage de Jean-Jacques et les débuts du culte révolutionnaire (1787-1791)*. Oxford, 1986.
Best G., *Honour among Men and Nations*. Toronto, 1982.
Blum C., *Rousseau and the Republic of Virtue*. Ithaca, NY, 1986.
Braesch F-R., *1789, l'année cruciale*. Paris, 1940.
Braesch F-R., 'Les pétitions du Champ de Mars', *Revue Historique*, 1923.
Buchez P-J-B., *Histoire de la Constituante*, 2nd edn. Paris, 1846.
Bus C. du, *Stanislas de Clermont-Tonnerre et l'echec de la Révolution monarchique*. Paris, 1931.
Cameron D., *The Social Thought of Rousseau and Burke*. London, 1973.
Caron P., 'La Tentative de contre-révolution de juin-juillet 1789', *Revue d'Histoire Moderne*, 1906-7.
Chaussinand-Nogaret G., *Mirabeau*. Paris, 1982.
Chaussinand-Nogaret G., *The Nobility in Eighteenth-century France* (Eng. trans.). London, 1985).
Chérest A., *La Chute de l'Ancien Régime*. Paris, 1884, 3 vols.
Cochin A. *Les Sociétés de pensée et la révolution en Bretagne*. Paris, 1925.
Coursac P. and P. Girault de, *Enquête sur le procès du Roi Louis XVI*. Paris, 1982.
Coursac P. Girault de, *L'Education d'un Roi: Louis XVI*. Paris, 1972.
Coursac P. and P. Girault de, *Sur la route de Varennes*. Paris, 1984.
Dansette A., *Histoire religieuse de la France contemporaine*, 3rd edn. Paris, 1965.
Doyle W., *Origins of the French Révolution*. Oxford, 1980.
Doyle W., *The Ancien Régime*. London, 1986.
Doyle W., *The Parlement of Bordeaux and the End of the Old Regime 1771-90*. London, 1974.
Dreyfus J., 'Le manifeste royal du 20 juin 1791', *Revue Historique*, 77 (1908).
Droz J., *Histoire du Règne de Louis XVI*. Brussels, 1839.
Egret J., *La Pré-Révolution française, 1787-8*. Paris, 1962.
Egret J., *La Révolution des Notables: Mounier et les Monarchiens*. Paris, 1950.
Egret J., *Necker*. Paris, 1975.
Flammermont J., 'Le Second Ministère de Necker', *Revue Historique*, 1891.
Forrest A., *The French Revolution and the Poor*. Oxford, 1981.
Freddi F., 'La Presse parisienne et la nuit du 4 août', *Annales Historiques de la Révolution Française*, 1985.
Furet F., *Understanding the French Revolution* (Eng. trans.). Cambridge, 1981.
Godechot J., *La Prise de la Bastille*. Paris, 1965.
Gooch R. K., *Parliamentary Government in France: Revolutionary Origins, 1789-91*. New York, 1960.
Goodwin A., 'Calonne, the Assembly of the French Notables of 1787 and the origins of the "révolte nobiliaire"', *English Historical Review*, 61 (1946).
Gottschalk L., *Lafayette between the American and French Revolution*. Chicago, 1950.
Gottschalk L. and Maddox M., *Lafayette in the French Revolution: through the October Days*. Chicago, 1969.

Gottschalk L. and Maddox M., *Lafayette in the French Revolution: from the October Days through the Federation*. Chicago, 1973.

Goubert P., *L'Ancien Régime*. Paris, 1965.

Goubert P. and Roche D., *Les Français et l'Ancien Régime*. Paris, 1984, 2 vols.

Gruder V. R., 'A mutation in elite political culture: the French Notables and the defence of property', *Journal of Modern History*, 1984.

Hampson N., 'The French Revolution and the nationalization of honour', in *War and Society: historical essays in honour of the memory of J. R. Western, 1928-1971*, ed. M. D. R. Foot. London, 1973.

Hampson N., *Will and Circumstance: Montesquieu, Rousseau and the French Revolution*. London, 1983.

Higonnet P., *Class, Ideology and the Rights of Nobles during the French Revolution*. Oxford, 1981.

Higonnet P. and Murphy J., 'Les Députés de la noblesse aux Etats-Généraux de 1789', *Revue d'Histoire Moderne et Contemporaine*, 1973.

Higonnet P. and Murphy J., 'Notes sur la composition de L'Assemblée Constituante', *Annales Historiques de la Révolution Française*, 1973.

Hulliung M., *Montesquieu and the Old Régime*. Berkeley, Ca, 1976.

Hutt M. E., 'The curés of the Third Estate: Ideas of Reform in the Pamphlets of the French lower Clergy', *Journal of Ecclesiastical History*, 1957.

Hutt M. E., 'The role of the curés in the Estates General of 1789', *Journal of Ecclesiastical History*, 1955.

Kates G., *The Cercle Social, the Girondins and the French Revolution*. Princeton, NJ, 1985.

Kennedy M. L., *The Jacobin Clubs in the French Revolution. The First Years*. Princeton, NJ, 1982.

Latreille A., *L'Eglise catholique et la Révolution francaise*. Paris, 1946, vol. 1.

Lefebvre G., *The Great Fear* (Eng. trans.). London, 1973.

Le May E., 'La Composition de l'Assemblée Nationale Constituante: les hommes de la continuité', *Revue d'Histoire Moderne et Contemporaine*, 1977.

Lever E., *Louis XVI*. Paris, 1986.

Ligou D., 'A propos de la Révolution municipale', *Revue d'Histoire Economique et Sociale*, 1960.

McManners J., 'Jansenism and politics in the eighteenth century', *Studies in Church History*, 1975.

McManners J., *The French Revolution and the Church*. London, 1969.

Margerison K., 'P-L. Roederer: political thought and practice during the French Revolution', *Transactions of the American Philosophical Society*, 1983.

Margerison K., 'P-L. Roederer: the industrial capitalist as revolutionary', *Eighteenth-century Studies*, 1978.

Mathiez A., *Contributions à l'histoire religieuse de la Révolution française*. Paris, 1907.

Mathiez A., 'Etude critique sur les journées des 5 et 6 octobre 1789', *Revue Historique*, 67 (1898), 68 (1899).

Mathiez A., *Le Club des Cordeliers pendant la crise de Varennes et le massacre du Champ de Mars*. Paris, 1910.

Michon G., *Essai sur l'histoire du parti feuillant: Adrien Duport*. Paris, 1924.

Neckeles, 'The curés in the Estates General of 1789', *Journal of Modern History*, 1974.

Oelsner Ç. E., *Notice sur la vie de Sieyès*. Switzerland/London, 1795.

Patrick A., 'The approach of French revolutionary officials to social problems', *Australian Journal of French Studies*, 18 (1981), no. 1.

Préclin E., *Les Jansenistes du dix-huitième siècle et la Constitution Civile du Clergé*. Paris, 1928.

Reinhard M., *La Chute de la Royauté*. Paris, 1969.

Roberts J. M., *French Revolution Documents*. Oxford 1966, vol. 1.

Rodmell G. E., 'Laclos, Brissot and the petition of the Champ de Mars', *Studies on Voltaire and the Eighteenth Century*, 1980.

Schmitt E. and Reichardt R. (eds), *Die Französische Revolution - zufälliges oder Notwendiges Ereignis?* Munich, 1983, 3 vols.

Söderhjelm A., *Fersen et Marie Antoinette*. Paris, 1930.

Stone B., *The French Parlements and the Crisis of the Old Regime*. Chapel Hill, 1986.

Sutherland D. M. G., *France, 1789-1815*. London, 1985.

Tackett T., *Religion, Revolution and Regional Culture in Eighteenth-century France*. Princeton, NJ, 1986.

Talmon J. L., *The Origins of Totalitarian Democracy*. London, 1952.

Taylor G. V., 'Non-capitalist wealth and the origin of the French Revolution', *American Historical Review*, 72 (1967).

Taylor G. V., 'Revolutionary and non-revolutionary content in the cahiers of 1789, an interim report', *French Historical Studies*, 1972.

Taylor G. V., 'Types of capitalism in eighteenth-century France', *English Historical Review*, 73 (1964).

Thompson E., *Popular Sovereignty and the French Constituent Assembly*. Manchester, 1952.

Vingtrinier E., *La Contre-Révolution, première période, 1789-91*. Paris, 1924, 2 vols.

Wick D., 'The Court Nobility and the French Revolution', *Eighteenth-century Studies*, 1980.

This book was completed before the publication of Murray Forsyth's *Reason and Revolution: the political thought of the abbé Sieyès* (Leicester, 1987) and the proceedings of the Chicage colloquium of 1986 (*The Political Culture of the Old Regime*, ed. K. M. Baker, Oxford, 1987) from which it would have benefited.

Index

Names of members of the Constituent Assembly are printed in capitals.